*the ice curtain, those
who established a bridge
of friendship between Magadan
and Alaska.*

LAWRENCE H.
KHLINOVSKI ROCKHILL

Alaska and Magadan

The Cold War and citizen diplomacy

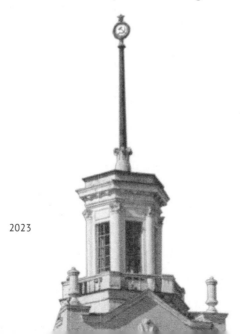

2023

PREFACE

This book is not meant to be a scholarly work on the history of the relations between Magadan and Alaska. In no way does it attempt to cover all the events and people that the author had the opportunity to interact with over the two years that he lived there and beyond. It is but a brief sketch of the life of one Alaskan who was lucky enough to be at the right place at the right time in the history of Alaska and the Soviet Union. This Alaskan is me and this book is my memoirs.

My love for the history of Alaska, and the history of Staraya Rossia (Old Russia) pointed me in the direction of the Russia of the Soviet Union, and I found that this was my fate, to see if I could be involved with others in helping to develop positive, friendly relations with people who we were privileged to share a common Russian heritage, and who were considered enemies of the United States, and who were our closest neighbors to the west of Alaska across the Bering Sea. I found myself not to be alone but surrounded by many Alaskans and Magadanians who shared the same desire, to try to put an end to the Cold War that made no sense to the millions of people in both countries. We wanted to melt the thousand-mile-long political iceberg, the Ice Curtain in the middle of the Bering Sea that separated us Alaskans from our Soviet friends in Magadan.

I went to Magadan as a professor of English, but also as a serious student of Soviet and Russian culture. My teachers were the people of Magadan, and my classrooms were wherever I was. I attempted to live the life of the Soviet person at the time. When shopping, the lines, and the stores were my classrooms, and my teachers were the other people in those

LARRY KHLINOVSKI
ROCKHILL PHOTO BY
PAVEL ZHDANOV

LARRY ROCKHILL DURING CLASSES WITH STUDENTS OF THE ENGLISH LANGUAGE DEPARTMENT OF THE MAGA-DAN STATE PEDAGOGICAL INSTITUTE. 1989 PHOTO BY PAVEL ZHDANOV

lines as well as the shop assistants. When I went for dinner with friends, their homes became my classroom, and my friends were my teachers as I learned what their lives were like and the joys and problems they faced.

Likewise, my students became my teachers showing me what it was like to be Soviet youth at that time in Magadan. After two years of living there, I returned to Alaska with my most important teacher, my beloved wife Lena, and continued my life-long love of learning about Russian culture and life. After arriving in Magadan in 1989, I felt so at home with my newfound Russian friends and students that I never really left, my soul had found its home, and it was only my body that had to depart at times over the years from the Motherland for other places, but always to return. I feel at home in Magadan! Ya Magadansky!

This book is a collection of memories related to the journey that led me to live in Magadan, USSR/Russia for two years, and the thirty years following. I have continued to travel to Russia to live, teach, and visit with my family and lifelong friends. I was the first Alaskan to move to the USSR and to live in the closed Soviet city of Magadan, from 1989 to 1991. It was an unforgettable and life-changing experience for me. At that time Magadan was a border region, and militarily sensitive, it was even closed to most Soviet citizens unless they lived there or had special permission. And it was to become my Soviet/Russian hometown.

6

Magadan came out of the blue and propelled my life into a sphere that I could never have imagined. As a youth growing up just thinking of going to Europe was the same as thinking of going to the moon. Magadan became my cosmos full of interesting stellar experiences.

The Gorbachev Era came to an end, but the results of Melting the Ice Curtain prevailed. Citizen diplomacy played a significant role in bringing the Cold War to a close. Many of my Magadan friends from those days have continued to be my close friends and will always be my close friends. But thirty years have passed, and now the world is once again in turmoil. War is never an answer to people's problems and as ordinary citizens came together across the Bering Sea to do what they could to end the Cold War, citizen diplomacy, we all must continue to come together around the world to end war forever. Mir I Druzhba, Vsegda- Peace and Friendship Forever.

DEDICATION

I want to express my sincere and heartfelt appreciation to my dearest Alyonushka, the lady with her daughter standing at the foot of the stairs that Saturday in October, who shared her wonderful Russia, her love, and her life, with me for the past thirty years that are filled with so many great memories of interesting adventures and challenges. Alyonushka is my Russian friend, and partner, my beloved muse, as together we trekked from Magadan to the Northern Caucasus, to Sergiev Posad and all around the Kolyma, and then across continents to Soldotna and Cambridge and Keizer. She was always there encouraging me to continue to write down my memories of those years, my never-ending Russian years, that filled up my book. At long last, it was time for her to edit all my writings into this final work.

ACKNOWLEDGMENTS

When I moved to Magadan from Soldotna very many people opened their hearts and homes to me and made me feel that this was to be my Russian hometown. Roman Tchaikovsky and his wife Luda made me feel like a member of their family. Roman was my supervisor and with a twinkle of his eye at times told me I needed to work a little faster on my book. Evgeny Kokorev was a dear friend and a true leader who reached out across borders and continents to bring students and teachers together under the guise of education and real friendship. Larisa Kokoreva was my colleague and friend and was always willing to help me understand this new system of higher education. Pavel Zhdanov was at the airport with the traditional bread and salt. He taught me how to love and appreciate the history and beauty of the Kolyma. Chairman Vyacheslav Kobets was the main person who said the original DA (YES), which opened the doors that made it possible for students from the University of Alaska and Magadan Pedagogical Institute to come together and for me to live and work in Magadan. His friendship continues. Lubov Shaitanova, with the support of Galina Maximova, led the first group of teachers and students who came to Soldotna Elementary. Vladimir Pecheniy was one of our very best supporters, first with our school exchange program and then the MPI and University of Alaska Exchange Programs. All worked hard to bring Alaska and Magadan students together and many came. Mayor Gennady Dorofeev provided me with a comfortable living arrangement, friendship, and a Komandirski Vostok watch. Tamara Vikhlyantseva created exhibits in her wonderful School No.1 Museum so that our coming together would be remembered by future generations. Dima Poletaev was a fellow first-year professor at MPI with whom I shared many of my concerns about teaching and Soviet life, but then he left for Moscow, and I lost track of him for many years. And now we found each other, I am very happy to say.

On the other side of the Bering Sea, there is my friend Bob Williams with whom I first wrote a letter that he sent to Don O'Dowd, the President of the University of Alaska suggesting an exchange program with Magadan Pedagogical Institute in a then Communist country. This was very unusual, but the President bought it. Bob, along with Professors David Smith and Perry Gilmore were pioneers, they being the first to come to Magadan along with being weathered in Anadyr and partaking in too many Mir i Druzhba – Peace and Friendship toasts and dinners. University of Alaska President Don O'Dowd and President Jerry Komissar, along with other UA professors like Jerry Mohatt, Vic Fisher, Chancellor Pat O'Rourke, Gunnar Knapp, John Tichotsky, Nancy Mendenhall, Dan Johnson, and Administrative Assistant Irma Jean Strickler all contributed greatly to initiating and the eventual success of the exchange program. A special mention must go to Professor Gretchen Bersch who has hosted more Magadanians in her home than any other Alaskan and outlasted most others in continuing to cross over the waters of the Bering Sea to work with the MPI staff for the past twenty-some years with her Teacher of the Year Program. The many host families that made it possible for students to afford to come in both directions were indispensable to the program. The members of the business community, Soldotna and Kenai Rotary Clubs, the Kenai American Legion Post, and the many parents who provided funds to support the students were also integral to the program. It was impossible with all the warmth of sincere friendship and the interest of these fine people, for the Ice Curtain to continue to separate us. And so, it melted.

I owe a great part of who I am to my loving and caring Mother Mary and Father Lawrence who met the challenges of raising an only child, and in part, the result can be seen in my book. I am eternally grateful to them both.

I want to also dedicate my book to all my family, friends, and colleagues who have been such an important part of my life during these unique times and have contributed directly and indirectly to the melting of the Ice Curtain and bringing Alaska and Magadan together in a spirit of peace and friendship. Sadly, here I must mention those who have passed away, including Professor Roman Tchaikovsky, Dr. Evgeniy Kokorev, Ludmila Tchaikovskaya, Lubov Shaitanova, Gennady Dorofeev, Vladimir Khlinovsky, Nina Khlinovskaya, Paul Hunter Rockhill, Dr. Lawrence Hunter Rockhill, and Mary Bernadine Rockhill.

Lastly, any errors or omissions are solely the shortcomings of the author and I take full responsibility.

CHAPTER ONE:
FROM CHILDHOOD TO THE SOVIET UNION

In Alaska, the Eskimos living on Little Diomede Island could easily see with their binoculars the Soviet soldiers only a few miles to the west on Big Diomede Island. Since a 1938 agreement between our two countries, Eskimos had been granted visa-free travel between the two islands to visit their relatives. It was after a visit by Eskimos from Little Diomede in 1946 to their relatives on Big Diomede that the Soviets closed the island and removed all the Soviet Eskimos that had been living there to villages on the mainland. The Alaskan Eskimo visitors were imprisoned by the Soviet soldiers for 52 days and then released to return home to Little Diomede. Afterward, only Soviet KGB Border Guards remained to guard the Soviet Mainland against an invasion by the United States. In 1948, the border was closed by the Soviet Government to everyone, including Alaskan Eskimos visiting their relatives. These actions precipitated an Ice Curtain across the Bering Straits and beyond, which closed the border between the US and the Soviet Union and prohibited any contact. Without any possibility of visiting our neighbors in the Soviet Far East, for many Alaskans, our curiosity was raised to an even higher level.

These were unique and intense times for the citizens of the United States and the Soviet Union. The Cold War was in full bloom and citizens of both countries lived in fear of a nuclear war. It was the era of Gorbachev and Reagan and their diplomacy. Maybe for us Alaskans, it was even more intense since we were the closest state to the USSR.

The two countries were only separated by 2.5 miles from Little

Diomede Island to Big Diomede Island at Bering Straits, just across the International Dateline.

Before continuing I would like to digress to an earlier time of my life that I feel is related to my interest in the Soviet Union of not so long ago. World War II was the greatest single event of the Twentieth Century, and the world of today is in part the result of that war. It was, shall we say, the time of my introduction to the Soviet Union and Russian culture which has been the main focus of my life for many years. The Alaska-Magadan Educational Exchange Program bears roots from the days of my youth in the 1940s and 1950s in Lodi, California, and San Gabriel, a suburb of Los Angeles, California. This was the time of World War II which was followed by the Cold War Era of the late 1940s through the 1980s.

Even as a young boy growing up during WWII, as the Soviets called it: "The Great Patriotic War", I had some knowledge of who was on our side, the side of the Allies. The faces of Hitler and Mussolini were well known to almost everyone reading the news stories in Life, the Saturday Evening Post, Time, and Newsweek, along with the daily newspapers and watching the Pathe News of the Day when attending a local movie theatre. I can remember seeing pictures in Life magazine of Stalin and the Soviet Red Army fighting the German Nazis at the Battle of Stalingrad in Russia. Each issue had many photographs of the war in Europe. The photos of actual battle scenes by combat photographers had a big influence on our imaginations as young boys growing up. We did not see or understand the terror of battle faced by these soldiers, civilians, both men, and women, but only the excitement and glory of conquering the enemy. And seeing all this, we too wanted to be soldiers, sailors, and airmen. At times, even the characters in some of the kids' comics in the daily newspapers dealt with the war.

Sometimes, on a Saturday afternoon, we kids would go to the local movie theatre, and often they would be showing a Hollywood war film with a patriotic bent. Usually, they would also show the Pathe News of the Day, which would contain footage of the war in both the Pacific and European theaters. Many people in Hollywood felt they were being patriotic and supportive of the war effort by making war movies. Even cartoons attempted to instill feelings of patriotism in those sitting in the audience. It seemed that Mussolini, Hitler, and General Tojo, the military leader of Japan during WWII, were always being chased and destroyed by Tom and Jerry, Donald Duck, and other cartoon characters.

There were advertisements before the main feature film encouraging people to support the war effort by purchasing War Bonds and saving old newspapers and metal pots and pans for recycling into war materials during salvage drives. Sticks of Wrigley chewing gum, like Juicy Fruit, were wrapped in aluminum foil and we kids would add the foil from each new stick into a ball and then later turn it in at the salvage drive. All metal was considered vital war material and this resulted in many items of daily use being made from plastic. This was the time when women found plastic dishware and containers coming into the stores to replace those made from metal. Kid's toy soldiers, which were once made of metal, were now being made from plastic and even pressed sawdust.

The government initiated a system of food rationing so that everyone would have an opportunity to buy items that were also needed for the war effort. My parents had food ration stamps and coupons for buying limited quantities of items like sugar, butter, coffee, flour, meat, and alcohol.

These were issued by a special government department. One of the health benefits of this program was that we were not consuming quite as much sugar in the way of cakes and cookies as we once did. But with limits being placed on such items as sugar, we appreciated each cookie even more than we did before the war. Gasoline and tires for automobiles were also rationed. My father was a medical doctor and received extra gasoline coupons because he made house calls to his patients, some of whom lived on farms out in the countryside.

Many of us were greatly influenced by what we saw in the movies, read in the press, and listened to on the radio. There was no television to watch in those days so an evening of home entertainment consisted of reading and sitting around the radio in the living room with other members of our family listening to our favorite programs. There was a wide selection of drama, music, and news. Listening to the radio provided us with the opportunity to use our imaginations as opposed to later watching television. It was during these times that we would engage in family conversations with each other around the dinner table and into the living room. We all wondered what the post-war world had in store for us and future generations.

In those days, our imaginations were our best friends and a big part of our everyday life. I had quite a collection of metal army toy soldiers that I played with on the floor of my room. How many battles did I fight on the floor of my room with a rug folded up to make mountains and val-

LARRY ROCKHILL PLAYS "WAR" IN THE FRONT YARD OF HIS HOUSE IN LODI, CALIFORNIA, 1942 KHLINOVSKI
ROCKHILL PERSONAL COLLECTION

leys? My little imagination was quite active, and I always divided my toy soldiers into the good guys and the enemy. Only the good guys were allowed to win the battles in my wars.

As young boys growing up during WW II, we usually played "war". When we played outside, fighting for our country in the vacant lots of our neighborhood, the war was as real as it could be, and the 'enemy'was just across the field in our imaginations. We could either be a soldier, a sailor, or a Marine. All of us had our small replica military rifles, play helmets, and cap gun pistols that went bang-bang. Some of these looked almost like the real ones. At times during the war rolls of caps were in short supply, and so you used them sparingly when shooting at the imaginary 'Jap' and German soldiers hiding in the bushes of the vacant lot across the street from my school. We even dug little 'fox holes'in the dirt to hide from the 'enemy' that was 'shooting' at us from the other side of the field. If you were lucky, you might even have a war souvenir, like a genuine army helmet or part of a soldier's uniform to wear. These were real treasures to any boy who was lucky enough to have one.

War was a prominent part of our lives growing up, even though there was little in the way of actual danger or fighting that any of us experi-

LAWRENCE H. KHLINOVSKI ROCKHILL

enced. On the West Coast, there was the shelling of the oil refinery tanks at Goleta, near Santa Barbara by a Japanese submarine that made big news at the time. But events like this were few in number. The war never really entered the United States in the same way it was felt in Europe, especially in Russia. There, millions of people were killed and whole cities were destroyed. This was almost beyond our imagination. We were fortunate, even though we still had grave concerns regarding the danger of spies and enemy agents working in the United States.

When I went with my parents to visit my mother's relatives in Southern California, sometimes my father would take me out to the Lockheed and Boeing airplane factories. We enjoyed watching the fighter planes take off and land on the runways next to the plants. My interest in old airplanes and flying goes back to these times. I knew the names of most US fighter and bomber aircraft during the war and have not forgotten them to this day. I still have the black plastic airplane silhouette identification models that my dad gave me then, such as a P-40 Curtis Kitty Hawk, a P-80 Shooting Star, our first jet fighter, and a P-38 Lockheed Lightning.

On one of these visits to our relatives in Los Angeles, I can remember seeing at night the searchlights scanning the sky in search of enemy aircraft. These may have been just practice drills, but they got my attention as a little boy and raised my anxiety level. Sometimes these drills were accompanied by the sounds of air-raid sirens blaring away. This had the same effect. At times, I would have bad dreams that we were being attacked by Japanese or German Nazi bombers and would wake up being frightened in the middle of the night. I would try to hide under the covers, and once woke up not knowing where I was. Distance from the fighting front did not seem to lessen the intensity of the fear of being attacked by the enemy in the minds of many Americans.

In 1944 I went with my mom and dad to visit my father's parents, Grandpa and Grandma Rockhill in Lebanon, Ohio. This was the first and only time I had the opportunity to know my grandparents. I am so glad that we have a family photograph of them standing in front of their house and watching me, their little grandson, riding his homemade scooter along the sidewalk. Ohio was not in the direction we tended often to go, and with the war on we stayed close to home.

We went by train from California to their home in Lebanon, where my dad grew up. It took several days in a compartment on the train, and

CHRISTMAS 1944, LODI, CALIFORNIA, MARY B. ROCKHILL, MOTHER, LARRY ROCKHILL, AND DR. LAWRENCE ROCK-
HILL, FATHER. KHLINOVSKI ROCKHILL PERSONAL COLLECTION

I have distinct memories of that trip. The military used trains for shipping soldiers from one station to the next and when a soldier would go on leave he often took the train. I was most impressed at seeing all those soldiers and sailors in their uniforms when we would go out of our compartment to the dining car for meals, or to get off the train for a brief moment when we came to a stop. The uniforms were very impressive, and I hoped that someday I would be able to wear one too, which I eventually did.

All houses had to have air raid curtains that would completely shut off any light coming through windows from inside the house. Local air raid wardens were responsible for patrolling the neighborhoods to make sure that no light was visible from outside the houses. This was very important so that no enemy aircraft would be able to see where the houses or other buildings were located. Some people had built underground air raid shelters in their backyards and filled them with emergency supplies of food, medicine, and clothing. I do not think that this was common, and I personally never knew anyone who did this. Even without an air raid shelter, people were encouraged to keep extra supplies of food and first aid supplies on hand in case of an emergency. Doing this was a challenge with so many foods being rationed. This was the time of the Victory Garden when people were encouraged to have a kitchen garden, grow their own vegetables, and make preserves in glass jars for the winter. Although there was little deprivation and/or suffering on the American homefront in comparison to Russia and other European and Asian countries, there was a great feeling of relief when news began to indicate that the end of the war was near.

Needless to say, when in 1945 the newspaper headlines read 'Victory in Europe 'and "Victory over Japan", millions of people around the world rejoiced.

LARRY ROCKHILL PLAYING "WAR" WITH HIS COCKER SPANIEL IN FRONT OF HIS HOUSE, LODI, CALIFORNIA, 1944.

My interest in the USSR and Russia continued to grow even after WWII. I knew that during WWII the USSR was one of our strongest allies in the fight against Nazi fascism. I could not understand how the world could change so drastically after the war came to an end. From being friends with the Soviet Union, we had become Cold War enemies, each with arsenals full of the most deadly weapons of mass destruction in the history of man. At this time of my life, my interest, anxiety, and fears were generated from the fact that the American press, and the media in general, were full of articles related to the buildup of nuclear weapons arsenals on both sides of the Iron Curtain. It was impossible to ignore the changing world situation as it existed.

Now there was a cloud of free-floating anxiety that hovered over the vast populations of the people in both the United States and the Soviet Union. It was certainly felt by me and my fellow students during my childhood when we were required to duck under our school desks when the practice air raid sirens went off on the last Friday of the month. We were all relieved when on the radio it would be announced that this was only a CONELRAD practice emergency broadcast – a part of the US Civil Defense System – and if it was a real emergency to stay tuned for further instructions. Now we had to get back to our lessons.

17

LARRY ROCKHILL, ST. FRANCIS HIGH SCHOOL, LA CANADA, CALIFORNIA GRADUATION PHOTO, 1956.

Around the age of twelve, my mother gave me a Zenith Transoceanic shortwave radio for my birthday. It was exciting to think that I would now be able to be in direct contact with other parts of the world, especially Europe and Russia. I was interested in being able to listen to broadcasts from foreign countries, and I used to stay up late at night with my short-wave radio next to my bed listening to Radio Moscow and the BBC Foreign Service, among others. But for some reason, Radio Moscow was the most interesting for me. Maybe this was due to the mystery generated by the Cold War of what lay behind the Iron Curtain.

It was Radio Moscow Foreign Service in English that provided me with the opportunity to hear about the life of the average person living in the USSR. Even though it was the official Party version, to me it was still of interest. There were a variety of different kinds of programs, some dealing with the life of Soviet people, others dealing with the history and culture of the Soviet Union. Since the Soviet Union consisted of fifteen different republics, there was a lot to learn. Although as a teenager I had been listening to foreign broadcasts on my Zenith short wave radio, it was later as an adult educator, during the 1980s that I developed a strong renewed interest in the USSR when Vladimir Pozner began to play an important role in helping Americans to better understand the people of the Soviet Union. He was one of the main journalists on Radio Moscow who tried to bridge the cultural gap between the US and the USSR. He had lived in the United States as a youth and was fluent in English and American culture. For some of us, he was the main person who could provide some idea of what was going on inside the Soviet Union. Often his main focus was reporting on the negotiations between President Reagan and General Secretary Gorbachev. During some of his programs, he would interview Soviet citizens and ask their opinions as to their lives under the Communist system. Of course, all respondents would only give positive statements about what it was that they liked. He would also take call-in questions from the West dealing with what some felt to be the oppressive nature of life in the USSR. He was later quoted to say that he never really lied about what it was like to live in the Soviet Union at the time, he just did not always tell the entire truth.

Although the war on the home front was something we had never experienced, we had little difficulty imagining the devastation that a nuclear war would bring to our cities and towns. We read articles in the press about the possibility of a nuclear war with the Soviet Union, and every last Friday of the month we listened to the wailing of the air raid sirens during the practice drills. Just walking along the streets of all major cities one could not help but notice that many public and private buildings had special Atomic Bomb Shelter signs on their outside walls to indicate that these buildings were where people should go in case of an atomic bomb attack from the Soviet Union. They were supposedly stocked with necessary food, water, and medical supplies to aid citizens in surviving an atomic attack. I think that when seeing these nuclear war symbols on the sides of public buildings many people wondered why our great world leaders were not doing more in the way of stopping the arms race. I often let the fear of a nuclear war enter my thoughts and I admit I was afraid and attempted to bury my fears in my subconscious where they would occasionally reappear.

How could the Soviet people, who had experienced the tremendous loss of 25 million lives, having entire cities destroyed during the Great Patriotic War, 1941 to 1945, who knew war as a real-life experience, have any desire to engage in a nuclear conflict with America? I eventually had the opportunity to discuss this question when I visited Soviet citizens in their homes. Many a time we sat around the samovar drinking tea in their kitchens and discussed the craziness of the Cold War. Of course, the average American, who for the most part only knew war from afar, felt the same.

How was it that I decided to initiate a Soviet Studies class that I hoped would eventually lead to an Alaska/Magadan Student Exchange Program? It was somewhat fate at the time that brought us together and all that followed. Fate in this case is named Mikhail Gorbachev. His peace initiatives and new policies of glasnost and perestroika changed the whole setting for international relations between the Soviet Union and the United States. After 1985, when he became the General Secretary of the Communist Party of the Soviet Union it became possible for ordinary citizens to play more significant roles in the connecting of people between the Soviet

Union and the United States. As always, citizen diplomacy played a major role during the entire Cold War. Since 1948 the Ice Curtain sat squarely in the middle of the Bering Sea. The challenge was: how to melt it and open the way to meet face-to-face with our Soviet neighbors and friends, to sit down around the samovar of peace and friendship, at last. It was both a time of great change and a time of great hope that our two countries would be able to come together and solve their problems without the use of weapons of mass destruction.

Strained relations with the USSR had been in the public discourse since the beginning of the Cold War, and it was impossible for this not to be in the back of people's minds from the number of articles appearing in the daily press and television news. Communism was presented in the US media as something to fear, that there was a need to put forth great effort to stem the tide of this 'menace to humanity', and the United States seemed to be the country that feared communism the most. In the United States, just the word 'communism' was so loaded with negative connotations that it alone struck fear into one's heart. Many felt that this reaction was somewhat exaggerated in the media. Across the United States, a feeling of paranoia was further generated by the Right-Wing Senate McCarthy Hearings and the John Birch Society. And since the United States needed to have a viable enemy to justify the billions of dollars spent on defense, the Soviet Union would due. The same situation existed in the Soviet Union. The United States was well suited to play the role of the enemy for the Soviet Union too, so they could justify their spending millions of rubles for defense.

To counteract these feelings of fear many private citizens, as well as some government agencies, put forth a great deal of effort and money to develop cultural exchange programs with the Soviet Union. There were, for example, music and dance exchange programs, where members of the Russian Bolshoi Ballet, the Kirov Ballet, and the Moiseev Folk Dancing group would tour American cities and perform to the appreciation of thousands. Artists from the US would in turn tour the Soviet Union and perform before enthusiastic crowds. There were also industrial/trade exhibitions that showed the development of new technologies by major industries. Although not many, there were some educational exchange programs where students from both countries were able to study at each other's schools and universities.

20

LARRY ROCKHILL AT HIS FLAT ON BOLDYREVA STREET ,MAGADAN. 1990 PHOTO BY PAVEL ZHDANOV

And, not least of all, there was a large movement of ordinary American citizens who wanted peace and friendship with the people of the Soviet Union. These were not just voices calling out in the wilderness, they were strong voices, heard throughout the country. These were the people who recognized that there was a huge difference between the hopes and desires of the average citizen of each country for peace and friendship, and the behavior of the leaders, who stressed that there was a grave danger of the possibility of a nuclear war on the horizon and stressed the need for an increase in defense spending. There were peace demonstrations in all the major cities where ordinary people, protested against the Cold War in general. It was universally recognized that a nuclear war was not winnable by either side and the destruction of mankind could be the result. In the end citizen diplomacy would have a significant effect in lessening the tensions between the governments of our two countries. Ordinary citizens were demonstrating because they would not give up hope that there would be peace in the world.

And there were those who graphically pointed out the tremendous persecutions and suffering that thousands of people had undergone in the Soviet Union under Stalin and beyond. People like Alexander Solzhenitsyn, Evgenia Ginsburg, Elinore Lipper, Varlam Shalamov, Michael Solomon, and others who had experienced the GULag first-hand, and had survived to let others know of the horrors. In the U.S. Robert Conquest

21

THE FOUNDERS OF SCHOOL EXCHANGES: VYACHESLAV KOBETS, CHAIRMAN OF THE REGIONAL EXECUTIVE COMMIT-
TEE OF THE MAGADAN REGION, AND LARRY ROCKHILL, A TEACHER, AT THE MUSEUM OF SCHOOL NO. 1 IN MAGADAN.
THE FRIENDSHIP, WHICH BEGAN IN FEBRUARY OF THE DISTANT 1988, HAS NOT STOPPED FOR 35 YEARS. PHOTO BY
PAVEL ZHDANOV

and Stephen F. Cohen were two of the main voices of the oppression of
the Soviet people under their Communist system. One must read these
works to more fully understand the feelings of the Soviet people concerning their lives under communism. This is also true of the suffering
and loss experienced by almost every Soviet family during World War II,
or the Great Patriotic War as it is known in the Soviet Union and the post-
Soviet Russian Federation, where over 25 million soldiers and civilians
died, and whole towns and cities were destroyed. Compare this with the
United States' loss of five hundred thousand casualties, with no cities or
towns being destroyed, and it should be easy to understand the Soviet citizen's concern for the defense of their Motherland. They did not have the
benefit of two great oceans as their east and west borders. The experiential background and concerns that the Russian people brought to the
world table for all to see were quite different from those of the US. We
must try to understand the concerns and mindset the Russian people had
during the Cold War by looking back into their history.

When I first moved to Magadan and visited with families over dinners in their homes, many conversations revolved around some of the differences and similarities between the two ways of life as we saw it. It was recognized that Soviet citizens lacked many of the personal freedoms enjoyed by people in the United States such as freedom of speech or the press as we know it, although, I explained to them that I felt that life in the United States was neither simple nor a paradise. They agreed and were quick to point out that they had certain state-subsidized benefits not available to people in the United States. These included free higher education and health care, state pensions for women 55 and men 60, subsidized food costs, housing, vacations to health resorts, and more. There were no known homeless people on the streets, and there was full employment, everybody had a job. And, as I often said, the true value of life cannot be judged solely by the consumer goods available on the shelves in the stores, although I fully understood the average Soviet citizen's concern over the often low quality of their consumer goods and the lack of consumer goods in general. What was important to the average Soviet citizen was the same as what was important to the average American: family, health care, education, enough food, good quality consumer goods, a job, decent affordable housing, peace, and friendship, and hoping for peace and a better life in the future. We all agreed that the standard of living for the average citizen of both countries was significantly different. As a result of our friendly discussions, while sitting around the samovar on their kitchen tables drinking tea, I experienced a closeness and bonding with these wonderful, warm, and friendly Soviet people. We all recognized the terrible situation we faced together in the Cold War and hoped that the peace talks between Gorbachev and Reagan would bring sanity in solving the differences between our two countries.

For a long time, there existed strong desires on the part of many Alaskans to work towards coming together with our Soviet-Russian neighbors across the Bering Sea. The Cold War was still on everybody's mind, although peace and disarmament talks were continuing between General Secretary Gorbachev and President Ronald Reagan. The Ice Curtain separating us loomed up in the middle of the Bering Sea as if it was a giant iceberg that was a thousand miles long. The thick chill of the Cold War prevented the Ice Curtain from melting, and it was certainly felt very strongly by those of us on both sides. The question on everybody's mind was how would we ordinary people be able to melt such a huge political iceberg? Yet there were many dedicated to this end, and we were not willing to give up

PROFESSOR VIC FISCHER WAS ONE OF THE MOST ACTIVE PARTICIPANTS IN THE UNIVERSITY'S STUDENT EX-
CHANGE PROGRAM BETWEEN ALASKA AND MAGADAN. 2011. COURTESY OF OXOTNIK PRESS ARCHIVES

just because of the present difficulties. This was to consume a major part of my daily life for some time to come, until February of 1989 and beyond.

Beginning in the mid-1980s the Governor of Alaska, Steve Cowper along with the Governor of Magadan, Vyacheslav Kobets were leading the way to open the borders of Alaska and Magadan to develop good economic and cultural relations between us. It was people like Jim Stimpfle of Nome and Bruce Kennedy, CEO of Alaska Airlines who had the idea for the Friendship Flight to Provideniya. Dr. Ted Mala, the first Inupiat medical doctor who led the way with the medical community. Vic Fisher, John Tichotsky, and Gunnar Knapp represented the Institute of Social, Economic, and Governmental Research at UAA in their travels to meet with their counterparts in Magadan, and I in a small way led a group of interested educators and students from the Kenai Peninsula School District.

By this time, classrooms were no longer places where students dove under their desks at the sound of air-raid sirens, and fallout shelters, with the familiar air raid shelter symbol on the sides of many city public buildings, were becoming less significant to the average US citizen. However, the threat of nuclear war was still on the minds of most people, adults, and children alike.

CHAPTER TWO:
SOVIET STUDIES CLASS, SOLDOTNA ELEMENTARY

It was quite clear when teaching Alaska History that we Alaskans shared a common Russian heritage. So, it seemed that with the Cold War being in full bloom it would make sense to develop a class on the history of the relations between the United States and the Soviet Union, with the focus being on the Russian Soviet Federative Social.ist Republic (RSFSR).

I think there was no other class with this focus in the entire state of Alaska. I began in 1986 to gather materials for my students to learn about the Soviet Union, which they had heard so much about in the media and the press but had little in the way of understanding what life was like for people living there. First of all, we needed to try and understand what the differences were since they lived under a socialist system and we lived under a capitalistic system of government. But the bottom line was how did this translate into people's daily lives? My students were particularly interested in what it was like to grow up and go to school in the Soviet Union.

The academic part of the Soviet Studies Program was the most important. I was fortunate to find a textbook on the Soviet Union that was at the high school level. There were chapters on the history, daily life, education, farming and industry, the economy, geographical regions, the fifteen different republics, etc. Reading this gave my students a fairly good idea of what it was like to live in the Soviet Union. Students were responsible for reading the text for information and then participating in

discussions of what they read. There were often articles in news magazines such as Time and Newsweek that were written by journalists who
were there on assignment. I added readings from these current magazines
and newspapers. It was a rather comprehensive program that also included several documentary films. The students were also required to
write a twenty-page research paper on any related topic they found of interest. This was a bit advanced, for most of them had not done this kind
of research report before. But it was good practice in getting them ready
for Junior High. I expected a lot from my sixth graders, and they were able
to achieve at a high school level.

But it wasn't until later on after I returned from the Intourist Hero
Cities tour in 1988, that I would be able to add many interesting Soviet
items with which I would decorate my classroom in a Soviet theme. We
visited quite a few stores during the five Intourist Hero Cities tours, and
I purchased many of what I consider to be unique and interesting Soviet
items which I would share with my students. Here I was able to bring some
real Soviet culture into our studies.

I have always felt that the more "real" you can make your lessons,
the more interesting they will be for the students. So, after returning I
brought into my classroom as much in the way of Soviet "stuff" as I could
from our Intourist Hero Cities trip to the USSR. I put Soviet political
posters, anti-war posters, pictures of Lenin, Gorbachev, and the Politburo,
anti-drug and alcohol posters, and large photos of Moscow and Leningrad,
on the walls of my classroom. Soviet toys, such as a small wind-up train,
dolls, toy soldiers, tanks, cars, and trucks were out where they could be
looked at and handled. A large Soviet flag with a red star, hammer, and
sickle hung from the ceiling in the middle of the room. This could have
been a little problem some years back during the time of the anti-Communist McCarthy Era. Soviet Army and Navy belt buckles and hats were
also on display, and the students enjoyed trying them on. But maybe the
most unusual for my students was the Russian electric samovar that I had
purchased in Moscow. Our classroom took on the appearance of a Russ-
ian/Soviet museum. I hoped that this would help put them into a 'collective 'mood where we would all work together. We were as immersed in So-
viet/Russian culture as it was possible to be without being there. But we
hoped that geographically this would change soon.

I had taken a Russian Language class at Kenai Community College and found myself at the beginning stages of being able to read, write, and speak Russian. I had bought several Russian Language programs and so with the help of my colleague Rick Mataya, who was quite fluent in Russian, I decided that it would be good for my students to take a beginning Russian Language course, too. It was highly unusual in Alaska for elementary students to take a foreign language. But I had the approval of my principal and the interest of my students. So, Rick Mataya and I introduced the Russian

ONE OF THE ADMINISTRATORS OF SCHOOL STUDENT EXCHANGES BETWEEN MAGADAN AND ALASKA RICK MATAYA. IN THE OFFICE OF THE DIRECTOR OF SCHOOL NO. 1 LYUBOV SHAITANOVA. JUNE. 1989. OXOTNIK PRESS ARCHIVES

Language to my sixth graders. First, they had to learn the Cyrillic alphabet, which was not a big problem for them, and one student memorized all 33 letters in one day. As we progressed, we would be able to name many objects in the area of our school and greet each other with simple phrases. For my students, it was interesting, enjoyable, and fit right in with our Soviet Studies Program. My students were pleased that they knew a little of a foreign language that few others in the community knew.

Every afternoon, during our Soviet Studies/Russian Language class, we would have the samovar filled with hot water and ready to drink Russky chai. Since the samovar was such an important part of Russian culture, I decided it would be a great symbol of our exchange, and we decided to call it the Samovar of Peace and Friendship. In Russia, the samovar was often at the center of family and friends coming together in the Russian kitchen to share meals, conversations, concerns, and friendship. None of my students were regular tea drinkers so we had to think of something that would be like Russian tea, for which we could use the samovar. We decided that instant tea flavored with Tang, the orange drink might work, and it certainly did. The students liked it very much. It was a big hit each day we had Russian Studies and Russian Language when each student took his/her cup/chashka to the samovar for Russky chai. Later, one of my best students, Megan O'Brien, majored in Russian Language and Studies when she went to the university. After graduation, she was able to get a position at a school teaching the Russian Language.

The traditional Russian samovar is an urn for heating water. There is a tube going down the center of the samovar that wood chips or charcoal are placed into and lit on fire. The surrounding area is filled with water and when the tube gets hot it heats the water. Then one pours the hot water from the spout on the samovar to dilute the strong tea concentrate in their cups. Modern electric samovars have a heating element instead of the heating tube in the center.

COMING TOGETHER:
GROUND ZERO PAIRING PROGRAM

Soon after this, I was able to contact Ground Zero Pairing, an organization in California that had some success in linking schools in the U.S. with schools in the Soviet Union. After connecting with the Ground Zero Pairing Program the possibility of my students being able to have some sort of personal contact with kids in Russia greatly increased and my Soviet Studies class took on a new meaning. My class began in 1986 and by 1987, after some discussion, we decided to put together a package of handwritten pen-pal letters, family photographs, pictures of our class and school, and an audiotape of my students singing some American and Soviet peace songs like Pust 'vsegda budet solntse (Let there be sunshine forever). Getting thirty students to write three personal letters to future pen-pals was a challenge. I knew that these young people were not in the habit of writing letters to anyone. Most did not have a clue as to the proper format of a personal friendly letter. I felt that each letter had to be just perfect with good penmanship and correct English. And so, this became an extended language arts lesson, and it took some time to get each student to write three nice personal letters to their future Soviet penpals. Of course, they had big hopes of receiving some letters in return. But with the distance and the Soviet postal system, this would take some time. Each package we sent required a small box and it was quite expensive to send them to a foreign country.

In the spring of 1987, with help in the form of addresses from the Ground Zero Pairing organization, we sent our first packages to School

No.1 in Magadan, a school in Ulyanovsk, Lenin's hometown along the Volga River, and one to Vladimir Pozner at Radio Moscow. Prior to our school year ending for summer vacation, no replies were received.

Of course, we had put a great deal of effort into each student writing three original letters to his/her future Soviet pen-pal. My students and I were anxiously awaiting any word from our neighbors across the Bering Sea. We had to wait until we returned to school in the fall of 1987 to receive our first reply.

At this time, it seemed that each day the main news stories settled around the peace proposals put forth primarily by General Secretary Gorbachev. President Reagan, of course, would then respond and

THE RUSSIAN SAMOVAR WAS A "SYMBOL OF PEACE AND FRIENDSHIP" FOR LARRY AND HIS STUDENTS. COURTESY OF PAVEL ZHDANOV

usually put forth some variation of the same theme. In our Soviet Studies classes, we were following these events very closely, as was the rest of the world. We would read and discuss the many articles in the newspapers and news magazines. Some issues of Time and Newsweek had articles about the daily life of Soviet citizens and the difficulties they faced living there. These articles were of particular interest to us in our Soviet Studies classes. Yet we still had hopes of receiving some personal communication from our Soviet counterparts in Magadan and elsewhere. One day, when we were watching live TV at the Gorbachev/Reagan Summit Meeting in Reykjavik, Iceland, the school secretary came and knocked on our classroom door. When I opened the door, she said that the postman had just delivered three letters from Russian students in Magadan. They were addressed to three of my students who were excited at being the first to get replies from their Soviet pen-pals. Roy Shapley, a reporter from the Peninsula Clarion newspaper came and took photos and interviewed my students regarding their participation in the first Soviet Studies class in Alaska. The letters from the three Magadan students were quoted in his newspaper article. Of course, the Russian students were able to write to us in English, since foreign languages were, and still are, an integral part

29

ONE OF THE MOST ACTIVE PARTICIPANTS IN THE SCHOOL EXCHANGES PAVEL ZHDANOV, WITH PENINSULA CLARION NEWSPAPER JOURNALISTS ROY SHAPLEY AND HIS WIFE JANET. KENAI AIRPORT, KENAI, ALASKA. FEBRUARY. 1992

of the Soviet/Russian system of education. Each letter was written in perfect English with information about themselves, their family, school, and city. Now, something real from the world of a Soviet student had entered the world of my students.

Unfortunately, one time in the great excitement of getting a large package full of letters and little gifts in the mail from students and teachers in Magadan, I inadvertently forgot to unplug the samovar, the water, and the heating element burned out. Samovars were difficult to come by at this time, as not at all available. Luckily, I had another one at home which I brought in, and we continued having Russki Chai.

Our goal was no longer just a dream since both Alaskan and Russian students had now shared something of themselves, something real, with each other. Each student desperately wanted to receive a letter from their pen pal in Magadan. Over the next several weeks, the letters would trickle in a few at a time. Each time the letters would arrive it was a time of great excitement for all of our class.

One week early in 1988 the Alaskan RAT-NET television satellite network broadcast 8 hours of live Soviet television to all of Alaska. This was a great opportunity for us to view what Soviet people watched on TV in

Future hopes:

Soldotna program aims for 'student summit'

their own country. We were able to see very clearly the differences between their TV programs and ours in the United States. There were no commercials on Soviet television and cultural programs including theater, classical music concerts, Great Patriotic War documentaries, and ballets from the Bolshoi and Kirov theaters. Soviet children's cartoons, of which there were many, had almost no violence such as was inherent in our Tom and Jerry cartoons. Many were based on classical Russian fairy tales. On the other side, there were many programs where there would be a long speech by General Secretary Gorbachev or a member of the Politburo. These programs were not the most interesting for the average Soviet person. Included here were some news broadcasts like Vremya, showing Gorbachev, a few Soviet feature films that showed life in the USSR, and several Soviet children's cartoons such as the classic, 'The Old Man and the Cow'. They were all a nice addition to my Soviet Studies Program and the students learned a lot from them. These Soviet television programs were broadcast over several days at rather inconvenient times, but that did not matter. I stayed up until 3 am and 4 am to video tape-record these programs for use in my Soviet Studies classes.

Although being able to watch live Soviet television was a step closer, we were still a long way from having the opportunity to visit with our fellow students and teachers in Magadan. However, there was one lady in her thirties living in our community who had grown up in Azerbaijan under the Soviet System. She was able to come to our class and tell us quite a lot about what it was like to go to school under that system and to live in Azerbaijan, one of the fifteen Soviet Socialist Republics. One of the main points she stressed was the high expectations that students had to live up to, and the teaching of a foreign language beginning in the early grades. She felt that many of the elementary classes she took were at a higher level than the ones we have in our schools today. There was rather strict discipline, and students were required to do much memorization in their foreign language classes. Mathematics was taught at a much higher level than in most of our classes. It was so interesting to have contact with a person who knew the Soviet system of education from experience.

The USSR was in effect a closed society where the government prohibited its citizens from free travel to most western foreign countries. Even within the USSR, its citizens were discouraged from contact with foreigners from Western countries. Only high government officials, those involved in cultural exchange programs, and the politically most trusted and carefully chosen regular citizens were allowed external passports needed to travel to a foreign country. Most of the cultural exchange groups traveling abroad were accompanied by KGB members who were required to keep a close watch on the activities of those traveling. See the movie 'Moscow on the Hudson' as an example. Several high-profile people decided to defect from the Soviet Union when they had a chance during a foreign exchange trip. The two ballet stars, Rudolph Nuriev from the Kirov Ballet in Leningrad and Mikhail Baryshnikov from the Bolshoi in Moscow were maybe the most famous.

One never knows what to expect and certainly, a big surprise was for us to have contact in our small Alaskan community with a person who was an actual dissident from the Soviet Union. This man had defected from the Soviet Union when on an official Soviet trip abroad to a European country. He was a Russian Language teacher at the US Army Language Center in Monterey California and was visiting the University of Alaska Anchorage when he came to Kenai. Rick Mataya met him and invited him to come to my class to talk about his experiences in the USSR. He was interesting in that he defected a few years prior and was considered a criminal in Soviet eyes. He told us that the results of his defection had a detrimental effect on his family back in Russia.

They were punished in various ways for his actions, and he was considered an enemy of the people. Interesting to note that he said when visiting the Kenai Peninsula, with all its display of Russian heritage, it was the first time he felt as if he was back in Russia. And he was, in the sense that the Kenai was Staraya Rossia, Old Russia of some years ago.

Later, during the Gorbachev era when things loosened up, it became easier for the Soviets to obtain an external passport and more people were able to go abroad. For most, before Gorbachev, it was not just money that you needed, but contacts in the right places where you could get permission to leave the country. By the 1990s almost anyone would be able to obtain an external passport. Being able to afford the expenses of traveling became the real barrier.

CHAPTER THREE:
1988 SOVIET INTOURIST HERO CITIES TRIP

I felt strongly that it was important for my Alaskan students to better understand what life was like for people living in the USSR and so in 1986 I developed and began teaching a class in Soviet Studies. But nothing could be better than a first-hand experience, with a visit to the USSR. The dream at this time was to work towards a real exchange program where we could meet face-to-face with Soviet teachers and students. But when and where were both still future questions that had no answers?

We wanted to see for ourselves just what life was like for the people of the Soviet Union. And so, my wife then, Nancy Courtright, and I made arrangements with Soviet Intourist, the Soviet travel bureau, to take a three-week trip to visit six of the Hero Cities of the USSR. These cities were Moscow, Leningrad, Minsk, Kyiv, Odessa, and Volgograd. All were given special Hero City awards from the Soviet Government for the role their citizens played in the defeat of Nazi Germany during the Great Patriotic War.

After flying from New York to Moscow via Paris with Aeroflot, we landed at Sheremetyevo International Airport and went through Soviet Customs and passport control. Our Intourist Guide Larisa was there to meet us and gave us a brief idea of what our time in Moscow would be like. We joined the rest of our small group of 11 and then boarded a bus that took us to the Cosmos, a rather modern Soviet hotel near the V.D.N.X. Exhibit of Economic Achievement. Once settled in our hotel rooms we headed back down the lift and out of the hotel door to the nearest Moscow Metro Station, put our five-kopek coin into the turnstile, and went di-

never seemed to be an issue with us. If anything, we may have felt safer there than walking around many major cities in the US.

Riding the Moscow Metro, maybe the most efficient and beautiful metro in the world, was very fascinating. Here more than a million people of all classes, backgrounds, and nationalities, rode to wherever they were going each day. The metro stations were truly works of art, with bronze statues and mosaic tiles depicting important events in Soviet history. Many had been built during the era of Joseph Stalin. Stalin called them 'people's palaces. It didn't take long for the Metro to go from the Hotel Cosmos to Red Square. Across Red Square from the Kremlin was GUM, the largest and finest department store in the entire Soviet Union. It is a beautiful late nineteenth-century building that housed shops selling all kinds of clothing and consumer goods. At the time of the Russian Revolution in 1917 GUM contained 1200 different stores. Then in 1928, Joseph Stalin turned it into an office building housing the committee responsible for the First Five-Year Plan. After Stalin died in 1953 it was again turned into a state department store. But now this was our opportunity to see under one roof many Soviet-made items that were in great demand and often in great deficit to most living in far-flung cities across the Soviet Union. GUM represented that abundance, which most people associated with living in Moscow, and for which so many Soviet people wanted to live in Moscow. However, a person had to have propiska, the housing registration, which entitled one to a job, health care, and education, and Moscow propiska was nearly impossible to obtain.

Soviet people traveled from across the country to shop at GUM and Detsky Mir, the children's department store not far up the street. We were fortunate to see them during Soviet times before in the 1990s they turned into shopping malls with mostly high-end Western designer clothing shops. Today one can hardly find anything in the shops in GUM made in Russia.

There were many different types of shops in GUM. Of interest to many tourists, and to me, was the availability of mechanical watches, both wrist, and pocket watches, made by Vostok, Raketa, and Slava. Watchmakers were still much in demand in the Soviet Union, along with good-quality mechanical watches. It was not difficult to find a watch repair shop if you had a watch with a problem, and it was not expensive to have your watch repaired. Battery-operated watches were also becoming popular with the Soviets back then. There were several old established fine Soviet watch companies. One of the most popular watches was the semi-military mechanical Vostok wristwatch called the Komandirsky. The only one we saw was at GUM on Red Square in Moscow and it was bought by our friend Hilton LaZarr. He was also a collector of Soviet military items from the period of the Great Patriotic War. I purchased an Amphibian, also made by Vostok, from another watch store and I still wear it today. I like old clocks and later was able to purchase two old Soviet desk clocks, a little Slava and a Sevani, both of which I still wind every day.

Another main interest of mine was the Russian samovar which to me was the symbol of a Russian family sitting around their kitchen table drinking tea, eating, and visiting. They were not available in most of the tourist Beryozka hard currency stores, or even in the regular Universam department stores. I just happened to find a shop in GUM that had a couple of regular brass electric samovars for around $15 each, so each of us bought one. A samovar did not fit into a suitcase with ease, so it had to be hand-carried. I preferred this as I did not want to take a chance on losing such a 'rare' item, which would play such an interesting role in my future Soviet Studies classes. To most Americans, they were a bit of a mystery, and to my students, a complete unknown. Today in our home there are five, two antique prerevolutionary wood-burning samovars and three Soviet electric samovars sitting out in all their glory. They are joined by my other interest of the times, ten Soviet commemorative podstakanniks, tea-drinking glass holders. Two other podstakanniks are silver and date from the 1880s and the 1890s, the time of Alexander III and Nikolai II, the last Russian Tsar. I have preferred to drink tea mainly from podstakanniks for the past thirty years and continue to do so.

Moscow provided us with the first opportunity to visit a working Russian Orthodox church. 1988 was the 1000th anniversary of the founding of Russian Orthodoxy by decree of Prince Vladimir of Rus and was being celebrated by many believers across the country. Under General Secretary Gorbachev things had become much freer regarding religion in general, especially towards the Russian Orthodox Church. After years of the Soviet government banning books that were on religion, one could now find in the state book shops many books dealing with this anniversary.

During our tour, we saw that there were still many old Russian churches closed and locked up, and if one inquired one might be told that they were just old museums, and not open to the public. We were pleased to see that not all had been destroyed. Interesting to note that since the Soviet Government was officially an atheist state, in the early days after the Revolution the Bolsheviks closed down and destroyed many old historic Russian Orthodox churches and confiscated all the religious objects made of gold and silver as well as valuable icons and vestments. Maybe the most well-known was the Khram Khrista Spasitelya (Christ the Saviour Cathedral) in the center of Moscow which was built in 1839-1883 and destroyed by Stalin in 1931, with some difficulty due to its sturdy construction. It was so well constructed that he had to use dynamite. In its place in 1960, was built a large outdoor swimming pool. Most of those churches that

IN HIS "RUSSIAN STUDIES" CLASS IN SOL-DOTNA ELEMENTARY , LARRY ROCKHILL TALKED ABOUT MANY ATTRIBUTES ASSOCI-ATED WITH LIFE IN RUSSIA, SUCH AS A BAL-AIAIKA, AND A SAMOVAR. 1989 PHOTO BY ROY SHAPLEY

were not destroyed were either closed and locked up, or used as storage buildings/warehouses, with very few being left open on a limited basis. A few were staffed by priests who had to conform to all the rigid rules laid down by the Soviets. During the Stalinist Purges, priests and nuns were often arrested and persecuted, then sent to the GULag forced labor camps, and some were just murdered as enemies of the state. Then forty years later times changed and after the fall of the Soviet Union, in 1994- 1996 the giant swimming pool was drained, and the new Russian Federation, along with the Russian Orthodox Church, constructed a replica of the old Cathedral on the same site. Christ the Saviour Cathedral had returned to the Moscow skyline in all its glory.

Fortunately, not all was lost, and one could find, if you looked hard enough, a church that was still open and operating although in a rather limited way. Not far, just around and behind the Hotel Cosmos was a rather small old church standing among the trees. After seeing it from the tour bus I decided to go there and have a look to see if it was open and if we could enter to see the inside.

There was a path and when we got closer, we noticed the beautiful traditional onion dome silhouetted against the blue sky of a summer day. This was an unexpected find, made our day, and allowed us to experience a real part of old Russia that was not Soviet.

The door was open, so we just walked in and stood at the back to observe the people. The first thing we noticed was the beautiful acapella voices of around ten women standing in the back singing softly. All were wearing long skirts and had traditional colorful Russian scarves covering their heads. There are no musical instruments allowed in a Russian Orthodox church. Candles were burning brightly in the holders standing in front of the icons of Bogomater '(Mother of God) and Spas (Christ the Saviour). Beautiful old frescos covered all the walls and the ceiling depicting the lives of Jesus and the saints. One could almost feel the ancient spiritual presence of Russian Orthodoxy. Most of the congregation consisted of older women, babushkas, some had small children by their sides. A few men of middle age also were present. The priest was standing in front of the iconostasis with smoke rising from the incense burner he was swinging gently from side to side while reciting prayers from the liturgy. Even though it was the time of Mikhail Gorbachev we wondered if any of these people were in danger of being persecuted for attending a Russian Orthodox church liturgy. During earlier Soviet times many people lost their jobs and were sent to far-off forced labor camps throughout the Soviet Union for being caught practicing their religion.

Not so many years (1993) later I was fortunate to be able to experience the waters of baptism from Otets Valentin, Father Valentine, in the St. Sergei Russian Orthodox Church on Little Communist Street in Moscow.

When we were touring with Intourist, we visited some of the many Soviet state-run book shops called Dom Knigi, the House of Books. The Soviet Union was the world's largest publisher of books, which were made available at very affordable prices to all citizens. At that time the literacy rate in the USSR was around 99%, the highest in the world. Most homes we visited over the years had a large number of books lining shelves along the walls of their flats. I think Russians read many more books per capita than the average US citizen. It was interesting to learn that many Soviet people I spoke with had read several American classic writers both in English and in translation. Steinbeck, Hemingway, Mark Twain, Jack London, and English writers like Charles Dickens and Somerset Maugham, were all rather popular with readers in the USSR. I do not think the reverse was true since I did not know many people in the US who had read the great Russian classics by authors like Tolstoy, Dostoevsky, Pushkin, Turgenev, Gogol, and others. Of course, all publishing was state-controlled, and all books had to be approved by Soviet state censors. Many of the foreign works in translation supported the Soviet socialist ideology.

I bought several books about the Soviet Union in English which were published by Raduga Publishers, their foreign language press: two Russian Language for Beginners programs with recordings, two Atlases of the Soviet Union, several maps of the Soviet Union and the world, and many Soviet propaganda posters: peace, anti-alcohol, pictures of Lenin, Gorbachev, the Politburo (the supreme policy-making body of the Communist Party of the Soviet Union), and of major cities such as Moscow and Leningrad. They added a lot of color and culture when hung on the walls of my classroom. And one day when we were walking around the Kremlin in Alexandrovsky Park a young man came up to me and asked if I would be interested in buying a black lamb's wool old- style Politburo hat that was popular in the 1960s and 1970s. I could not resist for a mere twenty dollars. Well, somewhat out of fashion to say the least, but did I care? No, it was an important part of the Soviet dress of not long ago. And to the dismay of my dear wife, I still wear it on occasion. The next day we went to the Lenin Museum on Krasnaya Ploschad'. This beautiful old red brick building was once the home of the Moscow City Duma before the Revolution of 1917. The museum collection consists of thousands of items connected to the life and death of the Founder of the Soviet Union, Vladimir Ilyich Ul'yanov (Lenin), including an uncountable number of busts of the Soviet leader. Busts of Lenin were readily available in all the tourist kiosks found along the streets, especially on the Arbat art streets. The Lenin Museum was not opened to the public until 1936, even though the collection was begun shortly after he died in 1924. Then it was closed again in the early 1990s and only again opened recently as the Museum of 1812. After his death, he was turned into a Soviet hero by those in power. We were fortunate to see several personal items such as the coat he was wearing with the bullet holes visible from the 1918 attempted assassination. His desk was set up as it would have been in his office when he was alive, and there was his Rolls Royce, which is interesting, and one would think not in line with the political philosophy of the day. It is an important collection that one must see if one is to try to understand the history of the Soviet Union.

After visiting so many interesting places in Moscow it was a bus ride back to the airport and our next Aeroflot flight to Volgograd. All flights were aboard Aeroflot passenger jets of the day and one did not expect too much. There were no First-Class seats in this classless society where everybody was supposed to be equal. Meals were very basic and non-existent on short domestic flights. Smoking was permitted at this time and made it unpleasant on occasion.

VOLGOGRAD

Our visit to Volgograd, known as Stalingrad during the Great Patriotic War, was of particular interest to me. Volgograd was and is today a modern Russian city with all its prefabricated cement apartment buildings. When we arrived, we registered at the rather old, but elegant Intourist Volgograd Hotel. Dinner that night was delicious beef stroganoff in the beautiful old Soviet-style dining room. The tables were set with the usual mineral waters. The waiters and waitresses were always friendly and never rushed us in our enjoying their tasty dishes. Not all the dishes served were Russian, most of the time we were able to choose some dishes from other Soviet Republics. From our hotel, it was a short walk to the Volga-Matushka, the Mother Volga in Russian literature and folklore, the mighty Volga River. The Volga River is the longest in Russia and enters into the Caspian Sea at its mouth near the city of Astrakhan. The Volga was and still is a vital transport route between central Russia and the Caspian Sea. In the later Soviet era and today, grain and oil are the largest cargo exports transported on the Volga.

Astrakhan, at the mouth of the Volga, is the city where Babushka Lena, my future Russian wife's mother, Nina Ivanova was born and grew up. It is rather well known for the large sturgeon fish that are caught in the Volga there and provides the very expensive black caviar one can buy at the House of Caviar on Piccadilly Circus in London. Mamochka, as we called her, knew well the fish processing plants as a youth growing up. She had to work in one of the fish processing factories to help her mother, Babushka Lena, support their large family who had lost their father to malnutrition after he had dug anti-tank trenches to protect Stalingrad from the advancing German troops. One day she took a big risk by supplying her underage younger brother with some fish to bring home to their starving mother and younger siblings. They were caught and let go but later that day good friends warned Babushka Lena that Nina could still be detained and prosecuted (her younger brother was not in danger of prosecution at that time). Babushka Lena convinced Nina to leave as soon as possible. Nina left for Moscow the next day and disappeared into the big city. There she became a student and graduated with a degree in Phytopathology and in a few years, with a Ph.D. in Agroclimatology, the study of climate and its effect on agriculture. I think she was far ahead of her time in her study of the effects of climate on agriculture. She also had a family with two daughters, who followed in her footsteps and became biologists. Times have changed since Mamochka grew up there in Astrakhan in the 1930s and now the sturgeon are a protected species, tightly controlled by the government, and much too expensive for most of us to buy.

The weather in Volgograd was sunny and warm. Each day before breakfast we would walk down to the beach along the Volga River for a morning swim. Often, we were accompanied by our new friend from Arizona, Hilton LaZarr, also a member of our tour, whose family heritage included Odessa and who shared our interest in Russian history. The Volga was just right for a wake-up swim since even the early morning hours were quite warm. There were also several other adults and even some local children enjoying the cool water. The water seemed quite clean and we could see little fish swimming close to the shore.

When we were not out on a tour we often just walked around the city and would go into the local stores and food shops to see what was there to purchase for the local Soviet consumer. It was interesting for us to try some of the available little food items like candy and some pastries. In each of the stores we visited, the shop assistants would use the old wooden abacus to add up the purchases of the customers. I did not see a modern electric cash register in any of the smaller stores. Most of the foods were behind the counters on shelves and one had to ask the shop assistant to get what one wanted to purchase. This was especially true in the little food shops scattered around the neighborhoods. Although state-owned shops, they resembled what we might call a neighborhood mom-and-pop shop.

Then on a few occasions, we were able to meet just by chance when out walking with some local Soviet people who wanted to interact with Americans and were willing to be more candid about the real situation they had to face on a day-to-day basis. Some were quite cautious about being observed talking to foreigners, especially Americans, so we would go with them and just sit on a park bench and talk. They had as many, or even more questions about what life was like in America, and so we also spent a lot of time giving them information about our daily lives.

Each of the Hero Cities had interesting memorials and museums dedicated to the Great Patriotic War. The Soviet government went to great lengths so that the Russian people would never forget the sacrifices made by so many of its citizens during the Great Patriotic War. These memorials were often quite large and impressive, sometimes with a tall statue of the Motherland. Often there was an honor guard posted in front of a war memorial consisting of Soviet youth, usually, members of the Young Pioneers wearing their red scarves with a little pin depicting the face of Lenin and the saying Vsegda Gotov - Always Ready. They would stand at attention, with some holding an old WWII military weapon in their hands. This was their patriotic duty. Often the war memorials would have pretty bouquets of flowers spread out at their base. It was a Soviet custom and still takes place today, for newlyweds on their wedding day to take and place a bouquet on the war memorial in front of the statues.

We were interested in visiting the Mamaev Kurgan (Mamaev Hill) war memorial on the hill overlooking the city of Volgograd. The Mamaev Kurgan commemorates the Battle of Stalingrad which was one of the bloodiest battles in the Great Patriotic War. The statue is named The Motherland Calls and is the largest free-standing sculpture of a woman in the world. The statue is all concrete and stands 85 meters from the base to the tip of her stainless-steel sword. Walking the 200 steps from the Volga River, up the path to the top of Mamaev Kurgan via the eternal flame, past the statue 'The Mourning Mother' with the body of a dead Soviet soldier lying in his mother's lap was a very touching experience. The 200 steps commemorate the 200 days of fighting during the Battle of Stalingrad. We stopped to see the names of all those Soviets who were killed during the battle. Such great sorrow there was for so many families. This battle was a major turning point in the war on the Eastern Front. It supported the eventual defeat of the Nazi German Army at the end of the war before the march of the Soviet Army to capture Berlin.

We took a bus tour of the city and some of the surrounding areas. In the city center, we saw an old bombed-out brick building that was left standing as a memorial to this battle that represented the impending end of Nazi Germany. This was the Pavlov House which was a symbol of the strong resistance of the Soviet soldiers during the Battle of Stalingrad from September 27, 1942, to February 2, 1943. Although only a small four-story building, it was here in this house that just 31 Soviet soldiers were able to hold out against the attacks of the German army for 58 days. It was occupied by a brave platoon led by Sgt. Yakov Pavlov, who commanded the platoon that seized the building and defended it during the long and intense battle.

The Museum of the Battle of Stalingrad was excellent. It was different from most military museums in the U.S., in that the exhibits were cases filled with the personal effects of individual soldiers, both men and women, who fought and died in the battle. Usually, there was a soldier's picture with the name of the person and his/her rank and organization placed alongside a medal, a watch, an ID card, an army belt, or some other personal item. There were also many photographs to give a realistic impression of the terror experienced by the many brave Soviets who fought and died here for the Motherland. We all owe the Soviet Army a big Thank-You, Spasibo, for the great sacrifices they made to help save the world from Nazi fascism during World War II.

I can say that this city left a distinct impression on several of us. We would have liked to have remained longer, but it was not possible. So, on July 4th we took our last morning swim in the Volga, breakfast in our hotel, and then the bus to the airport for our Aeroflot flight in a Tu-134 to Odessa.

ODESSA

Odessa was and is considered a major tourism city and an i.portant seaport on the Black Sea. During Soviet times, it was also known as the 'Pearl of the Black Sea'. The city suffered severe damage and sustained many casualties over the course of the Great Pa.triotic War. Many parts of Odessa were damaged during both its siege and recapture on 10 April 1944, when the city was finally liberated by the Red Army. It was the fourth city to be granted the status of Hero City of the Soviet Union in 1945. Today Odessa is a Ukrainian city of more than 1 million people. The city's industries include shipbuilding, oil refining, chemicals, metalworking, and food processing. Odessa was also the site of a Ukrainian naval base and home to a large commercial fishing fleet.

Here we checked into the Black Sea Hotel. We had some free time and decided to walk down under the hot sun to the Black Sea to take a dip in the cold choppy water. A hot day meant that the water would feel quite cool, a bit too cool for me. Many people were swimming and just lying on the beach sunbathing and enjoying being near the water. It felt so good to be back on the sea again, especially the Black Sea. After our little dip in the sea, we walked over to the beautiful Odessa Opera House and down the Potemkin Steps.

Our hotel was quite nice in a Soviet way and one evening we had dinner in the fancy dining room where there was live music playing with a small five-piece band. They played the pop music of the day such as the Lambada. Everyone was dancing and so we all joined in. You did not need to have a partner to dance with, whereas many women just danced solo. Even though not a lot of English was spoken, we all managed to communicate quite well since many had the same amount of English as we knew Russian.

In Odessa, we were very pleased to learn that two people from Magadan, with whom we had previously communicated regarding our coming to the Soviet Union, had arrived and wanted to see us. We were quite surprised that we were able to meet and visit with two English Language teachers from Magadan School No.1. They had come all the way from Magadan just to meet us.

Of course, we were so happy to meet Lena and Oleg Bushev. They presented us with several gifts, and we also shared things we brought with them. Although it was usually not permitted for ordinary Soviet citizens to enter an Intourist Hotel, we were able to make it possible for them to come to visit us in our room. We spent the entire two days visiting with them.

We were able to have some interesting conversations with them about life in Magadan and School No.1. They told us that there was also a strong interest on the part of the Magadan teachers and administrators in a future exchange program with our Kenai School District. Little did I realize that these two people would become my close friends and colleagues. Later they would both come to visit us in Alaska.

LENINGRAD

Now it was on to our next Hero City, Leningrad. Leningrad was an initial target of the Nazi invasion of Russia in 1941. The 900 Day Siege of Leningrad was the longest and most destructive of the Great Patriotic War. The city was isolated and food supplies became almost nonexistent ex-

DRINKING TEA AT OLEG AND LENA BUSHEV'S HOUSE. MAGADANIANS OLEG AND ELENA BUSHEV WERE PIO-
NEERS OF CONTACTS BETWEEN SCHOOL CHILDREN OF ALASKA AND MAGADAN, IT WAS OLEG BUSHEV'S STU-
DENTS WHO WERE THE FIRST TO REPLY TO LARRY ROCKHILL'S STUDENTS PEN-PAL LETTERS IN 1988. FROM
LEFT TO RIGHT: PAVEL ZHDANOV, LENA BUSHEVA, NANCY COURTRIGHT AND OLEG BUSHEV. MAGADAN. FEBRU-
ARY. 1989 PHOTO COURTESY OF PAVEL ZHDANOV

cept across Lake Ladoga, but only when the lake became frozen in the winter. More than a million Soviet citizens were killed in the siege, and thousands died from the freezing cold and starvation. Some were evacuated
to other cities in the beginning. On May 1st, 1945 at the end of the Great
Patriotic War, General Secretary Joseph Stalin declared Leningrad to be a
Hero City.

It is now known as St. Petersburg, which was its previous name during the 300-year reign of the Romanov Dynasty. It is a beautiful city, sometimes called the 'Northern Venice', and has more of a European flavor than
Moscow. Many of the very historic Tsarist-era buildings and Imperial
palaces were designed by Italian architects in the 18th century. Both the
Catherine Palace and the Alexandrovsky Palace in Tsarskoye Selo were
almost destroyed by the Nazi invasion of Russia and have now been fully
restored to their former glory. They are a must for anyone fortunate
enough to be able to visit this beautiful and historic city.

We stayed at the Pulkovskaya Hotel in Leningrad where I had the
chance to meet two young men who were waiters during our dinners.
Once when we were eating dinner, they asked if there was anything I
wanted that they could get for me. I said yes, I had wanted to buy two So-

viet Navy belt buckles and belts but did not know where they were available. So, they said, "net problem". I agreed to trade them two 90-minute audio cassette tapes of modern American rock music for the Navy belts. Then I realized that these tapes could be duplicated and sold as the latest US rock music to their friends and others for big rubles. They brought me two Navy belts and two Army belts complete with buckles, which were then going for around $100 each in the US. I was happy and so were they. They must have thought that they certainly got the better part of the deal as these military belts cost only a few rubles and were not hard to get there. Yet there was a big demand on the part of many people here, both young and old, for modern American pop music. I was so glad that these tapes were probably enjoyed by a great many Soviet youths who otherwise would not have had an opportunity to do so.

In Leningrad, we went aboard the Cruiser Aurora, a historical ship from the Tsarist era of Nikolai II, considered to be a symbol of the October Revolution of 1917 as was the storming of the Winter Palace, the seat of the Temporary government at that time. The siege of the Winter Palace began with the Aurora firing a shot from its cannon. It is well preserved by the state in its original condition and was manned by Soviet sailors. The interior of the ship is basically as it was during the Revolution, one of very few restored Russian Navy ships from that era. One of our group members was a retired US Naval officer and he had a great time exchanging some sea stories with the sailors. But when showing the Aurora officers his Navy ID card, he forgot to get it back before we left the ship. Sure enough, later that day our guide was contacted and was told that one of the Aurora officers would bring the ID card to him at our hotel.

We visited several historically important museums in Leningrad. I think my favorite was the State Russian Museum. This museum has the world's largest collection of Russian art and it was the first museum of Russian art begun by Emperor Alexander III in 1885 and housed in the Mikhailovsky Palace. The museum consists of thousands of art objects from the Gatchina, Winter, and Alexander palaces, from the Hermitage, and private collections donated to the museum. I particularly like the paintings of nineteenth and early twentieth-century Russian artists. Included were works by important artists such as Aivazovsky, Vasnetsov, Makovsky, Repin, Polenov, and Surikov. This museum, along with the Tretyakov Gallery Museum in Moscow, is my favorite museum even to this day.

We also took a hydrofoil ride down the Neva to the Petrodvorets on the Gulf of Finland. I never had the opportunity to ride in a hydrofoil so I was eager to experience this unusual watercraft. It was quite speedy, as it went up on its foils and "flew" over the water. Commissioned by Peter the Great, Petrodvorets is the oldest (1714) of the Russian Imperial Palace residences in Russia.

The palace has been completely restored since its almost destruction by the Nazi German army during the Great Patriotic War. As you walk up from the Gulf of Finland, seeing the large gold statues on both sides of the Great Cascade is a sight to behold. When walking through the garden one must be careful not to step on one of the secret stones that will turn on one of 115 trick fountains that will give you a nice cooling off on a hot day.

The interior rooms of the palace are magnificent with all their period furniture and ornate work on the walls, ceilings, and doors. Upon entering the palace, you encounter Rastrelli's very ornate Ceremonial Staircase, which is just the start of what you will experience along with the magnificent frescos of Aurora and Genius, and the many paintings and gilded statues. I especially enjoyed seeing in the dining room a formal table setting of porcelain dishware from the Imperial Porcelain Factory, complete with beautiful Imperial Russian silverware from the period.

LIFE AND LESSONS LEARNED IN THE USSR

During our Hero Cities tour, we were able to learn a great deal about the daily lives of the Soviet people. For many of them, it was not an easy life, flats were small and often crowded with extended families. People lived with the lack of many modern conveniences that most people in the United States took for granted. Not every family had a telephone, a washing machine, or even a refrigerator in their kitchen. Often there were shortages of many basic foods in the stores.

Central Planning also created problems, confusing what people really needed with what they, at Central Planning, felt the people needed.

Although some things were much less expensive, however when you considered the rather low salaries that most of the workers were paid, the consumer did not see these items as being such a bargain. Most food items were not only not considered to be inexpensive but took a major part of a family's monthly income. And when you consider that many foods were being rationed and many foods were not always available, the cost of the food was not the main consideration, availability was the main thing people thought about.

One example is that most books were much lower in price than the same kinds of books in the US. The Soviet State was able to use literature to its advantage in furthering the ideology of Lenin and Marx. Soviet women's cosmetics were also quite cheap, but their low quality was such that few Russian women would buy them unless they were all that was available. So, bringing even inexpensive US cosmetics like lipstick and perfume as little gifts was appreciated. In Alaska, one could go to the cosmetic department in a department store and ask for some free sample vials of perfume. Telling the clerk that they were gifts for Soviet women who had no possibility of buying perfume of such high quality would usually be enough to get several samples. When we stayed in the Intourist Hotels we would share a sample of perfume or an American Wet and Wild lipstick with the ladies who cleaned our rooms. There was often a dezhurnaya—a lady in charge of each floor-- sitting at the top of the stairs to check and see who was coming and going. Many were older ladies of retirement age, which was then 55 for women. They were pleased to receive such little gifts.

Clothing in the USSR was similar in that the quality was so often far below the standards in the West that again, women would not buy unless they could not afford better quality, or this was all that was available. Most women were quite aware of the fashions in the West from viewing foreign films on TV or in the cinema. There were also Russian women's magazines that would show the latest fashions in Eastern Europe. Bringing a copy of the latest US women's magazines such as Vogue, Harper's Bazaar, or Redbook to someone was considered a special gift. Some of the Soviet women's magazines had patterns for sewing garments that were of the latest styles. Sewing your own clothes was still popular with Soviet women at that time, and affordable. There were also ateliers employing a team of seamstresses where a woman could take a pattern and material for them to make the article of clothing for her. It was quite expensive but not outrageously so.

We learned that one of the most common Soviet complaints was the poor service from the sales clerks in the shops. It was not uncommon for customers to be ignored or spoken to rudely when inquiring with a sales clerk about an item from a display case. Sometimes you were made to feel like you were interrupting their eternal tea break or an important conversation and should come back later or maybe not at all. They did not get paid based on the number of goods they sold, or the profit the store made from sales, and to some, it just did not matter. But at times, if you were recognized as being an American, they would act as if they were happy to see you, were polite and tried to assist you in any way they could.

I have seen long lines of women waiting for hours and hours to get into a store that had just received a supply of women's leather boots that were made in Czechoslovakia or Hungary. These were considered to be far superior to the usual Soviet-made boots and were in great demand.

Kitchen appliances and television sets were also considered to be subject to serious defects and often in need of repair. Too often a TV set was the cause of an apartment fire. These, along with shortages, were some of the problems that Soviet consumers faced on an everyday basis.

This Hero Cities adventure was a much-preferred way to learn about the USSR/Russia than just reading books or watching films. It showed us that in many ways Americans and Russians are alike in the ways of people of the 20th Century. We all want the same as far as peace, a modern, safe, and comfortable lifestyle with all that that means as far as enough food, good housing, decent health care, a good job, etc. However, as we look deeper into the historical, cultural, and experiential background that each Soviet individual is made of, we should be able to understand that we are all different just as we are alike. If for no other reason, we should be able to understand that any people, society, or country that experienced the horrors of the Great Patriotic War could never see the world in the same way as people who knew the war mainly from afar when sitting in their homes in their safe communities that never even heard the roar of an enemy bomber flying overhead ready to release their bomb loads that would destroy people, homes and kill thousands. To understand the people of Russia we must look into their experiential and historical background that they bring to the table.

It was an unforgettable trip and made me even more determined to try to bring my students together with Magadan students. Now my concern was how to make this possible. Three weeks went by quickly and after touring the six Soviet Hero Cities it was time to leave this land we felt so at home in. But part of me remained, my little Russian soul.

CHAPTER FOUR:
GENNADY GERASIMOV IN ANCHORAGE
AND VYACHESLAV KOBETS IN NOME,
ALASKA, FALL 1988

In 1988 several interesting events took place concerning relations between Alaska and Magadan. Certainly, the one that received the most media attention was the Friendship Flight, sponsored by Alaska Airlines, which took Gov. Steve Cowper and other Alaskan politicians, businesspeople, and Alaska Native people across the Bering Straits to Provideniya in Chukotka. The main goal was to begin the process again to reunite Native families from both sides of the Bering Strait. This was the result of an idea that Jim Stimpfle had in Nome. Jim attempted to communicate with Soviet people across the Bering Straits by sending helium-filled weather balloons with peace messages attached. The Friendship Flight also had around thirty Alaska Natives aboard who were to be reunited with some of their long-lost relatives from Chukotka who also spoke Siberian Yupik. They had been separated since the closing of the border by the order of Stalin in 1948. The Friendship Flight, upon landing in Provideniya, had several people from Magadan asking if Larry Rockhill, or any of his students, were on the flight. This was because my class had sent so many Pen-Pal letters to students at Magadan School No.1. However, our time in the Russian Far East was yet to come.

In October of 1988 Gennady Gerasimov, Gorbachev's Chief Spokesman from the Ministry of Foreign Affairs, came to Anchorage to be the main speaker at the Alaska-Siberia Symposium, part of the Siberia Gateway Project organized by the Alaska Chamber of Commerce. There were about fifty people at this meeting from the Alaska State Chamber of Commerce, the business community, and two, Rick Mataya and I from the Kenai School District. We all had a chance to hear that exchanges between business people, people in Education, and the medical community would be supported by the Gorbachev Administration. This was very good news as far as our plans for a student and teacher exchange program that I hoped would take place in the near future. It was quite unusual for us ordinary people to be sitting around the table talking to a high Soviet official from General Secretary Gorbachev's Administration. This was another example of the role of citizen diplomacy in bringing together the people of Alaska and the Soviet Union. Later in the fall of 1988, I learned that in response to the Alaska Airlines Friendship Flight, Governor Vyacheslav Kobets of the Magadan Region would lead a delegation from Magadan and Provideniya that would arrive in Nome aboard the Russian research ship the Dmitry Laptev. This was at the invitation of Governor Steve Cowper and the Alaska State Chamber of Commerce, and I saw this as another possibility for us to be able to meet with people from Magadan.

Since my students had so many pen-pal friends in Magadan from School No.1, I was excited at the possibility of a meeting with Governor Kobets. I tried to think of some ways that we could help Magadan students and teachers to better understand our lives in Alaska. After some discussion with my class, we thought that the best way would be to raise enough money to buy a television set, a VCR, American videos (Disney cartoons and good films), Alaska Geographic Society journals, solar-powered scientific calculators, along with some classic American literature, to send back with the Governor of Magadan. Although we had only a short time to collect everything, I felt we could do it with some help from our friends. I contacted several local businesspeople and organizations, and they were interested and generous in helping us obtain these items to present to our new Soviet friends in Magadan.

I called my friend Dr. Ted Mala at the University of Alaska Anchorage (UAA) and asked if he thought it would be possible for us to meet with the Magadan delegation and present them with the gifts from my class while they were in Anchorage. He told me that the Alaska State Chamber of Commerce had all their time in Anchorage already scheduled. I would-n't give up and called my friend Jim Stimpfle in Nome and asked him if we could come there and make the presentation of our gifts for School No.1 to Governor Kobets. He said that would not be a problem, and that he would make arrangements for us to do a presentation when Governor Kobets and the Magadan delegation visited the new Nome Elementary School. This would be just fine, but now the question was how we could fund tickets for two teachers and two of my students to get to Nome. I called Bruce Kennedy, the CEO and President of Alaska Airlines, and VP Jim Johnson to explain what we were trying to do and ask if it would be possible for them to help us by giving my two students free tickets to Nome for this presentation. Bruce and Jim, of course, were both willing to help.

At this point, it seemed like I was on the go 24 hours a day. It was non-stop to get everything together by the time the Soviets would arrive in Nome. Fortunately, I had a lot of help from friends like Paul and Cheryl Miller who were very supportive in raising the needed funds to buy the TV and VCR and were always generous in sharing little gifts when we had student exchanges later. Bob Henning, owner, and Editor of the Alaska Geographic Society generously donated some thirty volumes of his fine publication. Parents, teachers, the Kenai and Soldotna Rotary Clubs, the Kenai American Legion Post, Charlie Weimer of FNBA, Sal Blakely of Sourdough Sal's restaurant, Linda the Manager at Lamonts, Mike Sweeny, and other members of the business community also contributed. We also bought Disney cartoons and some fine American classic films that we felt would be appropriate for Russian students. The solar-powered scientific calculators would also be quite appropriate for use in their school's math programs. Fortunately, Alaska Airlines did not put a baggage restriction on us, with all the boxes of gifts we were taking to Nome. This was also an opportunity for my students to write another 'Dear Soviet Pen Pal' letter and this time it would not take three weeks to go around the world to Magadan but would be personally carried directly to School No.1 by Governor Vyacheslav Kobets.

On September 8, 1988, the first Soviet officials to venture across the Bering Straits to Alaska since the borders had been closed by Stalin in 1948, forty years prior, arrived in Nome aboard the Soviet research vessel Dimitry Laptev. The entire Nome community came out to give our Soviet neighbors a true warm Alaskan welcome. Jim Stimpfle and his wife Bernadette, along with John Hadeland, Mayor of Nome, were right there at the front of the line to greet them. The Soviet delegation was led by

VIRGINIA HARVEY PRESENTS GIFTS FROM SOLDOTNA ELEMENTARY STUDENTS TO GOVERNOR KOBETS FOR MA-
GADAN SCHOOL NO. 1 ON SEPTEMBER 23, 1988. FROM THE FRONT PAGE OF THE NEWSPAPER "THE TIDES".
PHOTO BY ROY SHAPLEY, THE PENINSULA CLARION

Gov. Vyacheslav Kobets, a very forward-thinking Soviet leader. Included
in the Soviet delegation were government officials, journalists, and a few
Native people from Chukotka who had relatives on St. Lawrence Island
and spoke Siberian Yupik, including the well-known educator Anna Anain-
ina from Chukotka. It was hoped that this visit would lead to easier contact between Siberian Eskimo families living on St. Lawrence Island and
those on the Chukchi coast of Russia. The goal of both the American and
Soviet officials was to cooperate in opening up and developing future
business dealings, tourism, and commercial fishing, including educational
and cultural exchange programs. The next day after arriving in Nome the
Soviet delegation flew on Alaska Airlines to Anchorage to meet with Gov.
Cowper and the Alaska business community, as well as four people from
Soldotna Elementary School.

Rick Mataya and I took my two students and drove to Anchorage the
day the Soviet delegation arrived there from Nome. Fortunately for us, our
friend and journalist Roy Shapley from the Peninsula Clarion was able to
come with us and document our first meeting with his fine photography.
The night before we were to fly to Nome, we were invited to ex-Governor
Wally Hickel's home for a reception he held for the Russian delegation. Many

PROFESSOR OF MEDICINE, UAA, DR. TED MALA (LEFT) AND HEAD OF THE REGIONAL HEALTH DEPARTMENT V. LEBEDEV AT THE ANCHORAGE INTERNATIONAL AIRPORT. MARCH. 1989 OXOTNIK PRESS ARCHIVES

people were there from the Alaska business community as well as people from the University of Alaska including Vic Fisher, Gunnar Knapp, and John Tichotsky from the In.stitute of Social and Economic Research, and staff from Governor Cowper's office, including David Ramseur (See 'Melting the Ice Curtain' 2017), and Gina Brelsford who had helped us so much to get the of-ficial government approval for our future student and teacher education ex-change program. Governor Hickle had been Secretary of the Interior in the Nixon Administration and was very supportive of developing relations with the Soviet Union. It was a warm and friendly atmosphere for the Soviets and Alaskans to get to know each other. From the beginning, when meeting our new Soviet friends from across the Bering Sea, we were experiencing a bond-ing that for many of us would last a lifetime. Dima Poletaev was one of the main translators for the Magadan delegation and I asked him to translate for me when talking to Gov. Kobets. He is fluent in English and later we had some long conversations related to Magadan and Soldotna. I did not real-ize then that we would soon be close friends and colleagues as English Lan-guage professors at Magadan Pedagogical Institute.

This was the first time I was able to meet and talk with Governor Ko-bets. He was a person with whom I immediately felt comfortable talking, and we spoke at some length about the importance of bringing students from Magadan and Alaska together so that they could be the foundation for a future of peace and friendship between the youth of our two countries. I felt that he was a very sincere and progressive-thinking man who fit Gorbachev's spirit of Perestroika and Glasnost. Of course, he was somewhat familiar with our program because when our pen-pal package arrived at School No.1 in Magadan it had created quite a sensation. The arrival of our pen pal letters was an event that was covered by both the local TV station and the newspaper Magadanskaya Pravda.

We talked about all the possibilities for our students from both countries to interact in the future and that the result could only be mir i druzhba (peace and friendship). We also mentioned the presentation of gifts we would make the following day in Nome. This was the beginning of a long- lasting friendship that continues into the present. Not long ago Lena and I had the pleasure of staying with Vyacheslav, his wife Louisa, and their family in St. Petersburg. He was a great Soviet/Russian leader and played a large part in bringing our Northern parts of the world closer together. Now he is enjoying his well-deserved retirement in the beautiful city of Sevastopol in Crimea.

The next day the Alaska Airlines flight to Nome was full with the Soviet delegation, Alaska State Chamber people, Gov. Cowper's staff, two teachers, two students, and Roy Shapley from the Kenai School District. We had two days in Nome to discuss our future plans and to get to know our new Soviet friends before they would have to depart for Provideniya and Magadan. Fortunately, Jim Stimpfle had made arrangements for us to do the presentation of our gifts with Governor Kobets and his delegation in the new Nome Elementary School Library.

On the morning of the presentation, we took all the gifts over to the Nome Elementary School Library and carefully set them out on tables. We hung computer-made posters around the library walls that said, "Soldotna and Magadan Students for Peace and Friendship". We were all a bit nervous about giving a presentation to such an important international delegation. The four of us knew that we were privileged to be doing our little part to overcome some of the damage done to Soviet and American relations due to the Cold War mentality present in both our countries over the past forty years. Each of us went over what we were going to say in our speeches. I asked Dima Poletaev to translate my speech, and he said he would be happy to do this for me.

CHAIRMAN OF THE MAGADAN REGIONAL EXECUTIVE COMMITTEE VYACHESLAV KOBETS WITH VIRGINIA HARVEY
AND JENNIFER WAGNER FROM SOLDOTNA.ELEMENTARY SCHOOL. 1988 PHOTO BY ROY SHAPLEY

When the Soviet delegation arrived, we were ready and standing in front of the table with all the gifts. Both of my students, Virginia Harvey, and Jennifer Wagner had memorized their presentations in Russian and did very well. Governor Vyacheslav Kobets, Oleg Kulinkin, Mayor of Provideniya, Kirill Kasatkin, from the Ministry of Foreign Affairs Office in Moscow, Victor Timakov from Magadanskaya Pravda and other Soviet journalists, Chukchi, and Eskimos from the Nome and Provideniya area, and Nome teachers and residents, had gathered in the Nome Elementary School library. I addressed the group by saying that Russians and Alaskans, although being neighbors, had been separated by the Bering Sea Ice Curtain for the past forty years, and how important it was now to work towards bringing young people together in a spirit of goodwill and mutual understanding. Again, I stressed the symbol of coming together around the Samovar of Peace and Friendship. Then Rick Mataya gave his speech emphasizing the importance of taking advantage of the positive changes in the relationship between the USA and the USSR.

After this beginning Virginia Harvey and Jennifer Wagner gave their short speeches in Russian, and then they asked for Governor Kobets and Mayor Kulinkin to come forward. The girls pinned Soviet and American

58

ENGLISH TEACHER DMITRY POLETAEV, 1ST SECRETARY OF THE KOMSOMOL CITY COMMITTEE VALERY BARILOV AND LARRY ROCKHILL DISCUSS UPCOMING STUDENT EXCHANGE PLANS IN THE ASSEMBLY HALL OF SCHOOL NO.1, JUNE 1989. PHOTO BY PAVEL ZHDANOV

flag pins on the coat collars of the two men. Governor Kobets was deeply moved and gave Virginia a big Russian bear hug. After this Virginia became the Governor's adopted 'American daughter'. Virginia's photograph sits proudly on a bookshelf in his living room in Sevastopol. The gifts were presented to both men for them to take back to the schools in their respective cities. Governor Kobets expressed his deep appreciation for the TV set, VCR, and other items, and how much they would be enjoyed by the students in Magadan School No.1.

Mayor Kulinkin, whom we did not know would be there, also expressed his thanks for the items we presented to his school. We gave each other Russian bear hugs and kisses on the cheek in the grand Russian tradition. After the presentation was finished, we all headed over to the city auditorium to celebrate the coming of the Soviets. There was Eskimo drumming and dancing, and some of the Native folks from Provideniya joined the Alaskans in the dancing. Oleg Kulinkin even participated in some of the Eskimo Olympic games like the ear pull. This event included a citywide reindeer steak Bar-B-Q that was just delicious. A spirit of international friendship was felt by all those who were there.

LARRY ROCKHILL'S "RUSSIAN STUDIES" CLASS IS PREPARING FOR A MEETING WITH SCHOOL CHILDREN AND
TEACHERS FROM MAGADAN SCHOOL NO. 1. FEBRUARY. 1989 KHLINOVSKI ROCKHILL COLLECTION

It was so appropriate that Alaska, Staraya Rossia, should be the place where Russians and Americans could come together again after forty years of separation. Of course, the first separation took place on October 18, 1867, during the transfer ceremony on Castle Hill in Novoye Arkhangelsk, Sitka, when the flag of the Russian Tsar was lowered and the Stars and Stripes were raised, and Alaska became part of the United States. But it was in 1948 when the second separation took place by the order of Stalin.

THE DMITRY LAPTEV

The next day would hold some surprises for our small delegation from Soldotna. I wanted to make sure that the boxes of gifts for School No.1 were safely stored aboard the Russian research ship, so I asked Jim Stimpfle if he would help us get them out to the ship. He said he would take them out to the ship the next morning in his boat, and that we could go along too. We jumped at the opportunity to go aboard a Russian ship. But as things worked out it was much more than we expected. We were always

Food, Page E-1

named best in U.S.
Business, Page C-8

Whoopi thrives
on comic edge
Entertainment, Page F-1

Anchorage Daily News

ANCHORAGE, ALASKA

WEDNESDAY, JUNE 15, 1988

PRICE 25 CENTS

**BI seizes
entagon
cuments**

TRY A LITTLE SMILE FOR THE CAMERA, KIDS

Bernadette Alvanna-Stimpfle of Nome during the visit to the Siberian city of Providenlya.

United Press International/Terry Schmit

The Tides, September ??, 1988, Page 17

ЫЫ ИЗ

Photos
by
Roy Shapley

gram after her presentation Friday afternoon.

Rockhill and Governor Vyacheslav Kobetes say their final farewells.

ntum generated by the Nome visit, from
tiya has been compiling the entire program, from
ception through the present, to send out to national
media and networks. Eventually, he said, the pro-
will be brought together into a handbook documen-
the studies with a look into the future — student ex-
nges with Soviet schools. He's organizing a pres-
ation for teachers on how to begin a Russian studies
tion for the districtwide in-service program in Oc-
er, as well as a presentation for the Alaska-Siberia
ucation Exchange Committee, a statewide teachers'
anization. And the school administration has been
very encouraging and interested. They were elated we
uld pull something like this off."

Rockhill has been busy accumulating news stories,
tters and photographs into packages he wants to send
o "everyone from Reagan to Gorbachev, from (USSR
Ambassador Yuri) Dubinin to (Senator Frank)
Murkowski," encouraging support of student exchanges.

"We need to get kids involved in this; they have to
carry on what work we adults are doing today. And
Seldovia already has made tremendous inroads."

Recollections about the Nome trip tumble from
Rockhill, but "perhaps my fondest memory is personal
ly meeting someone as warm and kind as Governor
Kobetes. His reaction to us was unbelievable.

"It's hard to hate someone you've come to know and
learn to appreciate. How can you be enemies?"

opes for new beginnings

Far East may open for old friends, businessmen

over, a door was pried open, but it
to be seen for how long and just who
owed to go through.
Eskimos spoke hopefully of renew-
summer visits with old and
friends from Siberia, politicians
new diplomatic initiatives and
proposed joint ventures to help
town for cruise and airline

officials, however, appeared
ge too much too fast.
ld ever be calm," said local
or Starov of the plans for
Town development, he
ndent on tourism. Progress
n when it's time."

The flight takes place at a time when
glasnost is sending shock waves through
U.S.-Soviet relations, constantly redefining
the realm of the possible.

In 1983, the Soviets shot down a Korean
passenger jet that strayed into restricted air
space. Today, some of that air space is
routinely open to international air traffic,
allowing major carriers to fly shorter routes
between Asia and Europe and skip Anchorage refueling stops.

Dozens of new cultural and scientific ex-
changes have begun, including many between
Siberia and Alaska. This summer, Soviet and
U.S. scientists will meet in Sitka to ponder

See Page A-9, FLIGHT

See Page A-9, FLIGHT

THE ISSUE OF THE AN-
CHORAGE DAILY NEWS
DATED JUNE 15, 1988,
WHICH TOLD ABOUT
THE FAMOUS "FRIEND-
SHIP FLIGHT" AND THE
VERY FIRST MEETING
OF MEMBERS OF THE
ALASKA AND MAGADAN
DELEGATIONS

cloudy today with south-
ds to 15 mph, gusting
h in south Anchorage.
e low 60s. Chance of
night and Thursday.
hursday near 60.

	66
	51
	49%
	29.88
	62
	47
	85
	33

—C-11
—B-1
—C-1
—E-12
—C-5
—C-15
—B-5
—C-6
—C-6
—V-2

Baker resigns
as president's
chief of staff

By JAMES GERSTENZANG
Los Angeles Times

WASHINGTON —
Howard Baker, the
former Senate Re-
publican leader who
became President
Reagan's chief of
staff during the
height of the Iran-
contra affair, re-
signed his White
House post Tuesday,
citing his wife's poor
health.

He will be re-
placed by his chief
deputy, Kenneth
Duberstein, who formerly served as Reagan's
liaison with Congress.

Baker said that his plans to leave, ap-
first raised with Reagan several months
were prompted primarily by his desire
end more time with his wife in Tenn
and reflected no disagreement with the
dent.

Howard Baker

so glad that Roy Shapley from the Peninsula Clarion was able to come with us.

We drove to the Nome dock, loaded the boxes of gifts on board Jim's boat, and headed out to the Soviet research ship Dmitry Laptev which was anchored in the Nome harbor. The Dmitry Laptev was named after an early 17th-century Russian explorer of the Siberian Far East. When we arrived, we had to hoist the boxes up and over the side and onto the deck. Then we had to climb aboard via an accommodation ladder hanging over the side of the ship. Some of the crew then helped us to take the boxes below deck to a storage area. After this was done, we went to meet the ship's Captain, Vladimir Gurianov. Upon entering we noticed a picture of Peter the Great hanging on the wall of the Captain's cabin, but no photograph of Lenin. This seemed a bit unusual since he was a state official and the captain of a Soviet ship. From our conversation with Captain Gurianov, it seemed he had a deep admiration for Peter the Great and his opening of windows to the West. Along with this, he told us that it was Peter the Great who founded the first Russian Navy in 1705. With Captain Gurianov having traveled abroad he may have seen well beyond the closed borders of the Soviet society that he lived in at the time. This was still a time when few Soviet citizens were permitted to leave their country and travel abroad. However, now the window to the West was being slowly opened again under Gorbachev.

Captain Gurianov's cabin was not fancy but still quite comfortable with his desk, a nice couch, several chairs, and a coffee table. I had brought with me an American quartz wristwatch to present as a gift. When I gave it to Captain Gurianov, he said a special bolshoye spacibo, thank you very much, and then took his Russian mechanical pocket watch out and gave it to me as a gift. I was quite surprised and thanked him profusely. It is a nice memento from a Soviet ship's captain and the first visit of the Soviet delegation to Alaska.

Captain Gurianov was very friendly and made us feel very much at home on his ship. He invited us to stay for lunch and of course, we were delighted to do so. Galina, the main cook for the crew of the ship made sure we were well taken care of with delicious Russian food. This was the first time my students had tasted Russian cuisine, and they liked it. Captain Gurianov then brought out a bottle of fine Russian vodka. We toasted to 'mir i druzhba' between our two great countries. My young students were not old enough to partake in such a Russian tradition of toasting with vodka, however, Galina made sure they enjoyed that old Russian drink called lemonade, whatever the flavor. After our delicious lunch, Galina poured tea, and a box of lovely Russian dark chocolates was opened for us to enjoy. It was one of those rare meals that one will never forget. We were happy to have Rick Mataya, who acted as a translator, allowing us to participate in conversations with both Capt. Gurianov and Galina.

After lunch, we were invited to tour the research ship from the bridge to the engine room. And to our surprise, we were allowed to take pictures wherever we went. Not being a new ship, the bridge seemed to have the usual navigational instruments such as a gyrocompass, radar sets, and radios for communication between ship and shore. The helmsman stood behind a regular ship's wheel when underway, and there was a special chair for the Captain when he was on the bridge.

Since this was the last day the Soviet delegation would be here, we decided to just remain on board the ship and wait for our friends to board for their return to Provideniya. After the tour, we were invited to return to the captain's cabin for more Russky chai, and Russian dark chocolate, and continued our visit. As usual, there were many questions from Captain Gurianov about life in Alaska and the US. The time went by too quickly and soon we could hear the sounds of the people boarding. It took several small boats to bring out the entire Soviet delegation, accompanied by several of their Alaskan hosts. I do not think that any of the Alaskans were ready to see their newly found Soviet friends depart, the five of us certainly were not. I am sure this feeling was shared by our new Soviet friends too. Even though it had been just a few days spent together, deep, and lasting bonds of friendship had been formed. The time was getting short and everybody on deck was treasuring the remaining time they had with their friends, talking and toasting until their next meeting, of which nobody knew when or where would take place. There seemed to be no shortage of Russian vodka, and it was apparent that ties of friendship were getting stronger with each toast. Then the ship's whistle began to blow as a signal that we must get off the ship so they could get underway. People from both sides of the Bering Sea were exchanging last hugs and tears could be seen in the eyes of both communists and capitalists. It was a rather emotional time for most of us. Over the side of the ship and into the small boats we went. I remember standing next to John Tichotsky as

VIRGINIA HARVEY (SECOND FROM LEFT), JENNIFER WAGNER (THIRD FROM LEFT) IN THE CABIN OF THE CAPTAIN
OF THE SOVIET SHIP "DMITRY LAPTEV". CAPTAIN VLADIMIR GURYANOV IS ON THE FAR LEFT AND CHIEF COOK
GALINA ON THE FAR RIGHT. 1988 PHOTO BY ROY SHAPLEY

we all just stood there waving and saying our last goodbyes, determined
that they would never be real "good-byes", but only do svidaniyas, "till we
meet again".

Word did get back to us that Gov. Kobets returned to Magadan with
our gifts for School No.1 and that they were happy to receive them. Again,
the newspaper Magadanskaya Pravda and the local TV station covered
the story. More than thirty pen-pal letters went back with the gifts. Including the one that I wrote to the school Director Lubov Shaitanova
stressing the importance of continuing to work towards an exchange visit
of students and teachers from both sides to each other's schools. But with
no scheduled Aeroflot flights, this was still only a dream. Surely, now it
was more than just a pen-pal letter-writing program. We could put Magadan names and faces together in real time. We had been able to develop
a friendly relationship with Vyacheslav Kobets, Governor of Magadan, and
felt that he would help us find a way to come together. In our conversations, Gov. Kobets had expressed a desire to bring students from Alaska
and Magadan together as soon as possible. He gave us his promise that

he would support this type of program in the future. What more could we ask for at this point in time?

Keeping the relationship between us going via the American and Soviet mail systems was a challenge at best. It usually took an ordinary letter at least three weeks to go from Soldotna, Alaska to Magadan, Russia. The actual flying time between Anchorage, Alaska, and Magadan was four hours directly across the Bering Sea. However, it seems our letters were sent almost literally around the world via New York and Moscow to Magadan. It was difficult for the students on both sides to write a letter and then wait for such a long time, often as long as six weeks, to receive a reply. At times, due to the soft paper used in Soviet envelopes, some of the letters from Magadan arrived empty, without contents. But the students kept pressing onward. The Ice Curtain was slowly melting with the development of the warm relations between the young people of our two nations.

CHAPTER FIVE:
ON TO FEBRUARY OF 1989, MAGADAN
AND BEYOND FIRST VISIT TO MAGADAN:
PEOPLE, PLACES, AND EVENTS

In late October of 1988, back in Soldotna, I read in the Anchorage Daily News that Gov. Kobets was planning to bring a delegation of around 90 people from Magadan to Anchorage at the invitation of Gov. Cowper and the Alaska State Chamber of Commerce. This was to take place in February of 1989, only a few short months away. Since this would be on an Aeroflot charter, I saw it as an opportunity to invite some of our fellow teachers and students from Magadan School No.1 to come to Soldotna and meet with teachers and students at Soldotna Elementary School. I discussed this with my colleague Rick Mataya and my principal Dave Dickerson, and we agreed this looked like a real opportunity to have the first Soldotna-Magadan Educational Exchange. I sent off a rather long and expensive international telegram to Lubov Shaitanova, Director of Magadan School No.1, inviting 3 teachers and 3 students to come to Soldotna. I felt that our good friend Gov. Kobets would find seats for them, if possible, on his Aeroflot jet. It was towards the end of December when we learned that the exchange would be possible and we received our invitations from Magadan School No.1 for 3 teachers and 3 students from my school, Soldotna Elementary, plus our friend and journalist, Roy Shapley to come to Magadan during the time that School No.1's group of 6 would be at my school in Soldotna. Hearing so late in December that the exchange would take place did not leave much time to prepare for the first Soviet/Alaska International Educational Exchange meeting. It was almost too good to believe that this was happening.

It had been only two years previous that I had developed my Soviet Studies program, not that long ago. So, I selected three of my best students from that program to go with us to Magadan.

The three students I selected were at the top of their class both academically as well as being very responsible and understanding of what it meant to be representatives of their school and community. Virginia Harvey Miller was the oldest and had participated in our first meeting in Nome when Governor Kobets first came to Alaska to meet with Gov. Steve Cowper. This was the time when Gov. Kobets "adopted" her as his "American daughter". The other two were Maija Morganweck and James Cannava, both excellent sixth-grade students whom I knew I could depend on to be good student ambassadors.

But now we had just a few short months to prepare for the first visit of a Soviet delegation to our school and community. We couldn't forget that after all, Russia was a Communist country and we were officially still enemies. That the Russians were coming was big news for our Alaskan community where several articles written by my friends, and journalists, Roy Shapley and his wife Janet had appeared in the local Peninsula Clarion, and other articles about the future visit were published in the Anchorage Daily News. Their articles contributed a great deal to the support and the positive way our student exchange was seen in the community, and they both were an important part of our attempt to melt the Ice Curtain that separated us in the Bering Sea. Roy's great photographs from being with us on our visits from Nome to Magadan gave the reader a vivid idea of what interesting times we were privileged to experience. An international school exchange program like this would be something that would extend beyond the boundaries of my school and out into the wider community. Several parents of my students volunteered to host the teachers and students from Magadan in their homes. Business people said they would be happy to donate gifts and money to support our first Soviet positive press related to Gorbachev and Reagan discussing nuclear arms reduction, the feeling on the part of the community was very supportive.

Senator Frank Murkowski had been a big supporter of our coming together and developing relations with our friends from Magadan. He was one of the most active Alaska politicians in developing friendly relations with the Soviet Union and had been involved in the Friendship

DAVE DICKERSON, DIRECTOR OF THE SOLDOTNA EL-
EMENTARY SCHOOL ON THE KENAI PENINSULA OF
ALASKA, IS ONE OF THE MOST ACTIVE ORGANIZERS
OF SCHOOL EXCHANGES. 1988. OXOTNIK PRESS
ARCHIVES

Flight the year before. I asked him to see about the possibility of having President George Bush write a letter of congratulations addressed to the students of Soldotna Elementary and Magadan School No.1 regarding their soon-to-take-place meeting. A week before our scheduled departure for Magadan we held an all-school assembly where Senator Murkowski presented us with the signed letter from President Bush addressed to the students of Soldotna Elementary and Magadan School No.1, as well as a U.S. flag that had been raised over the Capitol Building in Washington, D. C. These would be included with the gifts we were taking. It was quite an exciting day with an all- school assembly and a visit from our Senior U. S. Senator. Now we just had to pack all of the gifts for our Magadan pen-pals and get ready to leave.

We so looked forward to this day (February 20th, 1989) when the delegation from School No.1 in Magadan would arrive at the Anchorage International Airport. We seven, my students: Virginia Harvey Miller, James Cannava, Maya Morganweck, and colleagues Nancy Courtright, Rick Mataya, and Roy Shapley were on our way to the Anchorage International Airport. We had left Soldotna early in the morning with our Soviet visas, all our baggage, and boxes full of gifts from the many Soldotna pen-pals in order to drive to Anchorage and be at the airport in time to check in all our baggage and meet Gov. Kobets and the delegation from Magadan School No.1 before they continued their journey to Soldotna. After a short wait in the airport, we heard that the Aeroflot Tu- 154 landed and they would soon be walking into the terminal. Then we saw them, and as the door to the terminal opened Gov. Cowper was waiting to greet them, along with many others from the Anchorage community. Walking through the door Gov. Kobets saw Virginia Harvey Miller, his new "American daughter" standing with our group and he first went over to greet her with a warm hug.

Then we all said a big hello to him, and he wished us all the best on our travels to Magadan. He said his wife Louisa was waiting to invite us to dinner at their home in a few days. Then we greeted Lubov Shaitanova, Direc-

SENATOR FRANK MURKOWSKI DELIVERED A LETTER SIGNED BY PRESIDENT BUSH FROM THE WHITE HOUSE CONGRATULATING THE STUDENTS OF SOLDOTNA ELEMENTARY SCHOOL AND MAGADAN SCHOOL NO. 1. IN THE PHOTO FROM LEFT TO RIGHT: JAMES CANNAVA, VIRGINIA HARVEY MILLER, LARRY ROCKHILL, MAYA MORGEN-WECK, SENATOR FRANK MURKOWSKI, NANCY COURTRIGHT AND RICK MATAYA. FEBRUARY 19, 1989 KHLINOVSKI ROCKHILL COLLECTION

tor, Irina Petrova, and Gregori Vaisenberg, both teachers, and students Lena Tulupova, Oxana Khavanskaya, and Ilya Koptilin from Magadan School No. 1. We told them that another welcome was waiting for them at Soldotna Elementary and we wished them a very enjoyable visit to Alaska.

Many people helped me to organize a special welcome program at my school when the Magadan Delegation would come to visit my classroom. Since I would be in Magadan, my colleague Betty Leonard would act in my place in meeting Gov. Kobets, the Magadan teachers, and students, and introduce them to my class. Bob Williams from the University of Alaska Board of Regents met Gov. Kobets in Homer and first took him to the Old Believer's village of Nikolaevsk, where he was the first high-ranking Communist Party official to ever have visited the Old Believer village. Here he was warmly welcomed, and being a rather low-key, friendly individual, he made a very positive impression on the Old Believers. He was also impressed with the successful adjustment that the Old Believers enjoyed in their new Alaskan home. It was a similar setting to a rural Russian peasant community where both sides of the streets were lined with wooden houses called izbas, and the vil-

THE FIRST SCHOOL EXCHANGE BETWEEN ALASKA AND MAGADAN. MEETING OF THE TWO GROUPS AT THE AN-CHORAGE INTERNATIONAL AIRPORT. FROM LEFT TO RIGHT: HEAD TEACHER OF SCHOOL NO. 1 GRIGORY VEIS-SENBERG, SCHOOL TEACHER AND TRANSLATOR ELENA BUSHEVA, ELENA TULUPOVA, DIRECTOR OF SCHOOL NO. 1 LUBOV SHAITANOVA, OKSANA KHAVANSKAYA. IRINA PETROVA, MAYA MORGENWECK, JAMES CANNAVA, ILYA KOPTILIN AND RICK MATAYA,. BACK ROW VIRGINIA HARVEY AND NANCY COURTRIGHT. FEBRUARY. 1989 KHLI-NOVSKI ROCKHILL COLLECTION

lage's church was sitting in the center of the village. Prior to my leaving for Magadan, I had spent quite a bit of time working with my students who would be greeting the Governor of Magadan, the Director of School No. 1, teachers, and the others when they arrived. Of course, they would be able to greet the guests with their limited Russian. We worked on special short readings from Russian literature and presented the gifts of little Alaskan treasures from our class to School No. 1. They were excited about being the only students in all of Alaska who would meet and host these special guests from Russia. All my students had written pen-pal letters and enclosed small gifts for their Soviet friends in Magadan that we would be taking. I felt quite good that our welcoming was going to be in the hands of my colleague Betty Leonard who was very much a part of this Soldotna-Magadan Exchange Program.

On the day Gov. Kobets, Victor Timakov from the newspaper Magadanskaya Pravda, along with a translator, Director Lubov Shaitanova, teachers, and students, our guests from School No. 1 arrived at Soldotna Elementary they were ushered into my classroom where my students, the Superintendent of Schools, Dr. Fred Pomeroy, Principal Dave Dickerson,

DELEGATION OF MAGADAN SCHOOL NO. 1 IN ALASKA: STUDENT ELENA TULUPOVA, TEACHER IRINA PETROVA, SCHOOL DIRECTOR LYUBOV SHAITANOVA, TRANSLATOR GRIGORY WEISSENBERG, STUDENTS OKSANA KHAVAN-SKAYA AND ILYA KOPTILIN. FEBRUARY 22, 1989 OXOTNIK PRESS ARCHIVES

and Betty were waiting to greet them. The presentation the students worked so hard on was warmly received. Gov. Kobets, and Lubov Shaitanova both said how happy they were to be able to come and meet the students that had shared so many pen-pal letters and little gifts in the past. In return, Gov. Kobets presented my class with many examples of beautifully polished Magadan agate and other special gifts.

Meanwhile, we were waiting in the Anchorage International Airport to fly on the return of Aeroflot flight 2315 to Anchorage which would take us to Magadan via Anadyr. This was a very historical event, being the first Soviet Aeroflot passenger flight to cross the borders from Magadan to Alaska and to bring Americans to the Soviet Union.

After saying hello and goodbye to our Magadan guests from School No.1 at the airport, we presented our tickets to the Aeroflot agents and walked down the stairs and out on the ramp where the big blue and white Aeroflot Tu-154 was parked. What a beautiful sight to behold. We walked over to the plane and there at the top of the stairs was an Aeroflot stewardess waiting to greet us and welcome us aboard. We walked up the stairs into the big cabin that usually holds around 160 passengers, but today would only hold our 10, including Jim Stimpfle, his wife Bernadette, along with their little daughter from Nome. We took our seats and felt pleased to even be aboard this historic flight. Nothing could ever replace this experience, Aeroflot Flight 2315, was a dream come true.

After takeoff, one of the friendly Aeroflot stewardesses came over to where we were seated and invited us to come to see the cockpit

MEMBERS OF THE MAGADAN DELEGATION AT THE ANCHORAGE CULTURAL CENTER DURING THE SOVIET-AMERICAN MEETING. 1989 OXOTNIK PRESS ARCHIVES

and meet the captain and crew. We were a bit overwhelmed by their openness. The captain of this Aeroflot flight was quite friendly and presented me with his First Officer pilot's wings and his Aeroflot black mouton lamb's wool fur hat as mementos of this historic flight. These are important historical artifacts from the melting of the Ice Curtain between Magadan and Alaska. We could hardly believe that we were flying over and above the Bering Sea Ice Curtain to join our Soviet friends in Magadan. As we looked out the window, flying over the water we could see the ice floes below. Two hundred forty years earlier there was a man named Vitus Bering, captain of the ship Saint Peter in service to the Tsar of Imperial Russia who was sailing in these waters exploring what would be claimed in the interest of the Russian Empire. And until October 18, 1867, these were the waters off the coast of Russian America.

When we touched down in Anadyr, we could look out the window and see Soviet fighter jets lined up along the runway, protecting the Soviet people from a possible attack from the United States. After we arrived at the Anadyr Airport Terminal and walked down the ramp from the plane, we were greeted by Soviet Border Guards in their special green uniforms armed with submachine guns.

This was the usual procedure to meet an international flight. There were no official Soviet Customs agents here, so the Border Guards had to act in their place. I am sure they had a grand time going through our luggage and boxes to see all the goodies brought by the Americans. Seems that maybe there was not much else for them to get excited about on another frigid and dark winter day in the Russian Far North.

AT THE SAMOVAR, LARRY ROCKHILL, RICK MATAYA AND BETTY LEONARD DRINK CHAI DURING A MEETING AT SCHOOL NO. 1 IN MAGADAN. JUNE. 1989 PHOTO BY PAVEL ZHDANOV

The Soviet Officials that met us were quite friendly and took us into the warm airport buffet where we were offered a nice selection of Russian foods like borsch, black bread, and hot tea. We had to wait a couple of hours for the Border Guards to go through our luggage and the boxes of gifts for our Magadan friends. But everything was new to us, and we were on the adventure of a lifetime.

We were then taken back out to the Aeroflot TU 154 and re-boarded for our flight to Magadan. It was the middle of winter and so only darkness was visible when looking out the window of the plane. Inside we were savoring each moment of this adventure to the land of the Soviets.

TRADITION OF BREAD AND SALT

We knew as we flew that soon we would be landing in Magadan but had no real idea of what kind of reception awaited us on our arrival. You can imagine what things were going through our minds. Then we landed at Magadan International Airport on this very dark and cold winter night to a very warm welcome from our Russian colleagues, many of whom

A STUDENT OF SCHOOL NO. 1 IN MAGADAN TIES A YOUNG PIONEER SCARF ON MAYA MORGENWECK, BOTH PARTICI-
PANTS IN THE FIRST SCHOOL EXCHANGE BETWEEN ALASKA AND MAGADAN. IN THE BACKGROUND IS JAMES CAN-
NAVA. FEBRUARY 21, 1989. PHOTO FROM THE NEWSPAPER "THETIDES" PHOTO BY ROY SHAPLEY, THE PENINSULA
CLARION

would become our lifelong friends, like Galina Maximova, Lubov Shaitanova, Vladimir Pecheniy, Pavel Zhdanov, Tamara Vikhlyantseva, and
Dima Poletaev as well as some of the parents that would be hosting us for
the length of our stay in Magadan. A small group of students from School
No.1 also came to greet their new friends from Alaska whom they would
host for the next eight days. Traditional bread and salt, on a beautifully
embroidered cloth, were offered to us as we entered the airport terminal.
Being the first ordinary American educators to visit Magadan, we were
rather unique, to say the least. It was as if we were some aliens who had
just dropped out of the sky. For so many years, Russians and Americans
on both sides of the Bering Sea had wondered what life was like for the
ordinary people of both our countries. And soon we would be able to find
out since we would all be staying with our Russian host families in their
flats.

   We were thrilled when we saw all those that came out to meet us. After our initial introductions to the administrators, teachers, parents, and students from the school district we boarded a bus that was waiting to take us

James Cannava, Virgina Harvey, Maija Morgenweck and Nancy Rockhill face questions from Magadan School No. 1 students during a school assembly.

For a week, we were the stars of Magadan.

Our tour bus drew crowds, cheerful waves and autograph- and momento-seekers. In the 10 below and colder air, people poured warm wishes, smiles and embraces upon us.

A delegation of six Soldotna teachers and students and Clarion Associate Editor Roy Shapley traveled to Magadan and spent a week in the Soviet Far North city. Larry and Nancy Rockhill, Rick Matiya, and students James Cannava, Maija Morgenweck and Virginia Harvey culminated a three-year project establishing contacts between Alaska and the Soviet Union.

Stories by
Roy Shapley

School girls in pinafores and with bows in their hair watch their American visitors.

School No. 1

School No. 1 in Magadan was our base, our common meeting place. The school was our prime reason for traveling to the Soviet Union. Teachers served as our interpreters and guides. Administrators cleared their schedules to accommodate our hectic itinerary; classrooms interrupted lessons so we could observe, for a few minutes, a Russian school day.

Our first day in Magadan began at School No. 1 with a student assembly. The student body was primed. We entered to a standing ovation, filing through a large hall packed with students seated on chairs and standing against the walls. The Soldotna delegation found its seats at a table facing the crowd while journalists jockeyed for position and a newsreel — not video — crew shifted lights.

We were all introduced to sustained applause. "We feel Magadan is our home," Larry Rockhill said in his opening remarks.

Outside the assembly hall, eager faces pressed against the doorways trying to get a view of the visitors, bright eyes shining with curiosity and excitement. Their emotions fairly shouted from behind the glass: our pen-pals...our friends from Alaska...students we've heard so much about...finally visiting our school...meeting my first American face to face. American clothes! Denim!

The Soldotna teachers and students fielded questions ranging from favorite foods to music, to American classrooms, holidays, pets, sports, clubs and how Magadan impressed the visitors.

A music class hosted us the first day, the teacher lecturing on classic composers and their work and, with his accompaniment

Continued on next page

to Magadan, 52 km from the airport in the town of Sokol. The bus had been specially painted with the words "Magadan and Soldotna Students for Peace and Friendship" on the sides in both Russian and English. Heading into Magadan we had an escort of police cars, red lights flashing, and sirens going, both in front of and behind the bus. To say that we were a bit amazed is an understatement. An official police escort for ordinary teachers from Alaska was much more than we could have expected. Sitting on the bus, everyone was so excited and talking a mile a minute with their newfound friends with one question after the other about what to expect. We did learn that it was late, and we would be taken to our host families so we could get settled for a big day that awaited us tomorrow.

In the past, both visiting scientists and journalists who had come to Magadan were lodged in the nice Communist Party Hotel on Ulitsa Lenina (Lenin Street) in the center of the city. Instead, all members of our group were to be housed with local families; whether with a teacher or with one of the parents of children from School No.1. This was the first time when foreigners were allowed to stay in a Soviet person's flat. In the past, even being caught speaking to a foreigner was discouraged by the Soviet authorities. For us this was a special privilege, especially being able to see how normal Soviet people lived and worked. We felt that staying with a Soviet family would be the best way for all of us to get to know and understand their way of life, which was one of our main goals. This also applied to our Magadan visitors in Soldotna.

Our Russian host parents did everything they possibly could to make us feel at home. And upon our arrival at their homes that night their first concern was to offer us something to eat in the grand tradition of all Russians. They adopted us into their families, and we immediately felt at home.

Even today some of the first students who participated in the exchange program remain in touch with their Soviet families from 1989. I

IN THE ALASKAN PRESS, MUCH ATTENTION WAS PAID TO THE FIRST EXCHANGE, WHICH BECAME HISTORIC. DE-TAILED PUBLICATIONS WITH NUMEROUS PHOTOS BY REPORTER ROY SHAPLEY WERE IN THE PENINSULA CLAR-ION, THE TIDES AND OTHERS. THIS EVENT WAS WIDELY COVERED BY THE SOVIET MEDIA IN KOLYMA AND CHUKOTKA. CAPTION UNDER THE PHOTO FROM THE NEWSPAPER 'THE TIDES' DATED MARCH 10, 1989: JAMES CANNAVA, MAYA MORGENWECK, VIRGINIA HARVEY AND NANCY COURTRIGHT ANSWERS QUESTIONS AT SCHOOL NO. 1 DURING A STUDENT MEETING. FEBRUARY 1989 have returned to my "Russian Hometown" Magadan many times over the past 30 years.

Coming from Alaska, a Soviet flat was quite different from the homes in Alaska that most people lived in. Experiencing this gave us a greater appreciation of how Soviet people were able to lead a warm and meaningful life without so much of what the ordinary American took for granted and sometimes what he/she could not live without. Soviet living space was usually at a minimum. We learned that some families had to make do with a one-room flat or even less, with a room in a communal flat setting. In a one-room flat, the main room was the living room, the dining room, and the bedroom. Usually, the couch would be made to fold down into a double bed, and bookshelves could be used as room dividers for a little privacy between where the parents slept, and the children slept. Soviet people learned to adapt to these living conditions and to make the best of them. Having a three-room flat was only a dream for most families here in Magadan. The waiting lists for flats could be long and some had been on one for several years.

It was a short night, and in the morning, we were up early because we wanted to see what the city of Magadan was really like. We just couldn't wait to get out on the street. The first impression was that it was cold outside, and secondly, it was a true Soviet city, a forest of two-to-nine-story prefabricated-cement apartment buildings with stores located on the street level and apartments situated above.

After putting on our warmest coats and hats, not fur as most people wore here, we walked from our guest's flats not far down Prospect Lenina to the central department store. Our guides were our new friends, two teachers from School No. 1. It was well below zero outside, and yet, in front of this major department store, Voskhod, mothers would park their prams outside the entrance with their infants swaddled warmly inside, leaving them to go inside to do their shopping. We thought this was bordering on the side of neglect, with the temperatures being so low. But it was the Soviet way mothers did things here, and they should know what they were doing since this was their home territory. We were just having a grand time exploring this wonderful Soviet city that was to play such an important role in the future lives of so many people from Alaska. There were so many stores just to drop into, and see what was available, along with the TV tower at the top of Prospect Lenina that looked a bit like a small Eifel tower, and from the top of the hill we could look out over beautiful Nagaeva Bay, and the Sea of Okhotsk in the far distance. We eventually visited places such as Okean, the fresh and frozen fish shop that was uniquely decorated with marine art on the walls, and lots of frozen fish in the cases, the little parks nearby, the Tsentral'niy Gastronom (Central Food Market), the Central Pharmacy, Dom Odezhdy (Central Clothing Store), and the City and the Regional Administration buildings.

Everything was new, and unusual for us from Alaska, and our eyes were wide open to take it all in. The only thing that we felt was like Alaska was the cold and the snow. Magadan was also interesting for us in that when we first began to explore the city out walking along the tamarack - lined streets with the short black fences showing a little polar bear, we didn't see any signs on the front of stores or buildings like we were used to seeing in Alaska, that would tell us what was in that building. There might be a small plaque next to the entrance with a name on it as there was in front of the Magadan Pedagogical Institute, Znanie ('Knowledge') Bookshop, the House of Political Education, a polyclinic, the Regional Pushkin Library, and the Magadan Regional Museum. There were no neon signs on the sides of the major department stores, food shops, clothing stores, children's stores, hardware stores, etc. Of course, the displays in the front windows, if there were such, would give you some idea of what was inside. It was not a big problem for those living there, nor for us, as we became orientated. However, many offices and polyclinics were often located behind residential apartment buildings, and one had to put some effort into locating them when one needed to go there. I had to get used to the house numbering system after I moved there but eventually found my way around without any difficulty.

One of the main differences that were readily apparent when we began to walk around the city was the political signs on some of the buildings. In Magadan, and throughout the country, the sides of the multi-story apartment building provided a large area where the Soviet government was able to display Socialist Realism art. Socialist realism was a form of Soviet art that was designed to depict the lives of the Soviet people and promote the ideals of the Communist Soviet state. This idealistic art focused on every phase of Soviet life, family, work, politics, the Communist Party, etc. It was developed for political reasons and meant to get the government's socialist message across to the people.

Aesthetics was a big part of this art. I remember one of my favorites was the depiction of Native people on the side of an apartment building that was the place where the Governor of the Magadan Oblast lived. It was

79

done in silver and showed scenes of Native life. Another one is a beauti-ful mosaic on the front of one of the middle schools in the town of Ola. Lenin was at the center of this quite large mosaic with his famous saying: "Study, Study, and Study". Both these examples of Soviet propaganda art are very attractive, and I believe they are still there. By the late 1980s, at the time we first arrived in Magadan, much of this art was disappearing from the public buildings. Although there were then a few examples still visible on buildings in Magadan, and in some of the surrounding com-munities, many of these imaginative and fine-looking historical art forms were destroyed during the late eighties and nineties.

When we were out walking along the streets, I can also remember see-ing a few Communist propaganda slogans along the tops of some of the buildings where in large letters were written such slogans as Glory to the Communist Party of the Soviet Union, Glory to all the workers, Long live Lenin, Glory to the Explorers of space, as well as the Soviet National Em-blems situated above the entrance of the regional and city administrations.

Near the bottom of Ulitsa Lenina was Lenin Square where outdoor events took place mainly in the summertime when many local farmers and others would bring their produce and dairy products to sell at one of the Food Fairs, and at other times there would be musical performances by local children's groups. This continues to this day. When I was living in Magadan there was a very tall statue of Vladimir Il'yich Lenin stand-ing in front of the unfinished fourteen-story Communist Party Building on Lenin Square. It had been under construction for several years, al-though work had stopped a few years before I came. At the request of the Magadan Pedagogical Institute, the University of Alaska sent some ar-chitects to Magadan to evaluate this building to see if it would be suit-able for use as classrooms and offices for the MPI. After a thorough ex-amination, the Alaskan architects submitted their findings to the MPI Ad-ministration, and it was determined that this building would not work well for educational purposes such as classrooms and offices. Several years later this large building was torn down, and the Lenin statue was moved to another part of the city. The beautiful Russian Orthodox Holy Trinity Cathedral /Troitskiy Sobor was erected in its place. In front of the Cathe-dral now stands a beautiful life-size bronze statue of St. Innokenti, who was a great Russian/Alaskan Missionary, and scholar who developed the first Aleut dictionary, and later became the Metropolitan of Moscow. I always enjoy strolling along the streets of Magadan, especially in the summertime during the period of the White Nights of the North.

SCHOOL NO.1

The next day School No.1 held an all-school assembly in their auditorium to welcome us. After arriving and hanging up our warm winter coats we were ushered into the auditorium full of children all dressed in their school uniforms. After being seated we listened to welcome speeches from Administrators, teachers, and students from both sides, and many gifts were exchanged. We had brought the letter signed by President Bush on White House stationery. The letter was addressed to both Soldotna Elementary students and Magadan School No.1 students, wishing them success in their first Soviet Magadan-Soldotna, Alaska student meeting. We presented them with the American flag that had flown over the Capitol building and a framed photograph of President Bush. We also brought many other gifts such as books, American film videos, and some unusual foods for the students in the cooking classes to experience. The most unusual was peanut butter. Nancy Courtright, being a Home Economics teacher, decided to bring some new foods to share with students and teachers in a Home Economics class. The foods were peanut butter and popcorn, which were unusual for the people at that time. When she had them taste the peanut butter, the students were not sure what to make of it. But in the end, Nancy, and her new foods were very popular with the teachers and students. She introduced some basic American food culture, the peanut butter, and jam sandwich, into the School No.1 community. We, in turn, received many nice gifts from School No.1 that would be treasured upon our return to Soldotna. They would be included in our 'Soviet Museum 'collection.

After the assembly, we visited many classrooms where lessons were taking place. The arrangement of the classrooms was not so different from ours in Alaska. One noticeable difference was that hanging on the wall of each classroom was a picture of Lenin, usually above the teacher's desk. This reminded me of my years in parochial schools in California where a picture of Jesus and/or a cross hung at the head of the classroom above the teacher's desk. These symbols hanging on the walls reflected the significance of these two different ideologies in both societies.

Here in the Soviet Union, Communist ideologies were a big part of the educational program, whereas in the Catholic schools in the United States, Christian ideology held an important place. In some ways, they both share many similarities.

We were favorably impressed with the comprehensive nature of the K to 11 educational curricula in each school. Their math, science, geography, and history programs were very good. Their foreign language program was excellent. We could tell this from the way the students were able to write letters and converse with us in English. Some of them had been studying English since the 4th grade. In each of the English Language classes we visited, we asked if the students had questions about life in the US and Alaska. Several students stood up and asked intelligent questions in their quite good English. Some were a bit too shy, and we understood.

We noticed that the students were all on their best behavior. They all stood up as a sign of respect as we entered their classes and then sat down when the teacher indicated. If they wanted to speak, they first raised their hands and spoke only when called upon. When speaking they stood up next to their desks. I initially thought they may be so well-behaved just for the visitors, but later I discovered that this was more of the norm than not. We envied them a bit as often, our classes in Alaska did not reflect such a high degree of order.

At this time the students in Magadan schools all wore uniforms. This was to change in the not-so- distant future after Magadan teachers returned from visiting schools in Soldotna. These students were all dressed in their blue school uniforms, many with their red Young Pioneer scarves tied around their necks, with the little pin picture of Lenin and the Young Pioneer motto of Vsegda Gotov – Always Ready. Little girls were wearing white lace aprons over their dresses and lace bows in their hair. They looked very pretty. Boy's uniforms were blue pants and a blue shirt with a dark blue sport coat.

One of the most noticeable differences between the schools in Magadan, and the schools in Alaska, was the discipline that teachers exercised in their classrooms. In Soviet schools, students were expected to always use strict self-control, and this was enforced by their teachers. During lessons, students were expected to pay full attention to the instructions and sit quietly with arms folded across their desks. No talking or whispering allowed. If a student wanted to ask a question, then she or he should raise her/his hand and wait to be called upon. When a student was in serious trouble, it was the threesome of the Director, the teacher, and the parents that they had to deal with. This may have been a significant variable resulting in a change in behavior.

English language classes became popular with the increased number of people being able to travel abroad, particularly to Alaska. From 1989 when we first visited School No.1, all the schools, and the students and teachers became aware of this new land across the Bering Sea as a place they would like to someday visit. Alaska was a popular topic in the public discourse, and many articles related to future relations appeared in the press and the media. And the fact that most Alaskans spoke English did not go unnoticed.

The English Language Program at all the schools followed the strict guidelines of the Ministry of Education. There was a strong emphasis on grammar, oral speech that was more like Oxford English than American English, and English Literature which included some American authors like Mark Twain and Jack London. Often students in the classes were required to memorize rather long passages of works translated into English. They learned English grammar in a more in-depth way than in most American elementary schools. Most of the teachers spoke with a bit of a Russian accent with the addition of an Oxford pronunciation.

The curriculum was from the Ministry of Education, and little deviation from the teacher was allowed. Creativity on the part of the students or their teachers was not fostered, and in most classes, Soviet ideology was the basis of the correct course of study.

A few schools had computers in a lab setting where a class could go for instruction in their use. These classes were an introduction to using computers. Not many students had a computer available to them at home. There also was a computer lab at the Magadan Pedagogical Institute where students took classes in information technology. Some of the college students did have their own computers at home. These were Soviet-made computers, and not so different from those found in the West. Soon computers were to be seen in many of the homes of the students as well as computer labs in all schools.

During our visit, we were surprised to learn that School No.1 had a museum and that we were part of it. The Curator was Tamara Vikhlyantseva, a teacher at School No.1. She has been a close friend ever since we first came to Magadan. Tamara designed several displays related to the Soldotna/Magadan Exchange Program. She was one of the main teachers who helped to organize our first visit. When we arrived at her school in February 1989, she invited us to come to see the Soldotna-Magadan exhibit in her museum. We were surprised to see so many pen-pal letters from my class, copies of the Peninsula Clarion with articles about our exchange program, and little gifts and school pictures we had sent to them during the year before our first visit. This is an excellent museum that has displays of important events and people who went to School No.1 from the very beginning. My wife Lena graduated from this fine school. We always look forward to visiting with Tamara and her husband Victor, a well-known ivory/bone carver, whenever we come to Magadan. Later on, Victor presented us with one of his beautiful bone carvings of a Mammoth that we have used in our Magadan displays.

At School No.1, I was asked by some of the teachers what kind of memento I would like as a gift. I was most impressed by the beautiful fur hats worn by both men and women in the Russian winter. They took my head size and in a couple of days when we were at a meeting in Lubov Shaitanova's office I was presented with a beautiful fur hat made from some mammal of which species I am not sure. I can only speculate the type of fur that was used, it is softer than seal, perhaps land otter?

The hat was in the style of an Astrakhan hat, like the hat often worn by Gorbachev, which was traditional in Russia. I still wear it, and it is a treasure with so many wonderful memories attached. There is nothing better than a fur hat in the Magadan winter to keep your head, and you, warm and toasty. I thanked them profusely and said many spacibos.

SOVIET WOMEN

We learned first-hand from our host families what the Russian homemaker could do with what she had to work with, and to us, this was just amazing. Few Russian women had all the labor-saving electric devices found in the average American kitchen, yet we always had delicious meals prepared by the women of our host families. These women usually had full-time jobs and spent time in long lines to buy food. They often had little or no help from their husbands with homemaking. Homemaking,

LARRY ROCKHILL WEARING HIS GIFT FROM MAGADAN SCHOOL NO.1, A "GORBACHEV-STYLE" FUR HAT. 1989.
KHLINOVSKI ROCKHILL COLLECTION

cooking, and taking care of the children were not part of a normal routine for most Soviet men. Coming home and resting and watching TV was
more their typical activity. No longer was this just something we read about
in a book or magazine, now we had seen for ourselves that this was the
case right here in Magadan. Although there were some exceptions, as we
were to observe in our host families. Times were changing, and the men
in our host families went out of their way to help their wives take good
care of their guests from Alaska. This was often the topic of conversation.

MEETINGS WITH TEACHERS

We had read a great deal in our Soviet Studies program about life in
the Soviet Union, but here we were experiencing it in real time. We began
the third day going at a rapid pace. There were around thirty schools in
Magadan, and all were curious to see these aliens that had dropped out
of the sky from an Aeroflot jet. It was not possible for us to visit all the
schools, so we had meetings where representatives from the different
schools could come to meet with us in a central location. Some of our meetings with various groups from schools and community organizations like
Komsomol, the Peace Fund, the Knowledge Society, and others, took place
in the Pushkin Biblioteka, the main city library. We would usually sit

...na Elementary School, the new year harbors hopes of
...er — and closer — contact with Siberian students and
...ers.

...th-grade teacher Larry Rockhill and district bilingual
...inator Rick Matija have been conducting a campaign
...ter writing and correspondence with Soviet officials,
...ian school authorities and individual teachers.

...this side of the Bering Sea, the two have been in touch
...Alaskan business leaders, elected representatives and
...taff of Gov. Cowper's Office of International Trade.
...efforts are smoothing the way for an Alaskan-Siberian
...dent summit" and an exchange of students and teach-
...th School No. 1 in Magadan.

...program has it's roots in Rockhill's
...room. A five-week block of school work in
...ted to Russian language, history and culture.
...ents are expected to write to school children
...eria and share the responses from their new
...pals with the class. Rick Matija, fluent in
...an, spends time with the class helping stu-
...with their reading, writing and speaking
...in the classroom. The program is in its third

...o of Rockhill's students, now attending
...tna Junior High, traveled with the two
...ators to Nome last September to meet with a
...t delegation on a reciprocal visit of the
...ndship Flight" from Nome to Providenya
...une. They carried gifts for their pen pals in
...dan and met Providenya's mayor, Oleg
...kin and Vyacheslav Kobtes, president of the
...tive committee of Magadan Oblast (pro-
..., the equivalent of a governor. The girls and
...viet men unofficially "adopted" each other.
...trip to Nome landed the girls and their gifts
...pages of Russian newspapers and on Soviet
...broadcasts. Kobtes sent a personal letter to
...na after the visit. (See excerpt)

...gadanskya Pravda, or the Magadan edition
...vda, carried an article called "An Image of
...dship" in its Sept 15, 1988 issue describing
...sit to Nome. Part of it read: "In the arena of
...ational politics the common understanding
...en political groups is the 'Image of
...ies.' Someday this attitude will outdate
...In its place will be an 'Image of Friends.'
...ve to believe this."

...ing the course of an Alaska State Trade and
...ship Mission to the Soviet Far East last Oc-
...Mrs. Lubov Shaitanova, Director of
...an School No. 1, traveled from Magadan to
...rovsk to discuss a student exchange with
...laskan officials. According to a letter
...ll received from International Trade staf-
...anna Brelsford, Shaitanova was "disap-
...d that the Alaska delegation did not include
...e in a position to officially accept an invita-
...participate in an exchange."

...er letter, dated Dec. 14, Brelsford wrote, "I
...rage you to pursue and exchange with
...l No. 1 with vigor...I support your efforts and

Future hopes:

Soldotna Soviet Studies Program plans for sum

Sixth-graders Malja Morgenweck, left, and Jenny Draper look over some of the latest gifts from Magad

At left, an article
issue of Pravda
entation of Virgini
Wagner's gifts an
Magadan School N
head of the newspa

(Special thanks t

— Репортаж —

ОБРАЗ ДРУГА

...встреча в клубе ...
...национальной школы № 1
...необычной. В актовом
...собрались почти вся
...нерская дружина, стар-
...лассники. На встречу со
...льниками пришел пред-
...тель исполкома Мага-
...кого областного Совета
...ных депутатов Вяче-
...Иванович Кобцев.
...адельской сцене — цвет-
... видеомагнитофон.
... дистанционного пуль-
... зорану побежали на
...ломые картины Севера
...льдами, белыми медве-
...горными прозрачными
... Это не Чукотка.

... мынешнего года в
...нии гостила делегация
...ото берега Берингова
..., и вот наш ответный
...на гидрографическом
...кан делегация при-
...озглавлял В. И. Кобец
...шей на Аляске три дня,
...много встреч. Прежде
...конечно, плановых, за-
...ск и налаживания свя-
...ических и советских
..., и возможные кон-
...рат освоении недр, тор-
...переработке кожевенно-
...за разговор с русским

...представителями кампании, ко-
...торая осуществляет спутнико-
...вую связь.

— Столько было встреч, что
...не удалось почувствовать себя
...туристами, — рассказывает Вя-
...чеслав Иванович. — На Аляс-
...ке, как в Магаданской обла-
...сти, полумиллиона жителей,
...половина их — в Анкорад-
...же. Побывали мы и в городе
...Номе. Знаете, что бросилось
...нам сразу же в глаза — непо-
...казная чистота, порядок. Чув-
...ствуется, люди берегут место,
...где живут. Улицы ухоженные,
...кругом палисадники. Подчерк-
...нуто уважительное отношение
...к собственности. А в школе
...нет и намека на то, чтобы
...что-то было разрисовано или
...попорчено.

...Есть на Аляске поселок Сол-
...дотна. Название его дано рус-
...скими первопроходцами. Два
...учителя и две школьницы при-
...ехали в столицу штата, чтобы
...встретиться с советскими людь-

...Школа из поселка с русским
...названием подарила первой
...магаданской школе видеомаг-

...нитофон и кассеты с фильмами
...об Аляске и диснеевскими
...мультфильмами.

...Одна из девочек спросила
...Вячеслава Ивановича:

— Можно, я буду называть
...вас русским папой?— И попро-
...сила передать коробку в кра-
...сочной упаковочной бумаге и
...письмо Юле Соколовой. Сколь-
...ко было удивления и радости
...на лицах ребят! Аплодисмен-
...тами встретили такую ин-
...формацию.

...Позже мы беседовали с
...Юлей. Осторожно развернув
...упаковочную бумагу, она до-
...стала батник с аппликацией на
...груди — в виде верны и над-
...писью «Аляска».

...Американскую девочку, ко-
...торая знает Юлю, и у которой
...теперь есть «русский папа», зо-
...вут Виргиния Херн. Она очень
...любит животных, дома у нее
...живут две собачки, две кошки
...и птичка. Юля тоже ухаживает
...за собачкой, и об этом она пи-
...сала своей американской по-
...друге.

...«Моя американская подру-
...га» — такое словосочетание

...стало уже привычным, хотя пе-
...реписке школьников из «Мага-
...дана и Солдотны меньше двух
...лет.

...А началось это так: пришло
...письмо с Аляски: отзовитесь. И
...адреса. Главная сложность —
...языковой барьер. Преподава-
...тель английского языка Олег
...Германович Вушев (он вел в
...Доме пионеров кружок страно-
...ведения) помог перевести пись-
...ма пионеров на английский.

...Вячеслав Иванович привез
...еще несколько адресов амери-
...канских старшеклассников и
...дружески посоветовал ребятам
...не оставлять без ответа ни
...единого письма.

...Есть в школе № 1 магни-
...тофонная кассета — звуковое
...письмо. В нем американские де-
...ти предлагают дружить и поют
...по английски «Солнечный
...круг». А вот еще интересные
...реликвии — школьные газеты.
...Небольшого формата, их раз-
...множают на ксероксе. Фото-
...графия в такой газетой тоже
...помещают. В одной из газет
...опубликованы портреты ребят,
...которые состоят в переписке с

...магаданцами. Улыбаются, в
...руках письма советских дру-
...зей...

...Галина Васильевна Баскова
...руководит КИДом шесть лет, а
...раньше клуб существовал лет
...пятнадцать. Но какая в нем
...шла работа — кружковая, не
...большие. Сейчас здесь стремит-
...ся воспитать деятельное отно-
...шение к международной друж-
...бе, ведь уже столько примеров
...народной «детской» диплома-
...тии. Кто не знает о Саманте
...Смит или Кате Лычевой? Мно-
...гие хотят на них походить.

...Надо трудиться для дружбы.
...Это понимают все.

...Имею в виду ярмарку соли-
...дарности. Одна девочка, на-
...пример, сшила фартук, отдала
...его на ярмарку и тут же сама
...купила его: просто так денег
...не берут. Надо ради дружбы и
...мира поработать. Кто-то слона
...выкроил из мела — двуногого,
...плоского. Все равно купили. А
...сие — шпилевка, из «Мурав-
...ки» вырезанного, — за две
...копейки. Важно, что все сред-
...ства пойдут в Фонд мира.

...«Образ врага» — есть такое
...понятие в международной по-
...литике. Когда-нибудь оно вы-
...живет себя. И заменой ему
...станет другое — «образ друга».
...Давайте будем в это верить.

В. ДАНИЛУШКИН.

Gifts from Siberian pen pals.

was impressed with Mrs. Shaltanova's commitments and approach to an exchange project."

Rockhill and Matiya are determined to meet with Shaltanova. They are trying to arrange to fly back to Magadan on the Aeroflot flight that will be bringing Soviet a rock group and Native dancers to Anchorage in February as part of a cultural exchange program.

Rockhill and his wife, Nancy, Matiya and three students will try to meet with the director and Magadan students, opening dialogue that will lead eventually to a "Alaska/Siberia Youth Summit Meeting" to be held this year — possibly in Soldotna — and to discuss a student/teacher exchange in September or October, Rockhill said.

"Our goal is to get on that return flight to Magadan," he said.

Matiya is working on submitting a grant proposal to the Alaska Humanities Forum to help offset planning and travel costs to set an agenda for a student exchange.

"We'd be a shoe-in (for a grant)," he said. "There are cultural, historical and future connections" with such a project.

Rockhill received a letter from Shaltanova around Christmas and said she was very enthusiastic about the exchange and is "leading the way. The students and teachers are very excited and she's finding out whatever information she can" about transportation, school costs and accomodations.

It's possible that the youth summit and the exchange could take place concurrently. The summit, Rockhill said, would touch on four themes: students exploring, through their different backgrounds, environmental concerns; common heritage of Siberia and Alaska; lifestyles today; and "what is their dream of the future as Alaskans and Siberians — what is their view of the very best possible."

And apart from the possibility of student exchanges and summits, Rockhill and his wife and

Excerpts from a letter to Larry Rockhill, Rick Matiya, Teachers and Students of Soldotna Elementary School, following Kobets' visit to Nome:

'After the trip to Alaska I arranged a meeting between the students and teachers of Magadan School No. 1. (The) children were very surprised and full of joy at hearing about the trip and your presentation in Nome.

I am very gald that between you and the Magadan school children a true friendship is intertwining. Let this friendship be not temporary. You have the desire to strengthen and develop it further, so that it carries over onto friendships between our regions and between our peoples....

Please accept sincere thanks and gratitude from me personally, and from the teachers and students of Magadan. We wish you success in your studies and in the development of our friendship.'

—V.I. Kobets, President, Executive Committee, Magadan Oblast, USSR.

Matiya are planning a 10-day tour of Moscow and Leningrad during spring break with about 12 students, he said.

The article at right, from *Magadan Komsomol*, a youth-oriented newspaper published in Magadan, relates pen pals' experiences from the Siberian side. Soldotna students are 'heartily studying Russian...suffice to say everyone there knows what is going on in the Soviet Union.' The story concludes with 'and now we're going to know all about Alaska. We're looking forward to the future.'

...otos by Roy Shapley)

...agadan's
...' pres-
Jennifer
...dents at
...he mast-

...r providing Russian translations. —Ed.)

СЛУЖБА НОВОСТЕЙ

ВИДЕОТЕКА ИЗ АМЕРИКИ

Год назад завязалась переписка между членами КИДа «Ровесник», что существует при первой школе г. Магадана более 20 лет, и школьниками американского города Солдотна, расположенного на Аляске.

Отправляем письма и получаем ответы мы на английском языке. Но ребята с Аляски усердно изучают русский в дружбе мистера Рокилла, и мы думаем, что скоро будем получать послания из США на нашем родном языке.

Школьникам Солдотна интересно буквально все — как мы живем, как учимся, как идет перестройка в Советском Союзе. Кстати сказать, они в курсе всех наших политических событий.

Недавно делегация представителей общественности г. Магадана и п. Провидения побывала на Аляске. Они встречались с жителями городов близнецов и показали, как раз в ту школу с которой мы переписываемся. Ребята очень обрадовались этой встрече и передали нам ценные подарки нашим ребятам — классами, сменами, а двум самым активным колядам — шестикласснице Юле Соколовой и восьмикласснице Оксане Ховжиской — пуловеры и шведки для каждой.

Узнав из переписки, что мы создали музей КИДа, американские ребята подарили нам 12 фотоальбомов, в которых запечатлены города Аляски, животный и растительный мир самого северного штата и его людей. Теперь мы будем знать все об Аляске.

Наши кидовцы сейчас горят желанием сделать ответные подарки друзьям из Солдотна, и мы очень рассчитываем на нашу будущую встречу, на которой настаивают и американские школьники. Дети хотят общаться, а значит — жить в мире.

Г. БАСКОВА,
руководитель КИДа «Ровесник» школы № 1 г. Магадана.

Пролетарии всех стран, соединяйтесь!

АГАДАНСКАЯ ПРАВДА

...н Магаданского обкома КПСС и областного Совета народных депутатов   • Цена 3 коп.

№ 221 (15899)   •   Воскресенье, 25 сентября 1988 года

ИНФОРМАЦИОННАЯ ПАНОРАМА

...июля 1935 года

around a big table, and they would ask us questions related to our educational system and daily life. There were usually several English Language translators that were with us, often Dima Poletaev, Lena Busheva, Lena Kostenko from School No. 1, and Mariana Podolskaya from the school in Uptar. All of them were fluent in English and did a great job.

Although the main topic of conversation seemed to focus on the American system of education, we also had many questions regarding their system of education. We were to learn that the Soviet system of education had many strengths and was considerably more advanced than ours in several areas, not only in the teaching of foreign languages but also in mathematics, geography, and science, at least at the elementary school level.

One day, the four adults in our group had to attend some important meetings with other teachers, so we decided that the Soldotna students and their hosts would enjoy going to the Bluebird ice cream cafe for a treat. We dropped them off there and said we would return in about an hour after our meeting. We had given them enough money for all the ice cream they could possibly eat. Our meeting took a bit longer than we had expected, and it was a little over three hours later when we returned to the cafe. They were not happy, even though they had eaten all the ice cream they wanted. All Russian ice cream was excellent, always being made with fresh cream and not with nondairy products, but for them, enough was enough, and Virginia, Maija, and James conveyed this message to us quite clearly.

These were the days when everything was new to all of us, and Western bubble gum and candy were special little gifts for the Magadan school kids. We also prized the Russian gum and candy they shared with us. They would save the wrappers from the candy and gum that we gave to them, likewise, we followed suit. These colorful wrappers could always be used as bookmarks. Not only candy, but a Soviet green milk bottle, a bottle of Soviet vodka, or a Pepsi Kola bottle with the label in Cyrillic were all treasures to take back to Alaska, even empty.

GIFTS

Small commemorative pins called znachki were very popular in the Soviet Union and were collected like stamps by all ages. These pins were usually worn on a person's jacket or just placed on a special cloth for display. They had many themes, such as peace, Lenin, Young Pioneers, Komsomol, logos of cities, Aeroflot, animals, historical people, flags, the 15 Republics, etc. They were one of the main little gifts we all received many times until the front of our coats looked like the medals on the chest of a war hero. We were able to bring Alaska flag pins and walrus pins to share. At the time, it was the 40th Anniversary of the city of Magadan and special pins with the Magadan flag had been made to commemorate the historic occasion. Now, these old pins are collector's items and are on display in the Regional Museum.

Our Soviet host families were more than generous in giving us gifts. Of course, we also had brought several boxes full of presents from Alaska for our host families, the teachers, the students, and the schools. Costco was well represented with Snickers candy bars, Folgers instant coffee, and summer sausage. Women's fashion magazines and car magazines were also popular gifts along with audio cassettes of modern American rock music. When visiting one had only to express an interest in something that was on the shelf in a glass-enclosed cabinet in a Soviet person's flat and it was taken off and handed to you as a gift. This could be embarrassing, and so one had to be careful of expressing an appreciation of some of the interesting things, such as beautiful ivory carvings from Chukotka, and pretty crystal on display in people's flats. Most people's flats were nicely decorated and very homey. Some had beautiful Asian carpets hanging on their walls for both decoration and a bit of extra insulation.

In Magadan, my students lived with their Soviet host family for the duration of the exchange visit. They were made to feel as if they were a part of the family. Even without language, warm feelings of friendship were easily conveyed by the host families. The host families would often spend as much as an entire month's salary on buying gifts for their Alaskan students to take home. My students experienced new foods, new ways of living in smaller spaces than they were used to, and not being able to communicate with a common language. However, a Russian mom is a Russian mom, and they were all very well taken care of during their stay. In the beginning, there was some anxiety on their part, but they did quite well.

Most of our host families lived in small apartments by Alaskan standards, along with many other differences. Knowing this, later many Alaskans would go out of their way to send gifts of food and clothing to their Soviet friends when they heard that somebody from Alaska was going on a charter flight to Magadan. In those days, one did not have to deal with a baggage

A JOINT PHOTO OF THE TEACHERS OF MAGADAN SCHOOL NO. 1 WITH THE AMERICAN DELEGATION. 1 ROW: DMITRY POLETAEV OLGA OSTAPENKO, LARRY ROCKHILL, RICK MATAYA, BETTY LEONARD, LYUBOV SHAITANOVA, IRINA PETROVA, OLGA KOPYLOVA, GALINA KHOROSHILOVA. 2ND ROW: EVGENY KRASHENINNIKOV, NINA MINICH, RIMMA GOLOVAN, TAMARA PRIMAKOVA, TAMARA VIKHLYANTSEVA, ELENA KOSTENKO, UNKNOWN, LYUDMILA LIPINSKAYA, LYUDMILA MISHKINA, OLGA ZENKOVA, PAVEL ZHDANOV, OLGA..., PETER HAPERSKY. JUNE 1989 COURTESY MAGADAN SCHOOL NO.1 ARCHIVES

weight allowance on a charter flight. Gennady, the Aeroflot Manager in Anchorage, was supportive of our student exchange program, and would always allow us to take as many boxes of gifts as we wanted to our Magadan friends.

Most Americans feel that it is necessary to reciprocate if one is given a gift. In some cases, this was difficult for us as visitors. Money was not valued in the same way by many Russians as it was by most Americans. I don't think the average Alaskan would consider spending an entire month's salary on a student visitor from Magadan. This being said I do know of some people who spent several hundred dollars in providing needed items when visitors came from Magadan. This reflected the closeness that developed between the Soviets and Americans at this time. My students went back to Alaska loaded with interesting Russian gifts from their host families, including gifts for their parents.

VIRGINIA HARVEY (MILLER) AND MAGADAN

The following is the essay that Virginia has shared with me to be included in this book:

"It was a brisk Alaskan February day in 1989 when I set off on an adventure that would test every ounce of courage, grace, and sheer tenacity that a 13-year-old girl could muster. I had been selected to be part of a small delegation of Alaskans to fly across the Bering Sea and embark on a mission to bring two countries closer together. We were going to the city of Magadan, a closed Soviet city that had rarely seen Americans, let alone American children and their teachers. I had no idea what would await us when our Russian-Soviet Aeroflot jet touched down. It was the trip of a lifetime, pushing me far outside my comfort zone, to forge new experiences and step into the unknown.

There were people crowded in the Magadan airport when we arrived, though I was bewildered as to why that was until we entered the terminal. Inside the crowds of people, especially children began holding out flowers and trinkets to greet us. All I could do was smile politely and say "spasibo" or thank you, one of the few words I knew in Russian. It was an overwhelming experience, the crowds of people's faces all focused on the new foreign visitors never to have set foot in their city before. After being introduced to the Magadan School No. 1 teachers and students, we were

92

swept away on a special bus filled with other children, to be delivered to the homes of our pen-pals, where we would be staying for the duration of our trip in this new land. Dozens of eyes stared at us over and around the bus seats, smiling, and giggling at the sight of the strangers in their country. I remember thinking about how they were just like us, just happy children, doing what curious children do. I couldn't figure out what all the fuss was really about. I was just an ordinary girl, really, no different from them, but in their eyes, I was somehow special.

Almost immediately upon arriving at my pen pal's home, it was apparently determined that my clothing choices were not sufficient for the extreme Magadan temperatures, even though I had just come from Alaska. Of course, here there would be far more walking outside to be done than at home in Alaska where you drove to virtually every destination. I was promptly outfitted with a beautiful fur coat, and sealskin mukluks to protect me from the harsh winter elements, much to my teenage dismay. But of course, no Russian mama would allow me out in the below-freezing weather like that without proper clothing. I felt like royalty in that tiny little flat. I was cooked for, bundled up, and rescued by candlelight when the power went out unexpectedly. We all did our best to communicate, using dictionaries and gestures, and somehow, we all got by on nods and smiles.

The days that followed were filled with formal events, and presentations, walking to nearby shops and parks, and visits to schools, and ice cream shops. I was happily reunited with Governor Kobets who had taken me as his "American daughter" when he visited Alaska the year before. We signed autographs like celebrities, were showered with gifts, observed children in school classes, watched special performances, and became witnesses to the everyday lives of the people of Magadan. I learned when just a child myself, that children truly are the same all over the world, regardless of race, ethnicity, culture, or country. The people of Magadan were gracious, generous, nurturing, and kind. They cared for me as they would for their own children, accepted me as a stranger in their land, and like me, saw that we had far more the same about us than different. I will never forget the experience of traveling to Magadan. It opened my eyes to the world around me, and that people who for years were viewed as our enemies, were truly neighbors all along. I had but a small role in melting the Ice Curtain, though I now know that loving my neighbors, even those separated by government and ideological differences, is what we were always called to do as citizens of this planet we all call home."

MAGADAN AND THE GULAG

The Magadan Oblast in 1989 was almost the size of the state of Alaska at 720000 square miles and was the center of the Stalinist forced labor network of prison camps, the GULag, administered by the Dal'stroy Trust (The Far Northern State Trust for Road and Industrial Construction). It was here in the Magadan Oblast that one of the most important concentrations of gold was discovered by geologists like Yuri Bilibin, and others during the geological explorations of the late 1920s, along with other valuable minerals including, at a later date, uranium. Although in the beginning free labor was used to extract the gold, soon it was decided by Stalin during the 1930s that the most feasible and economical method was to use political and common criminal prisoners in the mines.

In an interview at the time, Magadan Mayor Gennady Dorofeev was quoted as saying "We have not forgotten those people." and "We hope it will never happen again." This was the time with the new openness of Gorbachev's Glasnost and Perestroika that people living in Magadan were becoming more aware of the thousands of people that had passed through the Stalinist forced labor camps that were scattered throughout the oblast. Many of the prisoners succumbed to the extremely harsh working conditions, the bitter cold of minus 40C, and the lack of adequate food and warm clothing, not to speak of the severe depression of being isolated from the love of family and friends. For some Soviet people, learning of the GULag was shocking news, the untold persecution, and suffering on the part of so many 'political prisoners who most would say committed no crime. Others felt that even though it happened, Stalin was the very strong leader that the Soviet Union needed at the time to defeat Hitler in the Great Patriotic War. Many people had little or no knowledge of the buildings along Lenin Street being built by Japanese and German prisoners along with political prisoners from the camps. Even today with Magadan being a rather progressive and modern city the memory of the camps remains in the minds of many residents and those people outside of the region in the materik (or the mainland as many northerners would refer to the western part of the Soviet Union), who were once residents of the camps.

There stands today on a hillside just along the Kolyma Trassa (Kolyma Highway) at the edge of Magadan the Mask of Sorrow, as a monument to all the oppressed of the past. The Mask of Sorrow is a large monument looking out over the city of Magadan. The monument commemorates the many prisoners who suffered and died in the GULag forced labor camps in the Kolyma region of the Soviet Union during the 1930s, 1940s, and 1950s. It is constructed of a large cement statue of a face, with tears coming down from the left eye in the form of small masks. The right eye is in the form of a barred window. The backside portrays a weeping young woman and a headless man on a cross. Inside is a replication of a typical Stalin-era prison cell. Below the Mask of Sorrow are stone markers bearing the names of many of the forced-labor camps of the Kolyma, as well as others designating the various religions and political systems of those who suffered there.

8TH GRADE STUDENT YANA YURIEVA AND VIRGINIA HARVEY AT A MEETING IN THE HISTORY ROOM OF SCHOOL NO. 1. FEBRUARY 21, 1989

ASIR SANDLER

During the eight days we spent in Magadan we had the opportunity to meet with a great many interesting people from different walks of life. Gov. Vyacheslav Kobets had made arrangements for us to visit one of the most interesting people in Magadan. His name was Asir Sandler, and he had been a political prisoner in Butugychag, one of the most dangerous Stalinist forced labor camps.

This was the mine where some of the first uranium was extracted for the development of Stalin's atomic bomb program. We were surprised to be able to speak with such an interesting person when we thought the topic of the GULag was not usual for people to speak about out in the open.

One afternoon we four adults were driven over to Asir's apartment building not far from Melodia, the Soviet music, and the TV store. It was a usual Soviet four-story apartment building. We walked up to the entrance and rang his doorbell. He opened the door and invited us to come in. He was a rather tall and slim man of medium build. Asir was seventy-one years old at the time of our visit. He had expected us, and so in the Russian tradition had prepared tea and several delicious snacks.

We expressed our appreciation for his taking the time to visit with us

95

THE COVER OF ASIR SANDLER'S BOOK "KNOTS FOR MEMORY", PUBLISHED IN MAGADAN IN 1988

and to share with us his memories of the time he was a political prisoner. The GULag was a rather new area for most of us. He said he knew why he was sent to prison, for he had helped publish poems that were critical of Stalin. First, he was sentenced to death. Then he wrote a letter to the tribunal asking for mercy and his sentence was reduced to ten years of hard labor. His time in the Butugychag uranium mine might have been his most difficult, and yet he survived even with the exposure to the radiation.

Stalin died in 1953 and Asir was released in 1956 during the anti-Stalin campaign of Chairman Nikita Khrushchev. At first, he went to Moscow but found that having been labeled an enemy of the people, a former zek, (prisoner) he was discriminated against and so returned to Magadan where there were many others who shared his terrible experiences in the Kolyma camps.

He told us that for the ten years before arriving in Magadan, he had been transported thousands of miles across the country in railroad cars without any sanitation, water, or heat to prison camps in Azerbaijan, the Urals, the Russian Far East, Siberia, and then the Kolyma. He had first arrived in Magadan in 1948 aboard one of the Dal'stroy Trust prison ships from Vladivostok. Upon arrival, all the prisoners were marched through Magadan to a holding station. Then he was sent to hard labor in the mines of the Kolyma where he worked until 1956. The Kolyma uranium mine of Butugychag was known as one of the very worst places to be sent. Thousands of prisoners died from overwork, a starvation diet, no contact with family or loved ones, poor clothing when working in freezing temperatures of almost minus fifty degrees below zero Celsius, and exposure to radiation from the uranium. Yet as incredible as it sounds, some managed to survive.

During his time in the camps, he said that the prisoners had a difficult time communicating with each other. The guards were always watching and trying to observe any of the zeks thinking they could escape. Asir developed a system where he would tie knots in a string with each knot being part of a secret code. He shared this with his fellow inmates and then they could secretly communicate among themselves. After his release, he wrote a book about his time as a political prisoner called 'Knots for Memory'. He presented us with copies of his little book, and it holds a special place in our family library of Magadan memories. His picture, balls of string, and book are in a special display case in the Magadan Regional Museum Gulag Room. Asir gave me four of his original black and white photographs of Butugychag with his stamp on the back that we have used in our Magdan exhibitions in the past.

JOURNALIST ASIR SANDLER

Asir had been fortunate to assist the doctors in the camps, which allowed him not to work outside in the extreme cold and under the terrible conditions in the mines. After his release, he pursued a degree in medicine and was a doctor in one of the Magadan hospitals. Now he was retired and focused on his writing.

Another old friend of our family, a Professor at our North Eastern State University was Miron Etlis, a Jewish Psychiatrist. Miron was also a GULag survivor. He told us he was sent to a prison in Kazakstan in the 1950s when someone reported him to have told some jokes about Stalin. Many people who were sent to the GULag had been betrayed by a friend or foe. Many never found out who sent some sort of accusing letter to the local KGB and as a result, they were tried and sentenced to years of hard labor in the Stalinist prison camps. He also wrote a book about his memories of being a prisoner in the camps, one of which we placed in the Scott Polar Library at Cambridge University.

THE SOVIET RESTAURANT

For us Alaskans, it was always interesting to visit with friends and colleagues both in their homes or in the local restaurants. Going to a Magadan restaurant was quite different from going to one in the US. In Russia, it was not unusual for this to be a three-hour experience with dining, socializing, dancing, and some form of entertainment.

Often there would be live music for dancing. Children were not a common sight in these restaurants. One would never be in a hurry to eat and run in this setting. Even going to a restaurant for lunch often meant an hour or more experience, as there was often some waiting time between one course and the next. If you had to hurry this was not the place to have lunch, better to go to the college stolovaya (canteen).

It seemed at times that our hosts were trying to stuff us with food so that we would return to Alaska fatter than when we came. Wherever we went food was offered and they expected us to eat and enjoy it. There is no question as to the fact that we enjoyed these times, and everything was unbelievably delicious. One day we had a meeting at a restaurant with a group of teachers from one school at around 2 PM, and a three-course meal was served. That meant we were served zakuska, a salad, then soup, and then the main course usually with meat or fish, and potatoes.

Then at 5 PM we went to another restaurant and met with another group of teachers from two other schools where another full-course meal was served. Again, at 8 PM we had another dinner meeting with teachers from other schools, and after this meeting, we were told that Galina Maximova, Superintendent of Schools, would like to meet with us at the Globus Bar at 11 PM for another late-night dinner. We had been turned into eating machines. It was impossible for us to eat much at the last meeting, we were just too full. We could hardly move to raise a fork to our mouths. All the food was tasty, and we did enjoy all the different Russian dishes we were served, but we did have bodily limits.

Salted salmon eggs, called ikra, were usually on the table at each meal, and are considered a Russian delicacy. But to the average Alaskan, salmon eggs are something used for bait when on the stream fishing. In Russia, the most important part of fishing for salmon is being able to get fresh salmon eggs/roe. No Russian would think of throwing them away. When a female salmon is caught the eggs are handled very carefully, taken home, and prepared to eat on fresh white bread with lots of butter. In Alaska, many fishermen will toss the salmon eggs back into the bushes for the bears or ravens to feast upon. This was unheard of here in Magadan and hard for our Russian hosts to understand. In Magadan, a fisherman might catch a female salmon, take the roe, and then share the fish with the bears, not usual of course. Now, when we are in Russia we take advantage of being able to enjoy fresh salmon ikra on a slice of fresh white bread covered with butter. As in Alaska, eating salmon was a major part of many people's diets each summer and fall.

LAWRENCE H. KHLINOVSKI ROCKHILL

THE RUSSIAN BANYA

One of the most unique experiences for us was the day we spent in the Russian banya (bathhouse) in Snezhnaya Dolina, or Snowy Valley, a resort that was owned by the Communist Party. We went there by bus with several teachers and administrators from the school district. Snezhnaya Dolina is a small village along the Kolyma Highway on the way to the airport in Sokol about a 30-minute drive from Magadan. Here there is a cross-country and downhill skiing training center for Russian National teams to practice when not competing. There were also several Young Pioneer Camps for school-age children to participate in outdoor and nature study programs during the summers. It was a chilly winter day outside, but warm and cozy inside the banya.

The Russian banya is a very old tradition, and yet still enjoyed by many today. An old Russian proverb says, "The day you spend in the Russian banya is the day you do not age." It is said the banya has many health benefits. It helps to clean the skin and fights any sickness as well as helping a person to lose weight. I think that we should also include the fact that a visit to the banya can help a person to feel less stressed. This is also a place where people come just to socialize and visit. Men sit naked in the banya while sharing stories and making important business decisions. Women sit naked to gossip and share secrets about their relatives, kids, and neighbors. Beer (pivo) and vodka are also known to be part of a banya experience. This was a lesson in Russian culture and tradition that we all enjoyed.

The banya interior was cozy and attractive; the walls were mostly panels of beautiful knotty pine wood. There were several rooms including rooms for socializing, eating, and drinking. The main part of the banya is the heated steam room where there were benches along the walls at different levels to sit or lay down. When you enter a Russian banya you disrobe, hang up your clothes in a locker, and take a big sheet to wrap around yourself. Then when you enter the banya steam room you disrobe and go in naked. Upon entering the steam room there was some competition to see who would be able to stand the very hot steam while sitting on the top benches when the water was poured over the red-hot rocks. The higher you sat the hotter it became. I tried the top bench but soon had to move to a lower bench. Even here it was plenty hot for us who were not used to

A GROUP OF MAGADAN SCHOOL NO. 1 CHILDREN AT THE ENTRANCE TO SOLDOTNA ELEMENTARY SCHOOL. FEBRUARY 23, 1989 OXOTNIK PRESS ARCHIVES

this type of experience. It doesn't take long to work up a good sweat and then you know you are in a real Russian banya. There is a bowl of cool water and a sponge that is passed around for you to rinse off. After a while, you begin to feel calm and relaxed. Just outside the steam room, there were two large tubs about 8 feet long and 4 feet deep, one with cold and the other with warm water, to dip in after you finish in the steam room.

Usually, the banschik, a professional banya employee in charge of the correct use of the steaming rooms and steaming procedures and birch branches whipping experiences, is in charge of raising the temperature inside the banya by taking a ladle, dipping it into a bucket of water, and then throwing the water on the red-hot rocks at the end of the room. This creates big steam and instantly raises the temperature, especially at the higher benches. Those of us banya novices did our best to grin and bear it and stay on the lower benches, even though we were 'encouraged 'by the banya experts to go up to the top benches like 'real Russians'.

We were a little apprehensive at first because we heard that when you are in the banya you get beaten by the banschik with birch tree branches and leaves. We found out later that the banschik beats you with the birch tree leaves to distribute the hot air all over your body. This is only mildly painful and good for your health. It is also a lot of work for the banschik to stand up there and do this in such heat. I remember when Victor Vikhlyantsev was the banschik, and after doing his job he became one walking sweat machine. But we felt really good due to his hard work.

After spending some time in the banya, and then cooling down in one of the little pools, we would go and lounge around the eating area and have some of the delicious snacks that they brought. Our gracious hosts brought food and drink for everyone since the banya was an experience in eating and socializing, as well as roasting your body in extreme heat. Russian tradition dictated that there was a lot to eat with the spread of cucumbers, black bread, lots of sausages, smoked salmon and other fish, Russian dark chocolate, lemonade, and of course Russian vodka for the adults to be able to toast to long-lasting Soviet and American peace and friendship.

We had a special theme song that was popular during our visit called, not surprisingly, "Magadan". Someone brought a boom box that could play this song and other popular music like the Lambada. So, dressed in our Roman toga-like sheets it was up on top of the tables, and a chorus line of teachers acting a bit wild and dancing. It was always a time of good conversation about life in Alaska and Magadan, as well as what was going on between Gorbachev and Reagan.

The eight days that shook and changed our world went by much too quickly, and we had to get ready to say our sad goodbyes and return to Anchorage. Here was a place where we had developed real friendships with our Magadan hosts who had made us feel so welcome. Never were we at a loss for topics to discuss, interesting places to visit, events, or delicious food and drink. We all hoped that soon our efforts to melt the Ice Curtain would be successful, and we could come together like this more frequently.

On the morning of our departure, we five bordered our special bus and were escorted out to the airport by school and city administration staff as well as host family members and students. After checking in with our boxes of gifts from our new friends it was waiting until we were called to board the Aeroflot Tu-154 sitting on the ramp.

We were not very happy to be leaving, a gross understatement. There were some sad faces, but we also felt so happy that we had, at last, made our dream come true and were now convinced that this would not be the last time we would all come together.

CHAPTER SIX:
BACK OVER THE ICE CURTAIN TWICE

We had many meetings to discuss the possibilities of continuing the Alaska-Magadan Educational Exchange Program with Magadan administrators and teachers.

We returned to Soldotna feeling that the beginning of our dream to bring Magadan and Alaskan students together had begun. Now it was time to plan for the next step in our dream, the first real educational exchange program between Magadan and Alaska students. We wrote many trip reports and had meetings with Superintendent Dr. Pomeroy, who was incredibly pleased and supported our further endeavors. We had signed protocols with the Magadan School administrators to bring 40 students and teachers in both directions with a focus on ecological problems and research in both countries. Each student would select a topic of their interest, do their research, and prepare to share it with their counterparts when they participated in the exchange.

PROCLAMATION FROM THE ALASKA STATE LEGISLATURE HONORING THE SOLDOTNA - MAGADAN YOUTH EXCHANGE PROGRAM

Upon our return, we were surprised to receive a proclamation from the Alaska State Legislature "Honoring the Soldotna-Magadan Youth Exchange Program". It was signed by Samuel R. Cotton, Speaker of the House, and Senator Tim Kelley, President of the Senate with a gold seal and ribbon attached. This proclamation read,

The members of the Sixteenth Alaska Legislature take great pride in honoring students, teachers, and officials from Soldotna Elementary School and Magadan School No.1 for their efforts in spearheading a student-teacher exchange between Alaska and the Soviet Far-East Territory of Magadan Oblast.

The student-teacher exchange is a direct result of the Soviet Studies Program taught by Soldotna Elementary teacher Larry Rockhill and Rick Mataya, bilingual coordinator. The program, initiated in 1986, included a letter-writing program for sixth graders and teachers at Soldotna Elementary School to Soviet students and officials. In the fall of 1987 three letters arrived from students in School No.1 in Magadan expressing their desire to communicate with the Soldotna students. The intense interest of the Magadan students, school, and community in receiving letters from youth in Soldotna was detailed in a follow-up letter from a teacher in Magadan who described the press coverage in the opening of the letters and subsequent placing of them in a community museum.

Since the initial contact, numerous letters have been exchanged between class members of both schools on a personal level and between classes. When the Alaska Airlines "Friendship Flight" landed in Provideniya on June 30, 1988, the Alaskan delegation was repeatedly asked, "Where are the students from Soldotna?" The return (Russian ship Dimitry Laptev) of the "Friendship Flight" to Nome and Anchorage provided the first opportunity for the Soldotna youth to have personal contact with representatives from Provideniya and Magadan.

During a presentation in Nome (1988), Soldotna student representatives Virginia Harvey and Jennifer Wagner presented a formal invitation to the Soviet delegation for teachers and students from Soldotna and Magadan to come together to further enhance and deepen the spirit of further understanding, friendship, and humanistic potential of people on both sides of the Bering Sea.

In October of 1988, an official delegation from the Governor's Office of International Trade traveled to Khabarovsk to sign mutual agreements in trade, resource development, and education and cultural exchanges. During this meeting, an official invitation was sent from the city of Magadan to invite Soldotna youth to Magadan for a youth summit. The invitation was formalized in writing at the signing of the Alaska Trade and Friendship Mission to the Soviet Far East Trade Agreement.

This is the first time in Alaska's history that Alaskan students have been officially invited to participate in a student-teacher exchange program with the Soviet Union. It is also the first time in the Nation's history that United States students and teachers have been invited to Magadan. This project has been in the making for three years and has taken place due to the youthful desire and exuberance of the Soldotna and Magadan children. They exemplify to both the United States and the Soviet Union that the Ice Curtain between our countries can be slowly melted and that we can all come together as friends.

SIGNED: Samuel R. Cotton, Speaker of the House, and Tim Kelly, President of the Senate Gold Seal of the State of Alaska

Peninsula Clarion

Letter to the Editor, April 25, 1989

Magadan and Soldotna children show the way to hope for a peaceful future. To the editor:

Although after eight days of visiting Magadan at a whirlwind pace, one cannot come away with an in-depth knowledge of the city, its people, or their educational system, there are certainly many deep and lasting impressions that one does come away with. The deepest impression I believe we came away with was the warmth and friendliness of the teachers, the students, and virtually all of the people. Wherever we went we were greeted as though we were returning members of a family who had experienced a long separation. Open to us were not only their arms but their minds and their hearts. It was clear that they had gone to great lengths for our visit. After all, we were the first 'ordinary 'Americans to visit Magadan since well before the Great Patriotic War. Only a few journalists and scientists had received permission to visit this area before. For the most part, these visitors had little contact with the average citizen. Of some amazement to them was the fact that we were just average teachers and students. Several Soviet people commented that after talking with us their stereotypes of Americans seemed to vanish. It was the same for us. Yet, we certainly were not treated as though we were ordinary. Ordinary people do not travel with police escorts, receive beautiful gifts at meetings after meetings with high government, city, and school officials, or have demands placed on their time until the wee hours of the morning. Yet there was still neither enough time nor enough of us to go around for all those deserving people to have a first-hand experience with an average American. People meeting people is worth a thousand books. We spoke in assemblies, meetings, classrooms, and homes. There was not nearly enough time to answer all their questions, which ranged from the content of our social studies curriculum to what Soldotna was like as a place to live.

We sat around the heartbeat of their homes, the kitchen table, and drank fine Russian tea from a traditional samovar. They made us feel loved and accepted. We discussed free enterprise, childrearing, perestroika, education, glasnost, daily life, democracy, peace, and communism. We shared meals in their homes and slept in their beds, which were often given up for us. We were open and honest with each other. Neither of us had to tell the other about their countries' problems. We came together in a spirit of sharing and learning from each other. For them, Peter the Great's 'Window on the West 'had been re-opened. But now they found themselves looking east towards Alaska. Since few at this time ever had the opportunity to see life in the West for themselves, our friends at this time had to see life in the West through our eyes. We tried our utmost to be honest and truthful.

For the past three years, the youth in Magadan gained some idea of life in Alaska from the pen-pal letters they received from Soldotna Elementary sixth graders. Their letters provided the youth in both countries with what life was like for the other. But most of all it showed the great similarities between those of us separated by the Ice Curtain in the middle of the Bering Sea.

In Magadan, more often than not, both parents work. Most people loved pets, school work took up a lot of the students' time, stamps and pins were fun to collect and they liked to play sports.

Many Soldotna students were amazed at how much they had in common with Magadan students. It must have been the same in Magadan. Certainly, it is impossible to measure the impact of one student's letter. With how many people does a child share her/his enthusiasm and excitement upon receiving a pen-pal letter? In these past three years, several hundred letters of goodwill and friendship have been received by students in Magadan and Soldotna.

Несколько встреч с педагогами и школьниками Аляски

В ПЕРВУЮ школу 21 февраля приехали гости из Америки: педагоги Лэрри и Нэнси Рокхилл, Рик Мейайа, ученики школы средней ступени Вирджиния Харвей, Джеймс Кэнэвэ, Майя Моргенвек и репортер местной газеты Рой Шали, чьи усилия в немалой степени способствовали успеху в организации приезда группы в СССР.

Событие вышло далеко за пределы школы. Оно стало общегородским. Гости побывали не только в СШ № 1, они встретились с ребятами из других школ города, побывали в магаданских музеях, в Доме отдыха на Снежной Долине, побеседовали с представителями совет-

— Есть ли у вас школьная форма?

— Школьной формы у нас нет, но определенные рамки соблюдаем.

— Есть ли в вашем городе небоскребы?

— Небоскребы есть в Анкоридже...

Иссяк поток вопросов и начался обмен подарками. В дар гостям ребята преподнесли пионерские галстуки, а руководителю делегации, страстному коллекционеру Лэрри Рокхиллу, зная, что объект его увлечения — военная форма всех стран, хозяйка встречи Е. Нечипорова вручила матросскую форму нашего военно-морского флота.

— Берег Аляски, — сказал Лэрри Рокхилл, — называют еще Рус-

Нэнси и Лэрри открывают Россию

Когда три года назад члены клуба интернациональной дружбы первой школы Магадана опустили в почтовый ящик письмо с адресом: Солдотна, Аляска, США, Рокхиллам — на встречу со своими адресатами они вряд ли надеялись. Ведь между такими близкими населенными пунктами стоял занавес, воздвигнутый десятилетиями непонимания. И одним из чудес, подаренных народам США и СССР перестройкой в нашей стране, стало чудо встречи педагогов и школьников с Аляски со своими коллегами и сверстниками в Магадане

ских и партийных органов, журналистами газеты «Магаданская правда». В этих встречах принимала участие ваш корреспондент Екатерина Кузенко. Предлагаем вашему вниманию ее короткий отчет.

23 ФЕВРАЛЯ, 15.00 магаданского времени. Фойе областной библиотеки имени Пушкина заполнили ребята магаданских школ. Тут и танцевальный ансамбль в русских национальных костюмах из Магаданского Дома пионеров и школьников, и кружка по изучению английского языка, и хоровой детской студии, и те, кто просто пришли, чтобы пообщаться со своими сверстниками из Америки. Приветственное слово секретаря горкома ВЛКСМ Елена Нечипоровой, а затем — диалог между ребятами. Пусть их вопросы не кажутся вам наивными: слишком мало знали мы друг о друге, а поэтому школьникам интересовало все.

— Есть ли оценки в американских школах, если есть, едина ли их система?

— Да, есть. Только нам ставят не цифры, 5, 4 и т. д., а буквы — от «А» по «F». Система единая.

— Чем вы занимаетесь в свободное время?

— Занимаемся спортом, катаемся на велосипедах, читаем, любим баскетбол и хоккей, смотрим ТВ.

— Есть ли у вас пионерская организация?

— Пионерской организации нет, но есть организация скаутов для мальчиков и девочек и общества: пожарных, любителей природы и много других. Мы очень любим мероприятия, которые...

— Какие у вас отношения с учителями?

— Отношения с учителем зависят от нашего поведения.

— Сколько у вас уроков и какова их продол-

ской Америкой. Память о ее первооткрывателях хранится у нас до сих пор. Это были русские моряки. И, принимая подарок, я, вспоминая также о том, что в годы войны мы были союзниками, мы были с фашизмом, и наши воины пожимали друг другу руки на берегу Эльбы. Ваша страна открыла двери для нас, а наши сердца и двери всегда открыты для вас. И мы надеемся, что эти двери никогда не будут закрыты.

После процедуры обмена адресами между русскими и американскими школьниками, короткого концерта на английском языке я воспользовалась возможностью побеседовать с Нэнси Рокхилл. Гостья охотно откликнулась на мою просьбу.

— Нэнси, расскажите немного о школе, где вы работаете?

— Наша школа включает три ступени: начальную, среднюю и высшую. Я работаю в школе начальной ступени. В ней занимаются ребята от 5 до двенадцати лет. Младшие школьники — это детский сад, где проводится подготовка к школе. В наших классах занимается от 22 до 27 детей. Занимается с ними один педагог, который ведет все предметы, за исключением музыки, физкультуры и библиотечного

ете?

— В основном мы практикуем коллоквиумы. А вообще каждый учитель ведет занятия по своему усмотрению, все зависит от его индивидуальности, а также индивидуальности его учеников.

— Вы упомянули предмет «библиотечное дело», в чем его суть?

— Наши ребята к пятнадцати готовят доклады, конспекты, просто короткие выступления.

или есть еще и другие?

— Мы переписываемся со многими странами. И во многих уже побывали. Это очень расширяет кругозор ребят.

— Какие иностранные языки изучают ваши школьники?

— Начиная со второй ступени, у нас изучают французский, немецкий и испанский языки. Изучение языка — выборочно. Школьник может и вовсе не учить, а может — и не три. Все зависит от его желания и индивидуальных способностей.

— И последний, традиционный вопрос. Какое впечатление осталось у вас от нашей школы номер один, от самой поездки?

— Мы посетили многие страны. Но такого радушия, такого широкого участия взрослых не встречали нигде.

В ВЕЧЕРОМ того же дня в видеобаре «Меридиан» состоялась встреча педагогов первой школы с гостями из-за рубежа. Здесь присутствовали все взрослые члены делегации. Так случилось, что 23 февраля, день своего рождения, Нэнси отпраздновала у нас, в Магадане. О празднике, приветствиях, подарках, о том, как расплакалась наша гостья, растроганная горячим приемом, мы уже рассказали. Хочется передать ее ответное слово.

— Долгое время мы очень мало знали о вашей стране. Из переписки мы поняли, что в Советском Союзе интересуются нашей страной, что здесь живет народ, желающий доброго соседства с нами. Собираясь к вам в Магадан, мы готовились к встрече с друзьями, но на такой фантастически радушный прием не рассчитывали. Большое вам спасибо, друзья!

— На следующий день гостей из-за рубежа: репортера и заместителя редактора местной газеты «Пенинсула Кларион» Роя Шали и педагога, общественного деятеля Ларри Рокхилла — принимали в редак-

тересуются историей России. Он публикует не только в своем еженедельнике, но и на страницах анкориджских газет, и эти публикации сделали «набивого» Лэрри Рокхилла, борцу за мир и искреннему другу нашей страны. На вопрос об источнике знаний о нашей стране и интересе к ней Рой ответил:

— Когда я приехал в ваш небольшой город, я сразу заметил, что он общался живо интересуется историей России, хранит в памяти предания о первооткрывателях нашей земли, сам полуостров изобилует русскими географическими названиями. Все это возбудило интерес к вашей истории. В лице Лэрри Рокхилла, человека обширных интересов и глубоких познаний, изучающего русский язык, я нашел великолепного собеседника. Он и помог мне расширить свои познания. А когда пришло первое письмо от магаданских школьников, оно было опубликовано на страницах газеты «Пенинсула Кларион».

— Наши газеты тоже сообщали о переписке американских и советских школьников, то есть не зная об этом, мы сотрудничали уже тогда. А возможно ли сохранить связь между нашими городами, установив обмен газетными материалами?

— Вполне. Через спутниковую связи мы можем принимать ваши материалы, хранить их в памяти компьютеров. Все возможно, нужно лишь ваше согласие.

— Какие впечатления остались у вас от поездки в наш город?

— Журналист должен быть беспристрастным. Но видя множество радостных, приветливых лиц, в беседах с милыми людьми, слушая слова дружбы, оставаться беспристрастным очень трудно. По возвращении домой я сделаю репортаж о самой поездке, но точно передам и то, что здесь видел. Это будет главный репортаж моей жизни.

дмет «библиотечное дело», в чем его суть?

— Наши ребята к пятнадцати готовят доклады, конспекты, просто короткие выступления.

В первой школе мы посетили несколько уроков. От этого посещения впечатление осталось великолепное. А вообще, должна сказать, что мы слишком мало побывали в

ции газеты «Магаданская правда».

В вопросах наших журналистов к американскому коллеге —

НА СНИМКАХ:

The greatest potential for peace in this world lies in the minds and hearts of the children of the world. We as educators must ask what we are doing for the development of this potential for world peace. Educators and politicians must share the greatest responsibility for leading the way. The children of Soldotna Elementary and Magadan School No.1 have taken a big step in bringing our countries closer together in global unity. This effort on the part of these students led to an important first in Alaskan education. On February 20th, 1989, a Soviet jet, Aeroflot Flight 2315, flew the first Alaskans, three teachers and three students, and one Peninsula Clarion journalist to Magadan as part of the first Alaska-Soviet Educational Exchange Program. Coming east from Magadan School No.1 were the first educators and students to participate in such a program. It is hopefully only the first step in a long journey that will continue to lead to better understanding and peace in the world. Let us not forget that the children played a significant role.

Now a bridge has been built across the Bering Sea under the leadership of Gov. Vyacheslav Kobets of Magadan and Gov. Steve Cowper of Alaska. The Ice Curtain has melted, and the bridge is standing on a firm foundation of friendship and understanding. This bridge will permit us to come together to strengthen the foundation of peace and goodwill laid by the people of Alaska and Magadan. We have once again been united in our common Russian heritage. Now that this bridge of understanding and peace stretches across the sea, we must do all we can, on both sides, to bring the children and the teachers of Alaska and Magadan together to continue strengthening the bond of friendship. Our world depends on it.

In his recent letter to Virginia Harvey, James Cannava, and Maija Morgenweck, President Bush said, "Your visit to Magadan offers hope that the new spirit of cooperation and goodwill between the United States and the Soviet Union will continue to grow". If left to the hearts and minds of such fine young people like these there is no question but that it will grow and flourish.

The snow geese are flying again, carrying the spirit of Alaskan goodwill to Magadan. My spirit too is borne upon their wings.

Larry Rockhill, Soldotna Elementary School

THE PAGE OF "THE MAGADAN KOMSOMOLETS NEWSPAPER" DATED MARCH 5, 1989 WITH AN ARTICLE BY JOURNALIST SERGEY BRAGA "NANCY AND LARRY DISCOVER RUSSIA". THE PHOTOS WERE TAKEN BY VALERY OSTRIKOV

BACK TO MAGADAN — NEXT STUDENT EXCHANGE

After returning to the Kenai Peninsula Borough School District, Betty Leonard, Rick Mataya and I made arrangements to return to Magadan in July via Tokyo, and an Aeroflot flight from Nakhodka to Magadan. It took us two days instead of the original four-hour flight from Anchorage directly across the Bering Sea to Magadan. Overnight in Tokyo provided for a dinner out on the town and not much else. We landed at the airport in Sokol and were again greeted by our dear friends and colleagues and went to stay with host families. Finally, we were back in our Soviet hometown, Magadan, sitting around the chainik (teapot) in our friends 'kitchens drinking fine Russky chai and discussing our future plans. Costco was again part of the program with jars of Folgers coffee, Snickers candy bars, summer sausage, and other gifts.

The second day was back walking along the tamarack-lined Ulitsa Lenina up the hill to meetings with administrators and teachers. This was to be a short working trip with the focus on figuring out the details of what would be an exchange of 40 students and teachers. We had a lot to think about before this would take place.

We three spent the better part of the next few days in meetings with School District administrators and teachers, our new Magadan friends. Our first order of business was to discuss just what the next exchange would focus on. After some discussion, we all agreed that the most relevant topic would be the ecology of both respective regions. Now it was necessary to determine how best for the students to share the information that they would obtain from their research. We felt that the easiest way was for each student to present his/her research findings during school meetings that would be scheduled during their visits when they arrived in their host country. This would have to be set up by the hosting school staff before the student's arrival. When the students would present the results of their research findings, they would be discussed by those in attendance. So here it would have to be only upper-grade students from science classes that would be involved. We had ironed out the details as much as we could. After our meetings, the evenings were spent enjoying the White Nights and just relaxing and visiting with our friends. Magadan also is blessed with the White Nights of a Northern summer, and one finds many people out walking. Nagaeva Bay was not far away if one wanted to walk along the sea and enjoy the view.

A LARGE CRAB THAT WAS CAUGHT WHEN RICK AND I WENT OUT FISHING ON NAGAEVA BAY WITH GOVORNER KOBETS, MAGADAN, 1989. PHOTO BY PAVEL ZHDANOV

Now that the basics of the next student exchange program were settled it was getting to be time to again return to Soldotna and help the teachers and administrators get on with the actual plans for when the Magadan students and teachers would arrive. We again had to face leaving our dear friends, not easy, but with hopes of coming back in the not-too-distant future.

But who could refuse when being invited by Governor Kobets to go out fishing on Nagaeva Bay on a warm sunny day? So, two days before we were to fly back to Alaska, we readily accepted his invitation, and he picked us up and we drove to the Magadan seaport (Morport), where his boat was tied up and went aboard. Being out on Nagaeva Bay on a beautiful sunny day was a pure pleasure after two days of traveling in airplanes and being in a hotel, then three days in meetings. Nagaeva Bay is a Kolyma treasure. We all were successful at catching some fish, enough for our supper. Vyacheslav took the boat right up to the beach and we all jumped out. It

A DAY OF FISHING WITH GOV. KOBETS. SOON THERE WOULD BE FISH SOUP FOR ALL. 1989 PHOTO BY PAVEL ZHDANOV

was all ashore and our hosts, along with Pasha Zhdanov, quickly built a campfire on the beach and in a large pot placed the catch of the day for ukha, delicious fish soup. The usual driftwood table was set with black bread, veggies, cheese, sausage, and chai. Somehow, I remember there just happened to be a bottle or two of fine Russian vodka for the mandatory toasts of mir i druzhba to our two countries. We had become close friends with Vyacheslav Kobets who was always supportive of our program.

After spending the day fishing on the Nagaeva Bay, and a real Russian picnic, it was back to Magadan and a drive out the Kolyma Trassa to Snezhnaya Dolina to the Communist Party banya. We would now have a chance to just relax and visit as well as enjoy the Russian tradition of the banya, visiting, eating, and toasting. Not hard for us Alaskans to experience. After several visits to the steam room, and being encouraged by Vyacheslav, and his Russian friends, to be like real Russians and to sit higher on the steam room benches when he threw water on the red hot rocks, it was time for another toast and rest. We slept well that night as people do after banya. The next morning, we had the usual breakfast of what was left from the night before, well except for the vodka. Then it was back to Magadan since we had to get back to work ironing out a few last- minute details before it was time to depart from our dear friends again.

VYACHESLAV KOBETS, RICK MATAYA, DMITRY POLETAEV AND LARRY ROCKHILL (WITH HIS BACK TO CAMERA) OUT FISHING ON NAGAEVA BAY. JUNE.1989 PHOTO BY PAVEL ZHDANOV

After returning to Soldotna we met with Dr. Fred Pomeroy, other administrators, and interested teachers, and shared with them the results of our meetings with the Magadan School District Administration. They were quite pleased and said we should continue to set a schedule for the next Student-Teacher Exchange Program focusing on the ecology of both regions, Alaska and Magadan. This student-teacher program would continue next year and beyond.

CHAPTER SEVEN:
ROMAN TCHAIKOVSKI AND EVGENY KOKOREV

However, before leaving Magadan I had one last item on my agenda that I had to deal with. Being able to spend a year living in Magadan and teaching at one of their schools was always on my mind. Earlier I had mentioned this to some of my friends who were English Language teachers at School No.1. They suggested that I would be more valuable teaching at Magadan Pedagogical Institute (MPI) rather than in a secondary school, as one of the main deficits of the college English Language Program was that the students were not able to interact with a Native English-speaking professor. So, I took their advice, and the result was a life-changing experience for me. I made an appointment and went to meet with Dr. Evgeny Kokorev and Prof. Roman Tchaikovsky at Magadan Pedagogical Institute.

Magadan Pedagogical Institute dates from 1960 and is the main teacher's college in the entire region (oblast). Here students can major in all areas that are taught in both elementary and secondary schools, as well as Early Childhood Education. Each course of study is an intensive five-year program with no electives. Those students completing the five-year English intensive course of study know the English language in a far more in-depth way than most native English Language speakers in the US.

I walked over to the red brick building and up the stairs and first met with Roman in his office. He then took me to Evgeny's office in the new building. Evgeny, Roman, and I had an important talk about the possibility of developing an exchange program between MPI and the University of Alaska. I explained my idea of what might be accomplished with students and teachers coming to each other's institutions and both giving classes and taking classes. They were interested and suggested that I return and see if this would be of interest to the President of the University of Alaska. They invited me to come to MPI and become a professor in the Foreign Language Department. I said I would be very interested in doing this and would have to first propose this to the President of the University of Alaska and then if he approves, I will have to get permission from my Superintendent. It already being July did not leave me a lot of time to accomplish this. But I agreed and on I went.

Evgeny Kokorev, Rector of MPI was a professor of Sociology, a severely marginalized field of social inquiry in the Soviet times. He had recently moved into his office in the new building that had just opened. It was the usual office of an important Soviet administrator with a beautiful large wood desk in two parts, one part of the desk he sat behind, and the other part was a long table stretched out perpendicular to his desk for people to sit at when they attended meetings with him. He also had several desk telephones on his desk since multi-line phones were not available at that time and the more phones one had on their desk indicated how important one was. Just as you entered on the right was a tall bookcase that held several rows of books bound in blue cloth. These were easily recognized as a complete set of the works of Lenin. He said this was not his favorite reading material. Behind his desk was the flag of the Soviet Union, the flag of the Russian Republic, and the flag of Magadan, and soon there would be an Alaska flag too.

Upon returning to Soldotna, I contacted my good friend Bob Williams, President of the Board of Regents of the University of Alaska. Bob was part of our Magadan School Program and had met with Gov. Kobets during his visit to my school. I told him about my idea to have an exchange program between the University of Alaska and the Magadan Pedagogical Institute. He understood the benefits to students and teachers on both sides and said he would be glad to help. I suggested that we write a letter to Don O'Dowd, President of the University of Alaska, and present the program to him. The letter would be signed by Bob as President of the UA Board of Regents. Since the Board of Regents was essentially

GRETCHEN BERSCH AWARD CEREMONY AT SVSU. PROFESSOR OF SVSU ROMAN TCHAIKOVSKY, PROFESSOR OF THE UNIVERSITY OF ALASKA GRETCHEN BERSCH AND ASSOCIATE PROFESSOR OF THE DEPARTMENT OF FOREIGN PHILOLOGY EKATERINA SHERSTNEVA. DECEMBER. 2014 PHOTO BY PAVEL ZHDANOV

over the President of the University of Alaska, I thought that at least O'Dowd would give my idea some consideration, and he did. He invited me to come to Fairbanks and meet with him to discuss my proposal, which I did. After a thorough discussion, he agreed to my proposal and suggested that I accept the offer to return for a year to MPI and both teach and coordinate the UA-MPI Exchange Program. He offered me a position on the UA faculty, and so I accepted and then went to present this to my Superintendent, Dr. Fred Pomeroy in Soldotna.

After returning to Soldotna, I met with Dr. Pomeroy and we discussed the possibility for me to take a one-year sabbatical, and what would be both fair to me and the school district. We agreed I would not take a salary, but the school district would pay into my retirement and my health insurance. Then I had to find a renter for my house so I would be able to make my monthly house payment. I would be paid in Soviet rubles in Magadan which would not be of much help with my Alaskan expenses. However, I knew the Magadan experience would more than make up for the currency exchange rate.

IN 1993, THE BOARD OF TRUSTEES OF THE MAGADAN INTERNATIONAL PEDAGOGICAL UNIVERSITY AWARDED MR. LARRY ROCKHILL THE TITLE OF "HONORARY PROFESSOR OF THE MAGADAN INTERNATIONAL PEDAGOGICAL UNIVERSITY". PROFESSOR KOKOREV, THE PRESIDENT OF MGPU. PRESENTS LARRY ROCKHILL WITH THE DIPLOMA OF "HONORARY PROFESSOR" PHOTO BY PAVEL ZHDANOV

GETTING READY TO HEAD OVER
AND ABOVE THE ICE CURTAIN.

I received an official invitation from Rector Kokorev and was invited to come and teach English and American Studies at Magadan Pedagogical Institute. Now I had met with the President of the University of Alaska regarding a UA-MPI exchange program and also with my Superintendent. Both supported my proposal for the exchange program and so I made plans to take a one-year sabbatical to return to Magadan. I now had to apply for my Soviet visa with an invitation from Rector Kokorev. Whenever you applied for a Soviet visa you were never sure when and if it would arrive. I was fortunate and it arrived shortly before my departure on an Aeroflot charter for Magadan in September 1989.

Being not sure what to expect, I was surprised to see that I had been granted a single-entry, one- year Soviet visa. This was a separate piece of paper since they did not put a stamp on your passport. A one-year visa was unheard of at that time and even today not usual. However, I was later to discover the meaning of a single-entry visa.

115

Now that my hopes and dreams were coming true, I was a happy man. Soon I would be back with my dear Soviet/Russian friends that I felt so close to and experiencing new adventures.

I found out that Dima Poletaev had come to Anchorage to be a translator for a group of Alaskan business people going to Magadan. We met and made arrangements to fly together on an Aeroflot flight chartered by an Alaskan group. We flew on an Aeroflot An-24 from Anchorage via Provideniya, and Anadyr to Magadan. Most passengers were Alaskan businessmen who were traveling to Magadan to meet with possible clients to set up different types of import/export business connections. This was the time when Alaska was the closest place for purchasing and shipping consumer goods that were mostly unavailable in the Magadan region and had been for years. What was an ordinary consumer item for most Alaskans could be only a dream for the average Soviet person living in Magadan.

After taking off from Anchorage we flew north towards Nome where we headed out across the Bering Sea, to the coast of the Russian Far North. We soon landed in Provideniya, a small Northern seaport town of around 2000 people built on a bay of the same name. It is almost directly across the Bering Straits from Nome, Alaska. After landing we were invited to go into the terminal where it was nice and warm and enjoy a cup of tea and a snack. Here the Border Guards, acting as customs agents found and confiscated an English language book that probably had crossed the Soviet border for the first time. Dima brought the popular, and many would say not pornographic, book, 'The Joy of Sex' that he had purchased in the Book Cache, an Anchorage book shop.

Although the text was in English, the illustrations were internationally understood. He protested in vain, and I am sure that this book was not destroyed according to Soviet law but was one of the most frequently read books in Provideniya at this time. I was taking a few boxes of gifts from Alaskans to their Magadan friends, as well as my luggage and boxes of items that I would need to live in Magadan for the year. But nothing I had was to spark the interest of the young Border Guards as this little item.

Here, the Soviet Army Border Guards in their bright green uniforms had the responsibility and fun if you will, of going through all of our baggage. All the baggage of the Alaskan business people meant that the Border Guards would need several hours to go through it. What could be more interesting for these young Soviet Border Guards stationed in a far northern remote outpost like Provideniya than to go through a group's luggage full of American consumer goods that were not available to most people in the Soviet Union at that time? I am sure it was a rather memorable day for them. After waiting in the terminal buffet and having tea, coffee, and snacks, it was back to the Aeroflot An-24 and our flight to Anadyr.

Anadyr was the administrative center of the Chukotka Okrug with a population of around 3000 in 1989. The economic base of this region centered on the mining of coal, fishing, and gold. Much of the urban population was employed in the Okrug Administration, education, construction work, and the fishing industry. A significant part of the Native population was involved in the herding of reindeer, and some subsistence hunting and fishing, however, not in their traditional ways during pre-Soviet times. The Native population here, and across the Russian North, had experienced a high degree of acculturation and Russification. Most Native people in the rural villages and towns were organized and employed in state-run sovkhoz and kolkhoz collective farms related to fishing and hunting.

We only stopped in Anadyr long enough to refuel and have a cup of chai in the airport cafe. Then it was a four-hour flight to Magadan. The Aeroflot pilot and crew were friendly and invited us to come and spend some time with them in the cockpit. I was able to share an emergency strobe light with the pilot that my FAA friend Earl Craig had given me. I gave a few Alaskan souvenir flag pins to the other crew members. Again, it was a surprise to find such openness when we thought it would be a much more closed situation, especially for foreigners.

CHAPTER EIGHT:
MY NEW HOME, MAGADAN

Aeroflot was becoming my favorite airline and I soon arrived back in Magadan, USSR, with my colleague Dima Poletaev, on the 16th of September, 1989. This was the third time I had traveled to Magadan this year. Nice to be back.

DIARY: Arriving at the Magadan Airport we were greeted by my dear friends Professor Roman Tchaikovsky, Chair of the Foreign Language Department, and Pavel Zhdanov from School No.1. We loaded all our boxes and suitcases onto a Magadan Pedagogical Institute truck. Then we hopped in the MPI Volga sedan and headed the 52 Km to Magadan. Arriving at my new flat we took all my things up the three flights of stairs and set them inside. Some friends from School No.1 had come and prepared a nice welcome dinner for all of us. We sat down to a delicious chicken dinner, with my favorite trubach mollusk salad, which included a few vodka toasts to Magadan and Alaska peace and friendship. At last, I felt that I had come home to Magadan. (24 Sept. 1989)

My new address was Dom 5B, Kvartira 29 on Ulitsa Boldyreva (Boldyreva Street, building 5B, flat 29) in the city of Magadan, Russia, USSR. It was provided for me through an agreement between the Magadan Pedagogical Institute and Gennady Dorofeev, Magadan City Mayor.

Since this was the third time I had traveled to Magadan, I was somewhat familiar with the city since I usually walked wherever I had to go. Now, living here would provide me with the opportunity to know it as my hometown. Most apartment blocks in the Soviet Union were conveniently located near food shops and other stores, which made shopping rather easy, that is when the shops had what you wanted to buy. My flat was on the fourth floor of a typical four-story apartment block from the Brezhnev era, and it overlooked a small park filled with tamarack-listvennitsa trees, and to the left, School No.14. I had a great view of the low-lying hills beyond the little Magadanka River maybe a mile away. Soon these hills would be covered with termination dust since winter comes early in Magadan.

Moving from a three-bedroom, 1600 sq. ft. house in Soldotna, Alaska to a one-room flat in Magadan did provide some food for thought. I had been in several people's flats during previous visits to Magadan and so had a good idea of what my flat would be like. I realized that the contrast was going to be quite evident. I was ready to initiate a minimalist living program as one might do when moving to a monastery, although it was not quite that minimalist. The priority was to bring warm winter clothes, a few books that I could use in teaching, my Panasonic boom box with some of my favorite music tapes, an old Navajo rug that I liked, and some gifts I would need to share when visiting friends. All this was contained in one medium-sized suitcase and two medium-sized cardboard boxes.

When I walked in the door for the first time I was a bit surprised at how nicely my one-room flat was furnished. I thought it was a bit more than I needed, not minimalist at all. The kitchen was completely outfitted with all the pots, pans, and utensils I would need. There was even a set of GDR (German Democratic Republic) fine china, a gift from Rector Evgeny Kokorev that I would eventually take with me when I left to return to Alaska. My flat was a usual one-room Soviet flat where the main room was the living area, dining room, and sleeping room, and also, there was a bathroom, a toilet, and a separate medium-sized kitchen that had an electric stove, refrigerator and sink for washing dishes. There was also a small table that could seat four. The main room had a couch and two folding armchairs that would open up into rather narrow single beds. This was not the most comfortable since the arms of the chair/bed did not permit any sort of stretching out. The couch was situated along one wall and the other wall was aligned with dark wood bookcases and cabinets, some with glass doors. In front of the couch was a long coffee table that could be used for serving food. This furniture was all new, quite nice, and rather expensive by Soviet standards. The way my flat was furnished, and just the idea that I was given a flat of my own to live in, made me a bit uncomfortable. I think I would have been just fine, and maybe even better off if I had been living in a communal flat and shared a bathroom, toilet, and kitchen with other Soviet families. It would have also forced me to develop my Russian Language skills to a higher level. This flat was not only quite comfortable but also quite convenient when walking to the Institute. I tried to show my appreciation to both Mayor Gennady Dorofeev and Rector Evgeny Kokorev.

I knew that there were several communal apartment buildings in Magadan where people lived who had been waiting for months or even years to be able to move into a flat of their own. In a communal flat, a person or even a family usually has one room and has to share a toilet, bathroom, and kitchen with several other people who live under the same conditions. I knew two families who lived in this type of flat. It is not hard to imagine the potential for problems to arise between tenants under these conditions, especially when vodka was part of the problem. And there was always the question of who was responsible for cleaning this area or that area. It seemed that some people felt that if it belonged to everybody-communal property, then it really belonged to nobody and therefore not their responsibility.

All flats were state-owned and usually provided to the workers from their place of employment. My rent was 7 roubles per month which included water and garbage as well as maintenance of the flat and building by the state. Also, I had to pay my electric bill. During the Soviet period, people paid a much lower percentage of their monthly income for rent and utility bills than people did living in the United States. A usual percentage for rent could be around 5 to 7 percent of a person's entire monthly income. This was because housing was highly subsidized by the Soviet state. The same was true of public utilities, food, and consumer goods, although food purchased outside of the state food shops in the open markets, rynok, along the streets from private vendors, could be five to ten times higher than the prices in the state shops. For me living here was going to be easy to manage on my salary from Magadan Pedagogical Institute.

Heating and electricity came from the Central Heating and Power Plant. This meant that there was only one thermostat in the entire city of Magadan, at the Central Heating Plant. One of the benefits of central heating is that you never have to worry about running out of hot water

LARRY ROCKHILL AT THE WINDOW OF THE MAGADAN APARTMENT ON BOLDYREVA STREET. 1990. PHOTO BY VALERY OSTRIKOV

when taking a shower. The downside of that could be the two weeks in the summer when the Central Steam Plant shuts down for annual maintenance and you had to heat your hot water on the stove if you wanted to bathe. Another downside was that in the summer the heating to the flats was turned off usually in early May when the temperatures during the day exceeded a certain degree Celsius.

This meant that even though Magadan's summer temperatures could be rather cool, no heat was supplied to the flats until the drop in the outside temperature later in the fall. Summertime meant that sometimes a space heater could make the difference between being warm and comfortable or not.

Cement walls did not offer the best insulation against cold, nor from noise in the way of family arguments, or sounds coming from your neighbor's stereo record player. Some people decorated their flats with beautiful oriental carpets that they hung on the walls. These provided nice decoration, as well as insulation against noise and the cold of an outside exposed wall. This was never a problem for me. My neighbors were quiet, and rarely did I even know when they were home.

Most apartment buildings were constructed of prefabricated cement slabs. This meant that you lived in a solid floor-to-ceiling and wall-to-

121

THE DELEGATION OF THE MAGADAN REGION TO SOLDOTNA ELEMENTARY SCHOOL. FROM LEFT TO RIGHT ARE:
TEACHER NANCY COURTRIGHT, FOURTH FROM LEFT ADMINISTRATOR RICK MATAYA, CHAIRMAN OF THE MAGA-
DAN CITY EXECUTIVE COMMITTEE, GENNADY DOROFEEV, ENTREPRENEUR, VLADIMIR VASILCHUK, PRINCIPAL OF
SOLDOTNA ELEMENTARY SCHOOL, DAVE DICKERSON. MAY 1, 1990 PHOTO OXOTNIK PRESS ARCHIVES

wall cement box. One time in my flat I tried to hang a picture that I was
given on the wall only to find out that trying to drive a nail into a prefab-
concrete wall was virtually impossible, so I gave up. However, some people were able to drill holes in the walls and hang their pictures.

My flat was also usual in that the windows provided added air con-
ditioning both in summer and winter, by way of the separation of the window frame from the wall. This was particularly so in the winter, and whenever the wind blew, the cold air had no trouble entering between the
spaces in the wall. On windy days I had to wear heavy socks and keep my
feet up off the floor if I was to stay warm. Since Magadan is a windy city
situated between two bays, I put tape all around the windows to keep the
cold wind out as best I could. At times, even with an electric space heater
and the radiator on full blast, it was difficult to keep the room temperature near 15 degrees C.

I could look out my window to the left and see the smoke rising from
the coal-fired boilers at the Central Heating Plant. This was a good wind
gauge indicator. If the wind was not blowing, a bit unusual for Magadan,

then the smoke would rise straight up from the smokestack. Often was the time when the smoke coming from the smokestack was pouring out parallel to the ground.

Obviously, this indicated it would be a good idea to dress warmly when going out on the street. I usually looked out my window before heading downstairs and out walking to the Pedagogical Institute. Wind and Magadan were close friends and relatives, along with winter snows and minus temps, and rain and fog in the summer and springtime.

NEIGHBORS

As with any apartment living, to a certain extent peace and quiet depend in part on your neighbors. I was fortunate to have good, friendly neighbors. One of my neighbors was a local medical doctor, Vera, who was an ophthalmologist. When she knew I was not feeling well, she would come over and take my temp, and give me some helpful advice on what I needed to do. Of course, she had lots of advice that was straight from old traditional Russian health practices. Usually, these were tried and true methods that worked.

Another neighbor was a KGB officer, but I never had any concern that I was being watched by the KGB. Never was I knowingly followed or contacted directly. I never had any reason to think that my telephone was tapped. I noticed that the wires for my telephone did run down the walls of our stairwell and so were quite exposed. However, it did not matter since I was not interested in saying anything that would be considered objectionable to the authorities.

I had some curious experiences though, like the one below. One afternoon, after my last class I ran up the three flights of stairs to find a piece of paper tacked to my door. My colleague and fellow professor Dima Poletaev was with me and so I asked him what it was. He said that this notice was for an unpaid bill from the Electric Utility Enterprise. It stated that the amount due was for the past six months and that I was late in paying the bill. I was a bit surprised because this was the first time to my knowledge that I had received a bill. I have always tried to pay my bills on time, and so I felt bad that evidently, I was about six months late. We wrote down the meter reading, walked down to the local Electric Utility office,

JOURNALIST VERA TIKHMENEVA, MAGADANSKAYA PRAVDA, AND TRANSLATOR MARIANNA PODOLSKAYA ARE VISITING LARRY ROCKHILL IN HIS FLAT. 1990 PHOTO BY PAVEL ZHDANOV

and showed the man my bill. He asked me if I knew how to read an electric meter and I said yes. Then he said that the reading that I wrote down was the exact same reading that he had from six months ago when I first moved into my flat. Evidently, the meter did not work at all. I explained that I lived there by myself and that I usually cooked two meals a day and would be willing to pay whatever he thought I would owe. To my surprise, he said: "That won't be necessary, and we will just fix the meter and you can pay your future bill." I am sure his kindness was due to my being the first American to live in Magadan. In the US my electricity would have been turned off a long time ago unless I had made the required payment.

Some friends I knew also had a similar experience. As in the US, it was not unusual in the USSR for both parents to work. Both were working and very busy, including having to stand in long lines for food and other necessities, as well as having to drop off and pick up their child from kindergarten. Somehow their monthly rent bill had just gone 'unnoticed 'for ten months. Each flat had a booklet that you were supposed to take to the housing office each month and pay your rent. When they finally went to the housing office after having received a late notice, they were a bit ticked at having to pay a small additional amount in interest. Feeling that you were entitled to the basic necessities of life, from the state, was not uncommon for most Soviet people in those days. DIARY: My American Studies lecture for the fifth-year MPI students went very well. A fine group of students. I have a bad cold today and so took a pill. At two o'clock this afternoon Dima and I went with Gov. Vyacheslav Kobets to Arman, a collective farm-kolkhoz community about an hour in a Russian jeep from Magadan. They raise around 30,000 mink there for their furs. The farm also includes around 2500 cows and pigs. We visited the Arman Middle School and talked to the two English Language teachers and their students. The students were excited to see visitors from Alaska. We were their first American visitors. Very appreciative. This is an old school that was built in 1965. Nice kids. Gov. Kobets had a two-hour meeting in the community hall with no heat when it was -30c outside. Dima and I sat there and almost froze. Gov. Kobets was giving a political speech since he was running again for the chairmanship of the regional Magadan Oblast. The driver of our Jeep got stuck in the snow on the way home and we didn't get home until 10 pm. It certainly was an interesting day and my first visit to a collective farm. Got a nice letter from Anna today.

Magadanskaya Pravda had an article on the recent Rotary visit and my speech at the Primoskiy restaurant dinner meeting. (10 January 1990)

CHAPTER NINE:
LIFE IN MAGADAN IN THE LATE SOVIET TIME

I would like to share several of the more unique aspects of my living in Magadan during the last two years of the Soviet Union. I came here to learn what life was like for the average person and I was not disappointed. My lessons in Soviet life were there for me to experience whenever I walked out the door of my flat. But first I will enclose an article from Magadanskaya Pravda, and then an article in the Moscow Edition of Pravda on my early life in Magadan.

The following is an article written by the journalist Vera Tikhmeneva and published on 12 October 1989 in the local newspaper Magadanskaya Pravda (translation by Dima Poletaev)

'MY NEW ADDRESS — MAGADAN '

By this time no one is turning his head towards Mr. Rockhill in the streets of Magadan whispering: "Look, an American."

"Passport USSR". – this is what Mr. Rockhill carries in his breast pocket. Certainly, the passport is American, only the cover is Soviet, nevertheless, Rockhill is proud to show this document to his friends.

I have now received the ration cards for sugar and alcohol and now I feel like a full and equal citizen of Magadan – he laughs.

True, it's a joke, but we feel a bitter irony in it. "A survival experiment" – that is how I defined his idea of living in the USSR, in Magadan for a long time.

However, it cannot be called a pure experiment. The city executive committee, the leadership of Magadan Pedagogical Institute, his colleagues from the English and German Department, his friends, and the members of the informal public organization "Friendship Bridge" met Rockhill with true Russian hospitality and cordiality.

Larry Rockhill has a nice one-room flat with cozy furniture. All visitors admire a comfortable kitchen with a refrigerator.

While you can hardly purchase a stool, all the furniture stirs up in us to many emotions. For Rockhill, the feeling of spiritual comfort is created mainly by the consideration and care of his associates.

Going up the stairway and knowing well Rockhill's flat's number we nevertheless ask his neighbor if the American lives at this entrance and if he disturbs his neighbors.

It's a custom within a neighborhood to help with diverse trifles, to invite for tea or dinner without ceremony.

More than two hundred years ago the first Russian missionaries came to Alaska. They built schools and churches, taught the Natives reading and writing, and rendered needed medical assistance.

Now it is as if Siberia and Alaska have changed their places: teacher Rockhill will live in Magadan and teach our children.

When I shared this very thought with Rockhill he shook his head: he doesn't feel himself to be a missionary. His friends from Alaska called him the first emigrant to the USSR from the USA.

As far as Larry is a modest and delicate person, he will never admit to being called a missionary. But when one thinks about this, he actually is. He has taken the mission of goodwill – to make our peoples closer, to restore our common heritage.

We asked about the attitude of his associates in Alaska towards his intention to live a year in Magadan.

Larry made us merry: he showed by his mimicry the way his fellows took the news: What? Then he became serious and said: By my presence here I would like to change the situation when your people leave your country. I want to help you believe that your life can also be attractive. And I want people not to emigrate just from the USSR, but also from Alaska to Magadan.

Really, these are the ideas of a missionary. In the interview which lasted two hours, Larry was attacked with questions. We were curious about everything right up to the last trifle: What does he eat for breakfast? Does he join the queue if he sees things he needs in the stores? How does he do without a car?

You know that people say that in America, to overcome a fifty-meter distance, they must take a car and drive there.

This is what Larry told us about his first impressions of life in Magadan. - I get up at about seven. Then I have breakfast. Usually, I have tea, bread, and butter. I must be at the Institute by 0815. I prefer to walk which I enjoy, and it is better for my health. It takes me about twenty-five minutes to get to the Institute, and on the whole, I walk around two hours a day.

Good relations have been established with his colleagues and his students. It is mostly due to the head of the English and German Department Roman Romanovich Tchaikovski. The students are curious, communicative, and very interested in gaining knowledge.

You ask me why the teacher of an Alaskan primary school was given a job at the Institute? I have been a teacher at the University of Alaska. I have a Bachelor's Degree, and a Master's Degree, besides my teaching in Magadan, is part of a joint exchange program between the University of Alaska and the Magadan Pedagogical Institute.

Three hundred twenty rubles a month is a high salary. I am sure I will be the first American to open a bank account in the Magadan City bank, or as you say, I will get a savings bank book.

Usually, I go shopping in the food shops at Torgoviy Center, or in the food shop Neptune. I usually buy bread, butter, and milk. There is another food shop near where I live called Universam. I have been there, but I think I did not buy anything there. Some of my friends and fellow teachers, Lena Busheva and Lena Kostenko have been very kind and have prepared a few meals for me. I very much enjoy Russian borsch and pelmeni. I believe that someday I will master the secrets of Russian cuisine. I admire and respect Soviet women more and more for their art of cooking and their skills to prepare delicious meals with little variety of available foods and without many kitchen appliances. I am sure an American woman would have a difficult time under such conditions as you have here.

I watch TV very seldom, maybe thirty minutes a day. I have no time for that. I try to thoroughly prepare for my classes at the Institute and I am working on my Russian Language as well.

Learning Russian is one of my goals, which is why I prefer to watch and listen to programs where there is a lot of spoken Russian, like Vremya.

JOURNALIST VERA TIKHMENEVA FROM MAGADANSKAYA PRAVDA SHARES WITH LARRY ROCKHILL THE SECRETS OF RUSSIAN CUISINE. 1990 PHOTO BY PAVEL ZHDANOV

I try to be in bed by eleven. What do I see in my dreams at night? As a rule, my night dreams are a continuation of my daily thoughts.

I have a telephone and I have already spoken to Alaska and my family and friends.

I did not expect my living conditions to be so nice. I am quite familiar with the housing problems in your country, people waiting in a queue for new flats for years. I feel a bit embarrassed that I have been treated so well.

We know that the crime situation in our country could not be called very safe: there are many thefts of flats and various incidents in the streets. Your department colleagues told me they are going to set up an alarm system.

I am very often asked if I am afraid to live in Magadan that I feel like I should be getting afraid, said Larry, joking.

I can only say that I very much enjoy living in Magadan and I feel as if I have been living here for a long time. '

The next article was written by Victor Timakov, a journalist, and was published on January 4, 1990, in the Moscow Edition of Pravda. Translation by Dima Poletaev.

129

A TUTOR FROM ALASKA

On New Year's Eve, Larry Rockhill, a teacher of English finishes his first semester as an assistant professor at Magadan Pedagogical Institute. This could have just remained a fact in his biography except for one thing. Larry is a citizen of the United States of America, and the first foreigner teaching in a remote Soviet Institute. This also means that he will celebrate New Year's Eve in our country for the first time.

Born in California, a graduate of California State University at Los Angeles with a BA and MA degrees in Psychology and Education, he has been living in Alaska for many years. He began as a teacher of Eskimo students in a Bureau of Indian Affairs boarding school, then worked as a professor at the University of Alaska Anchorage. For the past few years, Larry has been teaching in the small Alaskan town of Soldotna. There on the Kenai Peninsula, a place closely connected with the history of the development of this part of North America by early Russian explorers, he thought it would be good to establish friendly relations with the neighbors living just across the Bering Strait. It was Larry who thought of building the bridge of friendship between Alaska and the Russian Far East.

Not so long ago, Larry was among the first Alaskans who visited the Bay of Provideniya and Magadan. It was during this visit that he proposed and offered his services as a professor to the Soviet Institute, Magadan Pedagogical Institute. Frankly speaking, this idea was not accepted by everybody with enthusiasm on both the Russian and the American shores. But Rockhill was supported by the President of the Magadan Pedagogical Institute, Professor Evgeny Kokorev, by the Administration of the Department of Public Education in Magadan and educational authorities in Alaska, by Alaska Governor Steve Cowper and by the Chairman of the Magadan Regional Executive Committee, Vyacheslav Kobets. As a result, a new professor was admitted to the English and German Department as an Associate Professor. The Magadan City Executive Committee, notwithstanding the difficulties in housing, provided him with a one-room flat with a telephone in one of the new districts of our city.

And now the examination period is approaching. According to the head of the Foreign Language Department, Professor Roman Tchaikovsky, the results are exceptionally good. "You must not spoil before you spin," he said. Both students and teachers have a rare opportunity for professional communication with their colleague, a native speaker of English. Mr. Rockhill does not speak Russian and this makes his classes even more effective. He also teaches conversational English. He also plans to lecture to students on the subject of American Studies. And what is most amazing is the student's progress is great. Even the weakest students have begun to speak after a short period of communicating with their new teacher.

And what do students have to say about their unusual new teacher? "Everyone dreams of having a teacher like him", says Dmitry Kharbanov, a second-year student. "We found a common language at once. Mr. Rockhill is an ordinary sociable and friendly person, and he is very popular among us." We met Mr. Rockhill at the Foreign Language Department of MPI before he was going to teach his class. "What are you finishing this semester with and how will you be meeting in the New Year"?

He said, "I will be with my excellent students and new friends. I am greatly impressed by my Magadan students and by their sincerity and hard work. I really enjoy working with such hard-working students."

Naturally, many things were unusual and difficult in the beginning. Shopping, lines, and shortages of some products caused and continue to cause some difficulties. Like all Magadan residents, he has been given his talonies, and food rationing coupons for sugar, flour, macaroni, tea, and vodka. In general, our American friend understands our problems though some of them take too much time which is chronically never enough.

TAXI, BUS, OR WALK

Before my arrival, I did not have much of an idea of what to expect in the way of the location of my flat. Magadan was a very compact city with most people living in four to nine-story apartment buildings situated close together on the top of the hill between Nagaeva and Gertner Bays. This was a Soviet-designed city with each building being placed to best utilize the limited space available. Everything was to be as convenient as possible for the people living in the flats. Food shops, clothing stores, polyclinics, hardware stores, post offices, kindergartens, and schools were all within walking distance for most people. Magadan was a walking city during Soviet times, with no traffic jams and very few stoplights at intersections, so I knew that each day I also would spend some hours on the street going back and forth to the Pedinstitute (Magadan Pedagogical Institute, MPI), shopping, and visiting friends.

This was to be a big change from the way I was used to going places. In the US most people haul their bodies around from place to place in a car. Going up and down three flights of stairs at the Institute and three flights to my apartment each day was an exercise in good health. I walked everywhere and had to carry my groceries in a bag of some sort. The result of two years of walking and going up and down stairs was to become quite evident from the size of my waist. When I returned to the United States after the first year some friends at the University of Alaska asked if I had spent time in one of the GULag forced labor camps.

In winter, walking to the institute was bone-chilling, and it was especially difficult when you were the first one out of the apartment building, since the snow removal people did not come early in the morning to clear the sidewalks, and the first ones out would be breaking the trail in the deep snow. The wind was often quite strong, and I had to drop into a shop at times to warm up my nose, cheeks, and ears when it was so cold. After I had my mink fur hat, I was able to be out in the cold wind in a much more comfortable manner. I had to put my ear flaps down when the wind was blowing in order not to have frostbitten ears and neck. I would use my wool scarf to cover my face and nose. Then when I would go inside, I was a mass of melting ice that was covering my beard. I would just run to get some toilet paper, when available. Then dry again I was.

The taxis in Magadan operated quite differently from the taxi service in the US. You could take a taxi to any place in Magadan for just one ruble. Of course, this was a bargain, to say the least.

Here, if the driver so desired, any car with any driver could act as a taxi. And for me, it was interesting to be able to ride in several different makes of Soviet automobiles such as the Volga, Lada, Zhiguli, and the little Zaporozhets. If you wanted to take a taxi someplace all you did was stand on the edge of the curb and hold your arm outstretched when a car approached. If the driver stopped, then you would just tell him where you wanted to go, and if he wished to go there, he would say to get in, and off you would go. I would usually give the driver money and also a small Alaska flag pin and introduce myself in my broken Russian: "Ya prepodavatel 'angliski yazik Magadan pedagogicheski in.stitute." (I am a teacher of English language at Magadan Pedagogical Institute). Sometimes they would not accept money from me as a goodwill gesture for my living there. Most people were very kind, and of course, one would have to be careful, especially women late at night, when deciding to take a taxi. However, it was a convenient system that I did not use very often since I usually walked. The buses were very slow, traveling up Prospect Lenina at a snail's pace. Walking was the best for my health and still is as I walk everywhere when living in Magadan.

Many high Soviet officials had cars and drivers assigned to them. When out walking you would often see several black Volgas standing in front of Oblispolkom (Regional Administration) and Gorispolkom (City Administration) waiting for some official needing to go someplace. When we would have meetings with Vyacheslav Kobets in his Oblispolkom office, afterward, he would usually offer to have his driver take us where we needed to go, and Mayor Gennady Dorofeev would do the same. Relatively few ordinary Soviet people had their own cars during these times since it could take several years to be on the waiting list, and you had to be able to pay the full price upfront. In those days all gas stations were state-run and very basic. No frills and no sign, but the gas pump was a big clue. You just pulled in, filled up, and paid the attendant, no credit cards were accepted.

SHOPPING

Shopping was not a new experience for me, but Soviet shopping had its unique character that I found very interesting and different from Alaska. I found shopping interesting not only for what was available in the shops, but also for what wasn't available, and both were to be experienced frequently. One day I went to a hardware store called Tysyachnik, the House of a Thousand Things, to buy lightbulbs. Here I saw a very unusual item for me, the largest samovar I have ever seen, for it would hold at least ten gallons of water. Even though I like samovars very much, I think it would have been a bit big for my kitchen table. It was for some commercial setting like a stolovaya, and very interesting. Crystal glass was very popular and could be seen behind glass cabinets in many homes and was usually available in major department stores. Clothing stores had the standard Soviet fashions for both men and women. The selection to choose from was not always so popular with women shoppers. I needed a dressier coat than the Alaska parka I had brought so I went to Dom Odezhdy, the House of Clothing. I looked at several coats and bought a very heavy black long wool coat for 500 rubles, over one month of my total salary. Who could afford these prices? It was times like this when I wondered about why the prices seemed so high even with the state subsidizing clothing. By visiting the different types of stores, I was able to get a better idea of what Soviet people could buy to make their lives a little more interesting, a little more colorful, or a little easier. And at times it was quite a challenge for them. I was able to see in Almaz, the main jewelry store, just what Soviet women could buy in the way of earrings, bracelets, necklaces, and watches and, compare with stores in Alaska. There were around five bookstores in Magadan at that time. They were interesting, and times were changing which was reflected in the subject areas that were available. The changes that were occurring were from mostly Soviet and Russian classic literature to what in the US could be called pulp fiction and self-help books. The department stores also changed greatly in a few months after I arrived, from being full of merchandise to becoming almost empty. I will now go into more detail as to the situation for the Magadan shopper at this time in three different shopping areas, consumer goods, the Souvenir Native art business, and food shopping.

A nice discovery for me was the Souvenir Store and Souvenir Factory; I found it to be interesting since I was somewhat familiar with Alaska Native art but had seen little in the way of Soviet indigenous art. I have a background in working with Alaska Native people and a long-standing interest in their indigenous art. Eskimo ivory carvers in Alaska are very well known and respected for their skill in carving Arctic animals from walrus ivory and bone which is popular with tourists and collectors. Eskimo, Athabaskan Indian, Tlingit, Haida, Simpsian, and Aleut people are all involved in basket making, skin sewing, bone, ivory, and wood carving. Their work is sought after by tourists and collectors from all over the world and is a very important part of the tourism industry for Native Alaskans.

In the Magadan Souvenir Store, I saw some beautiful and quite different Native art from what I had seen in Alaska. This is where many artists were working in their little areas on different floors of the building. When you walked around you could see artists making many unique, handmade items from wood, skins, reindeer antlers, walrus bone, walrus ivory, and mastodon ivory. Those items carved from antlers were amazing in that one could hardly tell them from being ivory, they were so highly polished. The carved and etched ivory pieces were excellent and in great demand by collectors from as far away as Moscow, Europe, and even China. One of the most popular carvings was of the wooly mammoth, a native of historic times in the Kolyma. Our good friend Victor Vikhlyantsev is a well-known master carver who gave us one of his beautiful mammoth carvings as a gift. These carvings, as well as other items, were made by professional artists both Native and non-Native. Although walrus ivory could not legally be taken to Alaska, carvings made from mastodon ivory, reindeer antler, and bone were legal. Some of the most interesting carvings were of groups of Chukchi reindeer herders standing beside their sled with several dogs and reindeer ready to pull the sled. Others were carvings of Eskimo people doing daily tasks, like hunting, dancing, and just standing on the ice with a little polar bear beside them. Some artists made interesting plaques from carved pieces of ivory, or polished reindeer antlers mounted on reindeer skin that depicted the Magadan flag with the reindeer, gold, and the sea at the bottom. These were quite popular. Another plaque like this was the depiction of a group of reindeer herders with dogs, sleds, and reindeer mounted on a reindeer skin and seal skin that you could hang on your wall.

One time we were invited to go to the Souvenir Factory where we could see the artists working on their items that would later be in the stores for sale. We watched several people, both Native and non-Native, that were carving and etching pieces of ivory, and others that were doing art with seal and reindeer skins. I was able to purchase a diorama of a group of reindeer herders preparing a sled for transporting some goods. This was all realistically done in reindeer antlers and mastodon ivory and mounted on the curving section of a reindeer antler. The carvings of the very delicate and fragile reindeer antlers that just fit into the heads of the deer are amazing. Governor Vyacheslav Kobets gave me a special gift as a birthday present during my first year living in Magadan, in November 1989. Now it is a family heirloom from a dear friend and unforgettable Soviet times.

Many examples of this art can be seen in our fine Magadan Regional Museum. We also have a book published in 1989 that illustrates the work

VISITING THE FAMILY OF THE PRINCIPAL OF SOLDOTNA HIGH SCHOOL KEN MICHEM. KEN WAS ONE OF THE MOST ACTIVE PARTICIPANTS IN SCHOOL EXCHANGES FROM ALASKA AFTER LARRY ROCKHILL LEFT FOR MAGA-DAN. FROM LEFT TO RIGHT: DANIEL, VICTOR AND SVETLANA VIKHLYANTSEV, MATTHEW, CHERI, KEN, KRISTINA, JEREMY, MEGAN MICHEM. AUGUST 10, 1993 COURTESY OXOTNIK PRESS ARCHIVES

of several Chukotka ivory carvers. One can also see an early 20th-century example of etchings by a Chukotka artist on a large walrus ivory tusk in the Anchorage Museum of History and Art.

SHOPPING IN MAGADAN: 1989 TO 1990

The years 1989/1990 were times of continuing change for the average Soviet consumer. The three main department stores in Magadan were Voskhod on Prospect Lenina, Chaika, down by the Central Bus Station, and Crystal, on Polyarnaya Street. The changes seemed to occur rather quickly; I would even say in a matter of a few months.

Seeing empty shelves in food shops was becoming a common sight. People were beginning to worry as to what to do, especially with a deficit in certain basic food items such as tea, coffee, flour, rice, macaroni, pasta, sugar, butter, some canned goods, etc. As one would expect, this caused some people to begin hoarding items just in case they were not going to be available later on.

STUDENT EXCHANGES BECAME ANNUAL AFTER 1989. IN THE PHOTO: THE MAGADAN DELEGATION OF SCHOOL.CHILDREN PERFORMS IN THE ASSEMBLY HALL OF SOLDOTNA HIGH SCHOOL. MARIA LEONOVA, A STUDENT OF THE MAGADAN SCHOOL OF ARTS, NOW THE ARTISTIC DIRECTOR OF THE MAGADAN MUSICAL DRAMA THEATER, IS IN THE CENTER WITH A GUITAR. FEBRUARY 1992. PHOTO BY PAVEL ZHDANOV

Some of the popular food items like canned saira-fish and shproty (smoked fish) were in short supply, while less popular kinds of canned fish were still available.

DIARY: The first snow, termination dust appeared on the hills this morning. The University of Alaska Fairbanks students began their student teaching in the Magadan City Schools today.

I taught two paras today and then had a meeting with journalists from the National Teachers newspaper. Not particularly important. Then Roman and I went to his flat. My student Thomas was already there. I joined him in helping Luda to make solenaia kapusta, salted fermented cabbage. It is a lot of cutting and squeezing the juice out of the cabbage. I received my talons today for butter, flour, sugar, tea, and vodka. There is no rice, flour, coffee, meat, chicken, eggs, or cabbage available now in our food shops, very bad for winter, a great problem. And also there are no canned tomatoes in our food shops. At times there are even shortages of bread and milk. Things are not looking good and so early in the fall. So many food items are not in our stores now. It is much worse here now than it was two months ago. Stores are becoming very empty now. (7 October 1990)

Meat in the state stores was going for 2 rubles per kilo, and of course, there was by definition usually a high percentage of fat and bone combined with a small percentage of red meat. Canned beef and pork were usually available but canned pork contained a lot of fat. With the uncertainty of which food items would be available in the future, even I, when I could find them, bought several extra and put some away in my cupboard for later. Fortunately for me, my friends were generous in sharing boxes of good tea since I gave up drinking coffee, which was not available anyway. For most people, it was a bit annoying when going to their local gastronome and not being able to find such ordinary items as flour and sugar, let alone coffee and tea.

Not only food items were being bought up and hoarded, but clothing was also being affected. It was interesting for me to walk through the stores to see the various kinds of consumer goods available since most of the merchandise was new to me. But things were changing quickly. I remember one day when I walked into the women's clothing section of the main department store Voskhod and saw that the whole section was depleted of all items of women's clothing. In a matter of a few weeks, this department became full of nothing but empty clothes racks with empty hangers on them, but no clothes. It became just a large empty room. There were no customers, and a few sales clerks stood around with nothing to do. Other departments also shared this same situation, empty shelves, and display cases.

The clothes had gone, but some were not far away, and they could be found on the sidewalk just outside the store. Everyday ladies could be seen holding articles of clothing when standing out in the cold on the sidewalk in front of the Voskhod Department store. These Russian women were the new capitalists and entrepreneurs of the times. They were holding previously purchased items of new clothing draped over their arms, some with new shoes for sale placed on the ground in front of them that they were desperate to sell. Desperate times called for desperate measures, and these were desperate times when these women were doing what in previous Soviet times would have been called speculation and was illegal. I do not think that the authorities made any attempt to put an end to them selling these clothes. They stood there day after day, out in the cold, intent on making a little profit for their efforts and investment.

In those days the laws of the Soviet Union forbade the purchase of any items and their resale for personal gain. Of course, this was a big part of the black market, the nalevo, under-the-table economy. The copying of my audio tapes of the latest American rock music by the Leningrad hotel waiters and then selling them was also against the law, but not uncommon. They could also be used to get items the waiters wanted in an exchange or barter. Sad to say, this was the only way that the Soviet youth could enjoy popular music that was normal for youth in the West. Even paying a private person to fix something like a broken toilet was considered illegal. The government owned the worker's tools and the worker's time. So, with a little bribe in the way of goods or money, the worker was happy to do the job nalevo and the person who now had a working toilet was happy too. The only party not pleased was the state.

For many, the change in the value of the ruble had created serious financial difficulties. Some lost their life savings in a rather short period of time. Seeing people selling their personal possessions when standing along the sidewalks was becoming a common sight in many Soviet cities and towns. In order just to get enough money to survive some people would spread a blanket out on the ground next to the sidewalk and place all kinds of their possessions on it for sale. I remember Valentina, a retired lady at the open market who was selling new socks along with many used books from her library of Russian classic literature for little money. Next to her was an older man who was trying to sell ordinary household tools such as a hammer, screwdriver, pliers, a vice, a small shovel, a flashlight, light fixtures, faucets, doorknobs, etc. Others were selling dishes, kitchen utensils, samovars, chainiks (teapots), cups and saucers, and glasses.

One had to feel a bit sorry for often these were older retired people living on a small state pension who had devoted their entire lives to developing Communism, which in turn was to provide them with a good life in their old age. Here, they were living in poverty after all their working years in hopes that their retirement would be comfortable when living on their state pension. A Soviet pension amounted to little money, and it was difficult to pay all their monthly bills, including the cost of the flat, electricity, and water, and then buy food. There would be nothing left over for either an emergency or for recreation. Since most people had always relied on the state to take care of them, few people tried to save up money for their retirement. Having a savings account in the local bank was not usual for many Soviet people. Now, without savings, along with the devaluation of the ruble, meant that whatever little money had been saved became worth almost nothing.

The Russian ruble went from an exchange rate of being parred with the British pound—$1.65 to 1 GBP in 1988, which was also $1.65 to 1 Russian ruble, to a progressive devaluation after 1989 of $1.00 = 1 ruble, to $1.00 = 6 rubles, to $1.00 = 50 rubles and eventually by 1992 to $1.00 = 1000 rubles. Some people close to me had in 1989 15,000 rubles in the bank when it was still worth about $15,000. Then 2 years later the exchange rate fell to $1 =1000 rubles, and 15,000 rubles became equal to around $15.00. This happened to very many people in the Soviet Union, not just to the elderly. It is easy to understand how upset and angry the people who had lost so much became, and how this forced many to try and sell whatever they could to just survive. Many Soviet people also lost their jobs with the closure of so many factories and enterprises. This was as true in Magadan as it was in Moscow. Today, as one travels from Sergiev Posad to Moscow on the suburban train you can see many old Soviet factories that are now just abandoned buildings, with no glass in the windows, no doors, and rusting heavy equipment sitting outside. The 1990s were extremely difficult times for many Soviet people. Here I agree with Professor Stephen F. Cohen, that we should place some of the blame for the severe economic problems under Yeltsin, and faced by the people of the Soviet Union on the advice coming from the United States where well- known economists and some of the experts in the Clinton Administration advised mass privatization take place.

Most people carried an avos'ka, a string bag in their pocket or purse when they went out on the street. One never knew what a person might find that had been in a big deficit and had suddenly become available. Ironically, this is the same string bag that was becoming fashionable in the latter part of 2010 in an attempt to get rid of plastic bags and be more environmentally friendly. But back in the 1990s, I carried an extra plastic bag or two for shopping. One day I was walking along the street near the central department store and I noticed a small group of women, maybe eight or ten all huddled together in front of the store. I knew they were not there relaxing and having tea together, and as I approached, I thought there must be something available that was in short supply. As I got closer and was able to look over the shoulders of some of the women, to my great surprise what did I see but toilet paper that had not been available in the stores for months past.

This was a much-preferred item to have in many homes to use the cut-up squares, pages of the local news paper, which were placed in the holder on the back of the door inside the toilet. I bought several rolls, then immediately called some friends to let them know what was available. If one found something that had been in a deficit that suddenly appeared in a store, most people would buy extra to share with friends and relatives. This did not happen to me often, but it was like a nice surprise when it did.

FOOD DEFICIT

TALONIES: A month after I arrived and began teaching at MPI I received, as did all Soviet citizens, food ration coupons called 'talonies'. These food coupons could only be used in the state food shops, not on the rynok or open market where private sellers sold dairy products, meat, fish, vegetables, and fruit. There were ration coupons for flour, macaroni, sugar, butter, tea, rice, meat, and vodka. I never saw coffee in the food stores; a small can of instant coffee was distributed twice a year by the worker's labor unions. This did not mean that you would be able to purchase a given item even if you had the coupon, for the store often did not have such an item. But it meant that if available, you could purchase a limited number of a given item with your talonies. Basics like potatoes, carrots, cabbage, bread, milk, and kefir were regularly available if one got to the store before all were sold out. I noticed that canned peas and a type of not-very-popular fish sausage were also usually available in the food shops. I had canned peas, boiled potatoes, and black bread for dinner quite often during my first year in Magadan. This reminded me of the times when I was a little boy during WWII when in the US many food items were rationed due to the war effort.

FRESH PRODUCE: As far as fresh fruits and vegetables were concerned, being in the north, we had a very limited selection available in the state food shops from November to February. And the selection available in these shops became less and less as the fall season progressed, and winter arrived. In order to compensate for what was not available, many people grew their own vegetables such as potatoes, cucumbers, carrots, and cabbages in gardens at their dachas. This was both for economic and for health reasons. Often it was a family activity, and sometimes more than one family contributed labor. When harvested the crops would often be shared between participating family members and friends. All food was expensive, and salaries were not high for most people, so this was one way of reducing food costs.

I always tried to buy potatoes, cabbage, and carrots that were grown in Ola, a small fishing town about 32 km from Magadan, where many people had small garden plots. Even though locally grown produce from Ola was more expensive, I felt the quality was quite good and I wanted to support our local growers. Due to the situation during these difficult times, almost 50% of all food products were shipped in from outside the area.

It is interesting to note how times changed after 1991 when the importing of products from China developed into big business, including the importation of fresh produce, fruits, and vegetables. This made fresh produce more available even in the winter. Yet, imported vegetables from China were not preferred by many because buying vegetables from China, where the chemicals used to grow them were unknown, there was always the concern for one's health. Whereas the family dacha gardeners could control the methods used to fertilize their crops as they grew. Yet, presently, many of the kiosks at Rynok Urozhai/Market 'Harvest', and the open market just across the street, purchase their produce from wholesale suppliers who sell them imported Chinese produce. Since local produce was usually more expensive, some people had to buy Chinese produce since it might be more affordable.

In the Magadan region, the climate makes it quite challenging to grow vegetables. The first snow, called termination dust, can be seen on top of the foothills in early October, and by December temperatures of minus 30C are not uncommon. The interior regions of the Magadan Oblast, being in a continental climate, experienced warm summer temperatures and were very productive for growing vegetables, but the winters were much harsher than the maritime climate of Magadan coastal areas. The more moderate coastal areas were able to grow vegetables until later in the fall before the temperatures dropped.

Every year many families would buy several heads of cabbage at the beginning of winter and make solenaia kapusta, a salted fermented cabbage, then put it in large glass jars and store it in a cool place for the winter. I remember when Tom, one of the UAA students, and I went to Luda Tchaikovskaya's flat and helped her cut up a gunny sack full of cabbages.

This was time- consuming and hard work. Here she had around fifty kilos of kapusta (cabbage), and we had to cut it all up, a little at a time. Then after it was cut into thin slices, salt was put on it, and then we took it in our hands and had to squeeze as hard as we could to get the juice to flow from the cut cabbage. This took some time, and our hands were not used to this hard work. Russian women have always been used to not having many labor-saving appliances in their kitchens and so had strong hands and wrists. Then it was placed into a big bowl with a little more salt and mixed up together with some shredded carrots. After this, we placed a large plate on top of the cut cabbage with some heavy weights to press down and squeeze more juice out of it. After a few days of fermenting, it went into large glass jars with lids screwed tight, and into a cool space to sit until used in the winter months. I remember Luda and several other friends shared foods like solenaia kapusta with me during the first winter I lived in Magadan. I liked it a lot and often had it for dinner with pelmeni and chorney khleb-black bread. I never missed American food and I never tired of eating good Russian dishes either. Friends like Luda Tchaikovskaya, Larisa Kokoreva, Alexandra Alishova, Natasha Berzon, Natasha Poletaeva, and others were very generous in sharing their wonderful Russian dishes.

Many families also picked brusnika-low bush cranberries and mushrooms. In the long winter months, brusnika was made into juice concentrate with added water when served. Brusnika berries were also used as a dessert and served with just a sprinkle of sugar on top. Some women made delicious brusnika pies and pirozhki. These berries provided natural vitamin C which in the past helped to prevent scurvy.

With most Soviet women being already overburdened with full-time jobs, plus taking care of their children and their families, they had little time for activities like going to the forest to pick brusnika. After the first frost, these berries were considered ready to pick. There were ladies who had the time to go to the forest to pick berries, often babushkas, that afterward could be found on the sidewalks sitting with several jars of brusnika berries, and some jars of brusnika juice for sale on the top of an overturned box. They were a little expensive, but you did not have to spend the time you did not have after a long day at work. This was a way for some older people who had the time to add to the little money they were getting from their state pensions. It was an example of a private enterprise that the state did not interfere with.

Once when we were out picking brusnika in the forest of list ven-nitsa (tamarack) trees near Ola we observed a big brown bear crossing the road not far from where we were. It was the only time I ever saw a bear in all the time I had spent outdoors in the Kolyma area. We were encroaching on his territory and so moved on to another spot. Brusnika berries are small, and it must take some time and effort for a big brown bear to get his fill. We used a special berry-picking spoon, like one we have from a Yupik Eskimo family, to make it easier and faster to pick. It took us quite a while to fill a five-gallon empty paint bucket but was always nice to be out in the beautiful wilderness area of the Kolyma.

Mushrooms are considered a delicacy and many Russian people go out to the forest in the fall after it stops raining to pick them. You have to know which ones are safe to eat as every year some people get very ill from eating mushrooms that they thought were safe, but which were very poisonous. My first year saw some friends sharing the bounty of their mushroom-picking labor with me in the way of jars of marinated mush-rooms. Sometimes we went out and were able to pick very nice safe mush-rooms, took them home, and had a delicious dinner of just mushrooms and boiled potatoes. Serious mushroom pickers often have their favorite places to pick and try to keep this information a secret.

RYNOK: The rynok -the market was the place where people could buy better quality fresh food products including meat, fish, vegetables, fruits, and dairy products from private sellers. It was situated next to a park not far from Magadan Pedagogical Institute. Here private people could be found selling their produce out in the open from around thirty tables in both summer and winter. Shopping and selling in the winter, when the temperatures drop to minus 20 C and below, could be a challenge for both seller and buyer. These people sold all kinds of produce, much that they raised and grew on their own private plots, from meat, beef, and pork, to all kinds of vegetables, and some wild berries. Although the prices were higher than the state shops, there was no lack of customers to be found, especially on the weekends and during the holiday season. One usually had to go pretty early on a weekend to find better-quality vegetables as well as meats.

It was interesting to watch in the meat section on the open market, as in the state meat shops, men using the main tool for butchering an animal carcass, the large traditional Russian hand ax.

Usually, the butcher block was a round section, about a meter in diameter, of a tree trunk. After hacking the carcass into large chunks of meat, they would then use a saw and a big knife to cut them into smaller pieces, some resembling roasts, steaks, and chops. The meat was usually not covered in either summer or winter. Summers, at times, included watching some insects having their share of the meat. As you walked through the meat section the sellers on the open market would be happy to hold a portion up so you could take a good look at it, and hopefully buy it for dinner. It was not unusual to see the heads of butchered pigs sitting on top of the meat counters. Although this was late in the time of the Soviet Union, there was a feeling of capitalistic competition among the sellers in the open markets reflected in the prices that were asked by the different sellers.

The state meat stores had refrigerated cases where pieces of meat and bone were all piled together. Here the meat was not cut and wrapped, it was just placed in the case as pieces of meat. The customer had to use her imagination as to what the shape of meat could be called, what part of the animal it came from, and what it could be used for in cooking. If you could see red on a bone, then that meant that there was some meat attached. Some pieces had a lot of white (fat), and only a little red (meat). I remember once when we wanted to buy reindeer meat and ask the sales clerk for certain pieces and not others. Of course, we were asking for better-looking pieces and not some bones where you could see just a bit of red sticking to them. Well, she said net, nothing doing, to take all the good pieces. You had to take the good with the bad, and so we got some nice pieces with lots of meat on them, and some not-so-good. Boiled reindeer stew was always a favorite of ours.

FRESH FISH: My first fall in Magadan reminded me of living in Alaska when fresh salmon would enter the Kenai River and become available in the grocery stores. But in Alaska, we did not buy salmon from the grocery store, we would go to the Kenai River, and catch our own winter's supply of fresh silver salmon to fill our freezer. We would get up at the crack of dawn, and all would go down to the Kenai River with spinning rods and Pixie lures, hoping that a nice big school of fish was just passing the spot where we were fishing. The main lure, although many fishermen used fresh bait of salmon eggs, was the shiny Pixie, and I can say I donated quite a few to the spirits of the snags that they got caught on at the bottom of the river.

This was quite different from fishing in Magadan. Although I never had the opportunity to go fishing in one of the local rivers, I just observed at times when on the way to Ola. Russian fishermen did not use a spinning rod if they were trying to fill their freezers with a winter supply of salmon. They would obtain a special license to be able to use a net to catch, they hoped, a lot of fish. This was an operation where it took several people, and a small boat, who would be involved in taking and setting the net out in the river and then having to haul it in when it became full of fish. Using a net was a much more efficient way of catching fish than with a rod and reel.

In the fall when I walked to the open market near the park, there was a small section where several sellers had different kinds of frozen fish just sitting in boxes with the price. These were usually fresh frozen fish that had been recently caught. I was able to buy a whole cleaned silver salmon weighing at least eight pounds for less than five dollars. The price of fish here was not cheap for people making rubles, but for me, compared to Alaska stores, it seemed like it was very inexpensive. I was surprised when I walked to the Tsentral'niy Gastronom (Central Store) and found frozen blocks of paltus, halibut, for a mere 70 kopeks per kilo. Not so in Alaska where this would be considered pure fillet of halibut, and sell for at least $15 per pound. And also, my newly acquired taste for the delicious krasnaya ikra, salmon roe, although a bit expensive, was being taken care of quite nicely. This was considered the most delicious part of the salmon and was taken care of accordingly. I was pleased to be able to have fresh salmon for dinner many a night, just like in Alaska.

LINES: Russian women were noted for spending a lot of time just waiting in lines for whatever food items they needed to buy to feed their families. And this was usually in addition to the hours spent at a full-time job. Lines were a significant part of the life of every Soviet woman. Some would just take part of their work time to go to a store when the lines may be shorter than during the mid-day. For many Russian women, it seemed like lines were always available, and that it was what they wanted to purchase that was not always available, even at the front of the line. A few times I stood in line for chickens, which were only available sometimes. This line had over 100 people with hopes of having a chicken dinner soon. The chickens were being sold out of the Neptune food store window on Gagarina Street right on the sidewalk. The long line kept getting shorter

LARRY ROCKHILL RECEIVED A GIFT OF A REINDEER HIDE FROM A EVEN WOMAN IN THE 10TH REINDEER HERD-ING BRIGADE OF THE STATE FARM 'IRBYCHAN'. 2016 PHOTO BY ANDREY OSIPOV

as the wait grew to two hours, and I slowly progressed towards the front of the line where chickens were being taken from boxes and placed in the customer's plastic bags. Now I was only ten from the front of the line, and I could almost taste fried chicken for dinner. Then when I was fifth from the front of the line to my dismay, I saw that suddenly, the chickens had all flown out of the boxes, and I had to leave with only the dream of a future chicken dinner. Another unforgettable lesson and Magadan experience to treasure.

This happened more than once to me. Eggs were also in big deficit most of the time, and lines formed when they were available in the food shops. It is interesting to note that the availability of eggs was directly related to the transportation infrastructure of the area. The egg farm at Dukcha was several miles away from the center of Magadan on the Kolyma Trassa. Eggs were brought to the Magadan food shops in trucks that were used to haul many kinds of products, including very heavy construction materials. The roads they traversed were often a fine collection of potholes.

When the eggs arrived at the shops, a good percentage of them were already 'scrambled' from the ride over the bumpy roads in trucks that had

147

virtually no suspension systems for hauling things like eggs. Eggs were sold in tens, not by the dozen. When you purchased eggs, they were just placed together in your plastic bag, so you had to be especially careful in handling these precious little items that had survived the bumpy ride from the Dukcha chicken/egg farm to the shop.

One item there were usually no lines to buy was Russian black bread which was just excellent. There were several different kinds available, and so most people did not make their own bread at home. It was made from dark rye since rye is a crop that does well in a country where two-thirds of the landmass is above 60 degrees north latitude, and wheat. Borodinski is another popular kind of black bread with a rather unique flavor, with coriander seeds on the top. Bread was sold both in bread stores and in the gastronomes. During Soviet times bread came unwrapped and unsliced. In some stores, you could take a large fork and press on the loaves to see if they were fresh. Soft loaves meant fresh loaves. The bread was just handed to the purchaser by the sales clerk when taken off the stack of loaves sitting out uncovered on the shelves from behind the counter.

Sometimes it was placed in small plastic bags before being handed to the customer. Self-service was available only in some stores, called Universams. In most smaller stores selling foods, the products were sitting on shelves behind the counter, and you had to ask the sales clerk for the items you wanted to purchase. This was the continuation of the Soviet policy of keeping people employed. Since the 1990s, more self-service supermarkets have come into being.

HAVING TO WAIT IN THREE LINES TO PURCHASE

Food shops, also known as gastronomes, were somewhat different from what we know in the West. Although as in the US, they were set up with each general type of product having its separate section. There would be a section for each of these: bread, meats, fish, dairy products, fruits, vegetables, dry goods such as rice, flour, and pasta, tea, beer, wine, and vodka, and in some stores, they also sold kitchen cookware. There was no advertising of products in the stores like in the West, since most products were part of the same company, the state. At times one might see a Soviet poster that encouraged healthy eating habits, or against the drinking of alcohol.

The interiors were very plain with most food items being placed on metal racks. Some food shops had shopping carts, but not all, and so the customer would just place the food items she wanted, such as packages of flour, sugar, rice, and most canned goods into the cart or the bag she brought. Then she would take them to the kassa line, and when it was her turn take them out, and place them on the counter where the clerk would punch in the cost of each item into the mechanical cash register. Then the cashier would total your purchase and hand you a slip of paper with the amount you need to pay. Now you put all your items back into your shopping bag and move on to the next sales clerk and present her with the cash slip and the money for the items. She would then give you a paid receipt and you could then take your purchases home.

Some food items needed to be weighed and then priced. These were mainly items like meats, cheeses, sausage, and some dairy products that were kept inside refrigerated display cases since these products had to be kept cold. The main differences were in the ways that the customer paid for the items that she wanted to purchase. Let us use sausage as an example. You would look through the refrigerated display case at what was available, and the price per kilogram. Then you would get into the line and wait for the sales clerk to assist you in your selection of sausage. When it was your turn, you would tell her what you wanted and the weight. She would then slice, weigh your selection, and give you a slip of paper with the price on it. Next, you would go to another line waiting for the kassa, give her the slip of paper with the price written on it, and pay for your sausage. You were then given a receipt that said paid. Now back to the first line to give the paid receipts to the sales clerk and pick up what you had originally selected. You waited in three different lines for the purchase of just one item. This system was often compared to the US where there was a large segment of the population of unemployed workers.

This is another example of the concept of full employment in the USSR. So here we have three people doing the work of one clerk in most Western stores. But then we must remember that this was the worker's paradise, and there was no recognized unemployment. Everyone supposedly had a job. It was not always the job one might have chosen for oneself, but a job. With housing, utilities, and food being subsidized by the state, even people on a low salary could usually maintain a decent standard of living. In the Soviet Union, it was against the law, and one could receive a fine or even go to jail for not having a job.

Even sales clerks went to postsecondary training institutes where they were trained and received a certificate for completing course-work before getting a job in a shop. However, one thing that seemed to be lacking in the curriculum was how to treat customers in a kind and courteous manner. But the need to have returning customers to make a profit did not matter here since all stores were from the same company, the world's largest corporation, the Soviet Union. At times I was even hesitant to ask a sales clerk for any help, fearing that I would get yelled at. Although, when some recognized me as being a foreigner, they went out of their way to be friendly. Often it was the foreigner in the Soviet Union that received good treatment and a fair deal when the poor Russian was treated rather poorly. I never felt good about this.

THE GREEN BOTTLE

During the time I lived in Magadan milk and kefir were sold in green half-liter bottles. These green bottles, as well as lemonade, vodka, and beer bottles, were all made in a large glass factory in the town of Stekolni, not far from Magadan. The word Stekolni means glass, and so does the name of the town where these were made. They must have had several hundred workers in this large glass factory. Unfortunately, when in 1991 the Soviet Union ceased to exist this factory closed down; being without state support all the workers lost their jobs. This was one example of the thousands of incidents that occurred across

LAWRENCE KHLYNOVSKY-ROCKHILL WITH A CLASSIC SOVIET MILK BOTTLE ON THE TERRITORY OF A FORMER GLASS FACTORY IN THE VILLAGE OF STEKOLNY. JULY. 2016. PHOTO BY PAVEL ZHDANOV the former Soviet Union at that time where factories closed down, and workers lost their jobs. It is now a vacant factory with hundreds of broken green bottles lying in piles around the old kilns.

When I wanted to buy milk and kefir, I would try to go early to the dairy section of Volna, the gastronome across the street from the music store Melodia near my Institute, hoping to buy some before the bottles of milk were all gone. This usually meant that I would have to go there right after my last para, and before four o'clock, to find some still available. To carry several of these green bottles of milk and kefir, enough to last a few days, was a bit of a task. First, there was some weight involved, and on slippery winter sidewalks, this could present a challenge. I usually bought three bottles of each. These would just fit into two of the big plastic shopping bags that people used at this time. Even in mild weather, when carrying them, you had to be careful of going up and down the many short stairs along the sidewalks. If carrying them too low one chanced to hit a bottle on the steps, and there you were with broken glass and milk all over the bag and on the sidewalk. It was a bit of a pain. Then after bringing them home, you kept them in the fridge, with limited space. I had never known kefir before living in Magadan and liked it a lot. Dairy products like this were very inexpensive in these times.

After you emptied a bottle, you had to store it and return it to the place where it would be recycled and used again. These green bottles just seemed to accumulate and spread out all over the kitchen floor. When it came to the point that it impeded walking safely in the kitchen without stumbling over them and breaking your neck, you decided that they must go. There was a *five kopek* refund on each bottle. I tried to find a young person who would take them to the recycling place and get the deposit for their effort. This was an early recycling program before this was so prevalent in the West. I ended up keeping three of these green bottles as mementos, and have them at home in Oregon where one still has the foil cap that was on the top of each one when purchased. Now I use them again when I make my kefir from dried culture.

Being situated in a far northern, extremely cold sub-arctic climate, with a poorly developed transportation infrastructure, agriculture was the Magadan Region's least developed economic sector, and one of the hardest hit after the collapse of the Soviet Union in 1991. The large Sovkhoz and Kolkhoz state and collective farms that supplied vegetables, meat, and dairy products to the entire region were disbanded. Today as you drive along the Kolyma Trassa you can see the big empty fields, empty barns, and sheds of the old dairy farms that once operated with hundreds of cows. It looks strange now to see the open windows of the barns without any heads of cows sticking out. Many older folks still remember the high-quality products from these dairies. Not far away were large fields where hay was grown to feed the herds of dairy cows. Some towns were purposely designed just to house the workers, and support the people needed for these agricultural enterprises that were located nearby. Although during Soviet times there were many fine dairy farms, there are no dairy farms producing dairy products here at present. However, some private people do produce dairy products such as tvorog (cottage cheese of sorts), cheese, kefir, sour cream, butter, and raw goat's milk on a limited scale that they sell in the open market. The open market usually has a special section of tables where people sell their locally produced dairy products.

A few enterprises continued to function that are still involved in the food-producing industry, including the Dukcha chicken and poultry farm, bread bakeries, a few fish processing companies, a sausage factory, and some private people who raise beef and pork on their small plots next to their houses in the rural areas. There used to be the Magadan Vodka Distillery, and the Pivo Brewery, but have both since gone out of business.

In 1989 Doug Drum, a businessman, and owner of Indian Valley Meats near Anchorage, Alaska brought a bread-slicing machine to the main Magadan bread factory thinking that pre-sliced bread would be a big hit with the local women. Doug also brought a lot of sausage processing equipment to a plant in Chaibukha where he had hopes of being a part of a joint venture with a reindeer sausage plant there. Doug planned to take his profit out in the velvet reindeer antlers that he would sell to the Koreans. Due to some local politics there, this did not work out and Doug lost a good part of his investment. His idea for the bread-slicing machines did not go over at all. Sliced bread gets stale much faster, and the tradition was, and is, to slice one's bread at home as used. He was very kind, and always thinking of how to help people in the Magadan Region to improve their way of life and doing business. Unfortunately, this became an example of cross-cultural misunderstanding.

CHAPTER TEN:
ECONOMIC TRANSITION OF PERESTROIKA

I want to give my impression as to what the deficit was like for the average Soviet person during the Gorbachev Era of Perestroika and Glasnost. It was a time when people on both sides of the Bering Sea were optimistic about change in the way of increasing the possibilities for coming together in the area of business. Times were changing and it was becoming more possible for private business people to import goods, and sell them in places like the Open Market, and small shops in the downtown area. Many business people in Alaska saw Magadan and the Russian Far East as developing markets for their goods. And Soviet business people saw Alaska as the closest area from which goods that had been in deficit for so long, now had the possibility of being imported and made available to the average Magadan shopper for a decent price and a profit.

Initially, stores in Anchorage like Costco played an important role in that, with charter and scheduled airline flights it became possible for people from Magadan to come to Anchorage to purchase goods to ship back. The demand was there and now it was time to make the goods available on the shelves of the stores in Magadan.

Since almost every Soviet store or shop was a company store, there was not much in the way of competition between stores, and most stores did not have to be overly concerned with the volume of sales, or how much profit was generated at the end of the year. However, manufacturers of goods did have to adhere to specific production quotas stipulated by Gosplan, the Central Planning Department in Moscow. Some people felt that the quotas were not based on a study of the need or the potential market for an individual item, but were arbitrarily set. Many were the times when the demand for an item such as good shoes, or winter coats far exceeded the supply, and people had to do without these important items that could have made their lives a little easier or more comfortable. This is not to speak of the toilet paper deficit such as it was in Magadan when I lived there. Most people just expected that this was the way it was, and so whenever an item that had been in deficit became available, they would purchase as many as they could and then let friends and relatives know right away.

Sales clerks in shops had little incentive to try to increase sales of any given product, for their jobs, did not depend on the number of sales they made, or the profit the store made from sales in a particular department. It was often said that the poor service provided by many sales clerks would not have been tolerated in stores in the West where the company was dependent on satisfied, returning customers that were needed for the store or company to make a profit. If the company did not make a profit, then there was no money to pay the workers, and it went out of business, and people lost their jobs. This was a lesson that was soon to be learned by many Russians who entered into the area of private enterprise after the so-called 'collapse' of the Soviet Union in 1991. The saying, 'business is business', soon became just as true in Russia as in the West.

Times were changing, and for the first time, Aeroflot International Airlines had competition from across the Bering Sea. Aeroflot was the leader, the pioneer so to speak, in providing the first important charter flights that brought government people, business people, and our Magadan and Soldotna school children together in 1989. In the early 1990s, Alaska Airlines also began scheduled flights from Anchorage to Magadan. And then Aeroflot began scheduled service between Magadan, Khabarovsk, and Anchorage. This service then expanded to Seattle and San Francisco, but later Anchorage was dropped due to a lack of passengers. A new era was born, and big changes were soon to come in the lives of the Soviet people in Magadan. No longer were they so restricted from being able to travel abroad. And the potential for being able to come to Anchorage, and to import new consumer goods that had long been in deficit became a reality with the melting of the Ice Curtain.

One of the main differences between life in the Soviet Union and the

US was the cost of basic consumer goods. What most Americans could easily afford was often expensive, and unavailable to most people in the USSR. An example of this would be a regular double-disc drive Panasonic boom box audio cassette tape player. I bought one for $50 at Costco and brought it to Magadan. The price for the average American was ordinary and affordable. But to an average Soviet teacher, the price of this boom box in rubles would be the equivalent of six months of their entire monthly salary. Most could not afford this with the high cost of food prices alone. I brought three as gifts for close friends who gave me something even more valuable, their friendship. I also brought several hand-held solar-powered calculators that were rare items in Soviet stores then. In the US they cost around $5 at the time. Their cost in rubles would be the equivalent of two months of an average Soviet person's monthly income. I gave one to the Business Office Manager at the Pedagogical Institute and she was pleased. Her usual method of computing the finances was done on an abacus. She and many shop assistants were quite speedy in computing in this way. This was the usual technology used by sales clerks in most of the small shops and the stalls in the open market. The cost of the above items in dollars is not related to their cost in rubles.

Walking to the Institute in the morning and going shopping meant that I was out in the winter cold quite often. A fur hat is a necessary item in the Russian winter, especially in Magadan with the cold winds blowing out of Nagaeva Bay, but at this time there were no really good fur hats available in Magadan shops, or even at the kiosks on the Rynok. However, a fellow English teacher, Anatoly Krashakov, from Beringovski in Chukotka, offered to buy one for me and bring it later when he returned to Magadan. At the time he was a translator for the Administration in Beringovski and was just visiting Magadan on business. The price of 450 rubles was high for an average Soviet teacher, being considerably more than even my one month's salary. My salary was 320 rubles a month in the beginning, but I had very little in the way of expenses due to living alone. In Alaska, my monthly salary was over $5000 per month. Not the sum I would be willing to spend on a fur hat. I gave him the money and, in a month, I had my new norkovaya shapka-mink fur hat. It has lasted me for the past 28 years, and I still wear it in Sergiev Posad, a town near Moscow where I now live when in Russia, in the winter.

Although this was a time when many Soviet people had money, the problem was that there was so little of value to purchase. It was a time of the big deficit, as we called it. Some people tried to invest in things that had intrinsic value like gold and diamonds. This was one reason that the Almaz jewelry store in Magadan had display cases that were often half empty. People with a disposable income rarely bought from the display cases in the front part of the store. If they had 'blat – 'an informal exchange of favors -they could purchase the more expensive and higher quality gold jewelry only found (sometimes) in the back room.

This was when the nalevo, under-the-table system of blat was a significant part of the Soviet economy. Blat was, in the words of blat researcher Alena Ledeneva, a form of informal agreements, connections, and exchanges of goods and services, to get what a person wanted or needed in exchange for giving something of similar value to the provider. It was widespread due to the serious deficit in ordinary consumer goods and services. Many people who had such useful connections were able to obtain scarce goods, and services not available to the ordinary person who had to rely on the availability under severe deficit conditions. It was a form of corruption that could be employed by anyone who had the resources and opportunity to do so.

Most often it was not just money that made such a difference in the daily lives of the Soviet people. Even with money, many people found that there was little to buy from the shelves and display cases in most of the shops. This was equally true of what was available in the food shops. You needed to have personal contacts with people who could provide you the opportunity to purchase things and services that you needed or wanted, and in return, you had to be able to offer something to them.

A prime example of this is my story of Pasha and the Three Pigs Shop (nicknamed 'Three Sveeny Magaziney'). One day as I was walking home from teaching when I noticed a long line in front of a small food shop, nicknamed 'Three Pigs Shop', situated by Torgovi Tsentr, the Shopping Center. I learned that they had received a supply of bottles of vegetable oil used for cooking and salads.

This had been uavailable, and in big deficit for some time. I called my friend Pasha and told him what I saw and that I would buy some for his family too, and I was willing to stand in the long line and wait my turn. He said that this was not necessary as he would call his friend who was the manager of a sporting goods store in the Shopping Center, who knew the manager of this small food shop. She would call the manager of the food shop who would let us in the back door to buy the oil we wanted, and so as not to have to wait in the long line. In a little while, we both went in the back door of the food shop and bought the allowed number of bottles of cooking oil. Pasha had a lot of contacts to get the things he needed, and in turn, could offer help to his friends too. This was the usual system, an underground people's economy, of sorts.

Pasha told me that it was a time of high crime in Magadan. Quite a few small businesses were starting up, such as small clothing stores, shoe stores, and those selling housewares from China, some being sold from the small, covered sections in the open market. Most were just family-run and obtained their merchandise from Chinese importers, the materik, and stores like Costco in Anchorage, Alaska. These businesses were often exploited by what was thought to be a 'mafia' type of people who offered a form of protection for a monthly fee. This eventually changed into large security firms like those found in the West. At this time, it was not unusual to see an armed guard posted inside the entrance of what would be considered just an ordinary retail store in the West, with little merchandise that one would consider to be of high value. Yet, a gold and diamond jewelry store would always have armed guards at the entrance.

When people from Magadan came to Anchorage, and they went to places like Costco and J C Penny, it only validated their feelings that the future held out the possibility for more changes for the better if we could just melt the Ice Curtain that was preventing the way ahead for a more pleasant lifestyle for the people in Magadan. They deserved better and had hopes that soon it would happen. But unfortunately, the collapse of the Soviet Union dashed their hopes to the ground under the Presidency of Boris Yeltsin. The 1990s would thrust the Russian people into terrible economic turmoil.

The Soviet Union ceased to exist in December of 1991 when Gorbachev stepped down as President of the Soviet Union, and Yeltsin became the President of the Russian Federation. Russia and other member countries of the USSR broke away, and it ceased to exist. Initially, there was hope, but under Yeltsin, things would get much worse. Russians experienced some of the most difficult times after 1991 when there was a severe economic depression not so different from the 1929 economic crash in the United States. Many, many people lost their jobs, and their life savings if they had any.

People were often forced to sell anything they had just to get some money to pay for their rent and food. Many factories closed, and some paid their workers with what they manufactured, such as clothing, tools, auto parts, etc. In the mid and late 1990s, people in Alaska were sending container loads of food and clothing to their friends in Magadan. Magadan experienced a severe shortage of coal for firing their boilers at the central heating plant one winter. People's flats were without the heat needed to just be comfortable. The milk in the cat's bowl on the kitchen floor of our family flat froze each night from the lack of any heat in the flat. These were exceedingly difficult times for almost everyone in Russia.

The decision by President Yeltsin to discontinue the state subsidies, and price controls on goods and services was a terrible blow to the average family. Prices of goods and foods skyrocketed, and it was uncontrolled capitalism at its worst. Millions of Russians were living below the poverty level without any help from state social agencies. Much of the blame for this terrible economic depression must lie at the foot of President Clinton's Administration, and the many American economic advisors, including the Harvard University economists who rushed to advise President Yeltsin and the Russian government to privatize so many parts of the government. The result as we now see was that the Oligarchs took advantage of this situation, and in effect took control of much of the national wealth of the country. The people lost all hope in the system that in many ways had provided them with a reasonably good life for more than seventy years.

CHAPTER ELEVEN:
TEACHING AT MAGADAN PEDAGOGICAL
INSTITUTE

Growing up in the US, the public media was at times full of the differences between our two political and economic systems, and ways of life. I had read many books such as 'The Russians' by Hedrick Smith of the New York Times, and 'Klass' by David K. Willis, along with countless articles from major news magazines. But reading about life in the USSR is not the same as being able to experience this on your own. And what I read was always somebody else's interpretation of what was going on there. I wanted to find out for myself what it was like to live and work in the Soviet Union. I was willing to move to Magadan and to take a sabbatical from the Kenai School District for two years and trade making US dollars for being paid in Soviet rubles. I knew the experience would be invaluable and this was a chance of a lifetime.

I had dreamed of being able to live and teach in Magadan, and now it was to be a reality. My teaching was going to be a whole new experience for both myself and the staff and students at Magadan Pedagogical Institute. Having taught for almost thirty years at various levels and cross-cultural settings, from the University of Alaska to elementary classrooms, from small-town Cordova to the Bureau of Indian Affairs boarding school at Mt. Edgecumbe, often with those having limited English language, gave me the confidence I would be able to do this well. My ten years with the Bureau of Indian Affairs helped me in working with students from other cultures, and experiential backgrounds, other than white, urban, and middle class. Now I would be immersed in the Soviet culture of the Russian people. I was to be both a teacher and a student for the next two years.

MAGADAN PEDAGOGICAL INSTITUTE

Even though I had only recently arrived, and was getting settled in my flat, I was ready to get to work. Though classes would not begin for some days because each year MPI students are expected to go out to the fields for a week or more to help harvest the cabbage crop before their classes were to begin, I was eager to see my class schedule and to meet my fellow teachers in the Foreign Language Department. I had to wait until cabbage time was finished before I would be able to meet my students, but not my fellow teachers. After breakfast, I walked down the three flights of stairs in my apartment building, up the little hill to Ulitsa Gagarina, and across town to Magadan Peda.gogical Institute. Most streets were lined with five-story apartment buildings with stores at the street level. Though there was no snow yet, it was a usual cool, rather windy morning for a walk. In about twenty-five minutes I walked up to the front doors of this four-story Soviet red brick building dating to 1960. There were some interesting designs in the bricks across the front of the building, but it was not fancy. There was a small unobtrusive sign next to the front double doors that let you know this was Magadan Pedagogical Institute.

As you entered the foyer through the front doors there was always a lady on duty sitting behind a small window to see if anyone needed any help. Behind her was the coatroom, a large area with racks where students could take off their heavy warm winter coats and hats, so they did not have to carry them around from classroom to classroom. On the right side of the entrance foyer, there was a large mirror that the students used when combing their hair, checking their make-up, and making sure they looked nice. To the side of the mirror was a pedestal on the top of which sat a large carved white marble bust of Vladimir Ilyich Lenin. We could never forget this was still the Soviet Union. Vladimir Ilyich Lenin was always the first to greet the students, and faculty each day. I climbed the three flights of stairs and met with Dean Roman Tchaikovski in his office. He said to come in, and so I did. We talked a little about what I would soon be doing with students in the nearby classrooms. Then we walked down the corridor to the English Language Faculty room where he introduced me to my fellow English Language teachers: Larisa Kokoreva, Dmitry Politaev, Natalia Filkova, Irina Bragina, and Margarita Martynyuk. It was a great pleasure to be able to work with such fine and dedicated teachers. I felt welcome right from the time of our first meeting.

Then Roman took me out into the corridor and showed me the raspisanie-schedule of classes for all the teachers in our department. I could see that this was going to be quite different from teaching in an elementary school classroom. I had a full schedule of paras. A para is 45 minutes of instruction and there are two paras per class session. I had two class sessions, four paras each day, one in the morning, and one in the afternoon. I would be teaching from the regular Soviet textbooks primarily English grammar, English Literature, and a class in American Studies.

However, it seemed that most of my fellow teachers felt that their students also deserved to have some time with the native English Language speaker and so they often invited me to come to their classes when I had free time. I must say that my free time was quite limited by the demand for my time at the Institute and visiting English language teacher's classes in the city schools.

All the teachers in the Foreign Language Department were well-versed in their language specialty. My colleagues knew the English Language in a far more in-depth way than the average college professor in the US. It is interesting to note that some of the teachers were graduates of this department and were doing graduate work under the supervision of Dean Roman Tchaikovski. It would be unusual for an American university to hire one of its graduates. But I must say that with the intense and rigorous study that they went through, they were well qualified to teach in our undergraduate program. They were very disciplined and dedicated professionals. Every week or so we would have a Foreign Language Department meeting to discuss any impor-

THE BUILDING OF THE PHILOLOGICAL FACULTY OF SVGU. MAGADAN. 2010. PHOTO BY PAVEL ZHDANOV

tant information or concerns from the Office of the Dean. My fellow teachers had many questions about the difference between the University of Alaska system, and our Magadan Pedagogical Institute. There was a lot to talk about since Magadan Pedagogical Institute was all new to me, and I and the University of Alaska were both new to them. It was a very lively little department at times, a fun place to be with my colleagues who became my good friends. There was a strong feeling of comradery amongst our group of English teachers. I continue to keep in contact with several of them to this day. I can say without reservation that this was the most interesting time of my career in education.

With the Foreign Language Department located on the fourth floor of the old Institute building, we had a daily exercise program up and down-stairs because there was no lift in the building. The Foreign Language Kafedra took up the entire fourth floor with offices and classrooms. We six English language teachers shared an office of our own and a secretary, and each of us had our own desk. Roman, the Dean, had a separate office and two secretaries. Our classrooms were shared, and so, for the most part, were not decorated in any interesting way. Some did have student-made posters, and a few had travel posters of England.

To some extent these classrooms and offices were like many others of the same vintage, one size fits all. The interior walls between the classrooms were made from regular cement blocks, almost the same as an exterior wall. A lot of work when making changes in room sizes. The windows were a Soviet version of double glazing. This means that there were two actual panes of glass that were separated by at least 8 inches in the thick exterior walls. To open or close, you had to deal with two windows. This was an attempt to have better insulation since the air space between the two panes of glass should keep the warm air in, and the cold outside air out. However, being a bit old, somehow the window frames did not always fit into the wall very tightly. At times, they provided a bit more in the way of air circulation than most of us wanted, especially on cold, wind-blown, winter days when papers would fly off the student's desks from the wind coming in through the cracks in the window frames. There were days when we all had to wear our coats inside the classroom to just stay warm. The steam radiators along the walls seemed at times to hardly be even warm. In the fall, the Central Heating Plant did not turn on the heat until there were a certain number of days with the temperature outside being below a certain degree Celsius. So not only were our classrooms a bit cold, but people's flats were a bit cool too.

The English Language Kafedra office was the center of our lives at the Institute. I had brought as gifts to the Foreign Language Department an Alaska flag and an American flag that are both still hanging in our office. It was not uncommon to see indoor houseplants on windowsills in an office, and we had several in ours. Some were quite large and must have been growing there for a long time. Each office had a chainik, electric tea kettle, and teacups and saucers stashed away in a cabinet. When there was a break between paras, or at lunchtime, out they would come and anyone that wanted could help themselves to a cup of chai, and often some sweets that one of the teachers had brought into the office. There was always a tort and sweets brought to celebrate a teacher's birthday. A rather nice bakery was not far away from our institute. This may not have been to our advantage, but it sure was nice to have a tasty sweet with tea during breaks.

One must remember this was still the Soviet Union in 1989, and we did not expect that our little Pedagogical Institute would be as up-to-date as say the University of Alaska. When I first arrived at MPI the secretaries in our Foreign Language Department were still using old manual typewriters.

Before I left Soldotna, I went over to the School District Salvage Department and saw that several IBM Selectric ball electric typewriters were to be salvaged. I ask if it would be possible for the school district to donate three of these typewriters to the Magadan Pedagogical Institute. The answer was in the affirmative, and so I now had to pack these machines into boxes that I would take with me when I went to Magadan. Upon arrival in Magadan, we took them up to our department, and it was like bringing space-age technology to the secretaries. They were appreciative, to say the least. We did have to include very heavy converters for the electrical power in Russia is 220. Luckily for me, I was flying on an Aeroflot charter flight, and there was no weight or baggage limit. I knew the Aeroflot Station Manager in Anchorage, Sergei V. Balaur, and he was supportive of our student exchange efforts and tried to help us in every way he could, including the price of student airfares.

The technology that we teachers in Alaska enjoyed, and took for granted, was far ahead of what Magadan teachers had to use at MPI or in

ALAN MILLER, A TEACHER FROM THE KENAI PENIN-
SULA, WHO WAS ENGAGED IN SCHOOL EXCHANGES
UNTIL THE EARLY 2000S, PICKED UP THE BATON OF
LARRY ROCKHILL. ALAN MILLER TRAINED IN ROS-
TOV, THEN IN MOSCOW AT MOSCOW STATE UNIVER-
SITY, DESIGNED HIS CLASS IN THE STYLE OF THE
USSR. 1990. PHOTO COURTESY OXOTNIK PRESS
ARCHIVES

their schools. In most Alaska schools Xerox machines and Xerox paper for teacher use were just part of the regular budget and were not rationed.

However, in Magadan, teachers in the schools and at the Pedagogical Institute were using multiple sheets of carbon paper to make duplicate copies of pages of lessons, and tests they wanted for their students. I have seen teachers using up to ten sheets of carbon paper to make ten copies of a page of lessons for their students over and over again. This was such a time-consuming task, but carbon paper was the best that they had back then. Carbon paper had long been gone in most schools in the US.

There were very few Xerox copy machines in the Administration office at MPI, and they were not to be used by teachers, only the office staff had access to these machines, and they were restricted for use in making copies of documents. In another institute, the cord for the Xerox copy machines was locked up each weekend lest somebody desired to make copies of some forbidden information. This was soon to change, and most Magadan schools and our Institute had copy machines for use by the teachers as well as the administration.

My teaching style was somewhat different from that of my colleagues. Their approaches and teaching styles were quite strict and formal. This set the tone for their high expectations from the students and the discipline found in their classes. The results of their high expectations and discipline could be seen in the very high quality of the student's work. The classroom settings that I observed were never at that time any way close to the informal atmosphere seen in many college classrooms in the US.

Upon the professor entering the classroom, all the students would stand up and remain standing until told to be seated. The teacher would usually sit behind a desk or stand behind the rostrum when speaking to the class. My dear friend Larisa Kokoreva always greeted her class with "Good morning comrades", tovarishchi, in true Soviet style. Larisa was an excellent teacher and had high expectations for her students and they achieved accordingly. I decided to be different and a bit more relaxed.

We all followed the curriculum guide as far as the textbooks that we were using with the students. My main focus was on reading and discussing English Literature, conversational English, and American Studies. I certainly did not have the in-depth knowledge of English grammar that my colleagues possessed.

The first day of teaching was an introduction to myself, who I was, and where I had come from. I also had the students introduce themselves to me. They were an open and lively group, and we soon became friends, not just a teacher and a student. These were the finest, and most hardworking students I have ever had the privilege of teaching. I can say that from the first meeting with my class, I felt a closeness that would not go away. I decided right then that it was important for them to get to know me as an individual, and not only from behind an imaginary wall or desk.

When I was teaching, I usually walked around the room and spoke to individuals, often at their desks. Sometimes I would sit on their desks, and get upfront and personal. This was of course not at all what they were used to, and in the beginning, they did not know what to think of this new teaching style. However, I felt that I could convey a lot more than just information by relating to each student as an individual. I did not want them to see me as just another teacher giving out information, but as a real person, an ordinary American professor, an individual who tried to convey that he cared about his students as individuals. In this way, I think I was able to do both, teach, and become a friend to the students in my classes. Even today I still have contact with some of my former students as adults.

Discipline was never a problem in my classes. The students were for the most part always serious, interested, and engaged in what we were discussing. Of course, this was an unusual situation for them to be with an American professor. They knew they were a unique group. and they enjoyed what we were doing in class, and I certainly enjoyed being their

LARRY ROCKHILL TEACHES A CLASS IN THE FACULTY OF PHILOLOGY AT MAGADAN STATE PEDAGOGICAL INSTI-
TUTE. 1990 PHOTO BY PAVEL ZHDANOV

teacher. My home group was a group of 10 bright, first-year students. Such
an ideal language class of this small size would not usually exist in a US
university. With a small group, it was possible to interact frequently with
everyone. These 10 students were at the top of the more than 100 students from the Magadan high school graduates who had taken the comprehensive written and oral exams to enter the Institute. They were ex-
ceptional in many ways.

My home group classes were unique in more ways than just the fact
that they had a native English Language professor. Each day there was a
short break between the two 45 min. long paras. In my home-room class,
as soon as the end of the para bell would ring, out would come the chainik,
plug it in, and in a few minutes, we would all have a cup of hot tea with
some little pastry that one of us brought that day. This would be a short
time of just talking and visiting about whatever anyone wanted to discuss. After ten minutes or so, the cups were emptied, and the chainik was
put back in the cupboard well hidden. Somehow Roman Tchaikovski heard
about this little activity, and one morning we came in and found our
chainik gone. It was a mystery, but soon solved, and I had to go and explain to Roman that we were not wasting time, just 'doing English 'over
a cup of chai. He gave in and our chai program continued.

I developed my lessons following the guidelines from the Soviet textbooks that the students were using. Here the stress was on what I would call Oxford English. My teaching was focused on reading, and then discussing in English the passages from classical English literature. These were interesting excerpts taken from a particular work by a famous English author such as William Somerset Maugham, who was a favorite author of many of my students. We would read the passages, and then discuss them among ourselves. They were also required to memorize passages from the texts and to translate them from English to Russian. Each day they had to answer comprehensive questions from the text as their homework.

Here was the English language put to practical use, for the students had to read, and give their impression of the work in English. For me, this too was interesting, both the passage and even more so the comments of the students related to the subject matter. Even though these were first-year students, they were able to do quite well in analyzing the readings in their second language. At times, this resulted in long and interesting discussions. I was quite impressed with some of their analytical skills. All in all, after our regular work from the lessons in the textbooks, we did spend quite a bit of time conversing with the focus on them listening to me speak on the subjects they were interested in learning about. One of my main tasks and one that was appealing to, and desired by my students was listening to a native English language speaker. This is one of the main deficits found lacking in most of the English Language programs throughout the Soviet Union.

Many of their questions were on the differences between our two systems of higher education. In the Soviet Union, most university and college students went to the 11th grade and then graduated from high school. The program at MPI was a post-high school five-year course of study. This contrasts with our usual four years of high school before graduating and going on to study in a four-year college program in the US. They were interested and surprised to find out that the University of Alaska students were able to have electives within their major coursework, as well as having to take required subjects. My MPI student's five-year English course of study was a prescribed list of subjects with no chance of adding or deleting any classes. And, there were many other differences between the two systems of higher education. For example, all my MPI students received a monthly stipendiya of 90 rubles a month and paid no tuition or fees for living in the dormitory. Education was free to all in the Soviet Union up

167

to and before any post-graduate studies. Students did not have to buy their textbooks; they would just check out from the college library the required textbooks they would need for the classes they would take during a semester. They were responsible for taking care of and returning these books when finished with them.

To make our classes a bit more real and unique, I developed some simulation activities for them to act out. One was a restaurant situation where they had to take the roles of a waitress and a customer. I brought several menus from some restaurants in Alaska, and they had to greet and present the menu to the customer and then take the person's order. Some of the choices on the menu were quite new to them, but this gave them practical experience in using English in a simulated real-life setting.

I would at first demonstrate how this would be done in a real-life situation and then explain what an ordinary Alaskan restaurant was like. Going to a restaurant in Magadan was a different experience than in the US. Later on, I used as an example, shopping in a US grocery store with empty cereal boxes and cans of vegetables. They were the shoppers and would have to take their items to the kassa, have them tabulated, and then pay for them. All this required them to converse in English with their fellow students in the class.

To be honest, as far as the real situation in the United States was concerned was the way my American Studies classes went. I felt it was important for them to understand the real US situation rather than the official interpretation given in their press and television, or for that matter the way the American media portrayed life in the United States. Every country tries to put forth its best picture of how they want others to see them. I did watch a couple of Soviet documentary educational films on life in the US that focused on such problems as homelessness, alcoholism, poverty, violence, etc. These were serious problems, true, but only part of the big picture. They realized this to some extent.

The reality was that at this time most of my students felt that the US was perfect, and the USSR was in serious decline. However, I never tried to make it look like the US was superior to the USSR. I was open and often stressed that the US had many positive aspects, but also many failings and problems, and was far from perfect. Often, I would use examples of the racial prejudice against black people, and how they were treated, in the present and the past, as well as the terrible treatment, some say genocide, against the American Indian, and the prejudice in the South-west against Mexican people. This was shameful, and not always dealt with, even in American History textbooks. Sometimes, I felt that if people gauged life in the US by what they saw in American films on TV, where they saw so much violence and killing, they would not let their children go there. We also at times distorted life in the Soviet Union in the documentary films shown in the US. The US media tried to make the difficult lives of so many Soviet people the focus, not to speak of the lack of personal freedoms that people in the US often just took for granted. I felt that the BBC films of life in the USSR tried at least to be factual and balanced, and those were the ones I used in my Soviet Studies classes.

I brought several audio cassette tapes with the latest American music. My students would often borrow these tapes, then listen very attentively and write down the lyrics. One of the most popular was a children's tape titled "Alaska Is the State for Me". When the first Rotary Clubs arrived from Alaska, we had a welcoming lunch at the Institute and my students all sang "Alaska is the State for Me", and it was a big hit with the Rotarians. The Rotarians were duly impressed with the way that our students were able to converse with them in English. Our students greatly enjoyed being able to converse with so many Americans at one time in one group. It was a first that would continue as many people from Alaska would be coming over to Magadan during the next two years and beyond.

Due to the generosity of Chancellor Patrick O'Rourke of UAF, and the expertise of Dan Johnson from Nome Community College, we had a large-screen TV and satellite dish antenna installed at MPI. This made it possible for our English language students to see live Alaska television programs and some good American films, and to listen to a variety of the English language being spoken by many different actors. It was very popular with the students and on Saturdays with children in the community. The program was supported by one of our fine administrators, Stanislav Penievskiy. This was where the American video cassettes were put to good use.

Some students who had money from their parents were able to live in rented flats, and some lived at home. However, most students lived in the college student dorm. The dorm rooms were not at all spacious and there were up to eight students in some rooms with just a bed and a locker for themselves, and a communal desk or two for studying. This was more of a challenge for the girls since they had to find a place to put all their make-up, combs and curling irons. Usually, this was on the desks that were designed for writing and studying. The girls had their priorities. Students were able to decorate their rooms, as young people do, with posters and self-made art. It was communal living Soviet-style, with little in the way of space or luxury. But the price was right, and you did not have to be well off to attend college. And when you graduated you were not burdened with a college tuition debt that would take you years to repay.

The college stolovaya was the cafeteria where many of the students ate lunch or had snacks. It was open in the morning from the time classes began until late in the afternoon. Although the main meal served was at lunchtime, one could just drop in anytime for a cup of tea and a pastry. Here you had a group of fine women cooks who prepared all dishes from scratch. This was in great contrast to our US college cafeterias where pre-prepared meals were usually served. The women cooks did a fine job in preparing a nice selection of rather tasty dishes. You could buy a three-course lunch for one ruble. This was the time when the kopek still had some value, but not anymore for sure. I often ate here with my students where we could just sit and engage in a normal conversation between friends. Roman warned me that I might die if I ate in our "terrible" stolo-vaya. It was a joke, of course. I was living alone and so this was my main meal of the day, and an opportunity to interact with my students outside the classroom. I thoroughly enjoyed the variety of Russian dishes freshly prepared, and the price was right.

The menu was quite varied from day to day. It consisted of the first course of freshly prepared soup and the second course, a variety of Russian salads. The third course consisted of the main dishes such as meat and fish cutlets, pirogi (small pie), fried fish, pasta, meat pies, or other Russian dishes such as pelmeni. The final course was some sort of dessert in the form of a cake, cookies, pudding, a sweet pastry, etc. There was also black bread, white bread, tea, and compote available. If you went around one o'clock, after the second para, there was often a long line. Except for soups and the main dish, this was self-service with all foods sitting out on the counter shelves to take and place on your tray. Today it would not even be close to one ruble for all this since there are no state subsidies involved.

The students that I had the privilege of teaching at the Institute were the very best in all my thirty years of teaching. They were brilliant, very serious, and hard-working. They were the top students who had applied and passed the state comprehensive entrance examination to get into the Institute. They wanted to learn and to learn even more than what was in the course of study. We had extra meetings where we would get together as a group and have lunch or meet at my flat in the evening. Our conversations were about life and what the world had in store for them to live under the conditions of the Soviet Union at that time and to try and guess what the future held for them. There were several students who later took degrees from the University of Alaska, and some who stayed in Alaska to marry and work. Irina Alishova and Dina Nekrasova, both excellent students, graduated from MPI and took classes at the University of Alaska Anchorage. Gleb Tchaikovsky was one of my very best students, and at the top of his class; after graduating from MPI he received an MBA from UAF. Anna Tokaeva is another example of an excellent student who also studied and received an MBA after graduating from the Institute. Many of our students were fluent enough in English to be able to act as translators for Alaskan businesspeople who came to Magadan.

I did many things with my students outside of the classroom. Sometimes they invited me to come to their homes if they lived outside the dormitory. On one occasion I was invited to the birthday celebration of Taras Korolyuk at his home. He also invited several other students from our group. I remember this was the first time I tasted okroshka, a traditional Russian cold soup made with kvas and filled with sausage, cucumbers, hard-boiled eggs, and green onions. It was delicious and is now my favorite. His mother also made a special lemon torte which I wanted to get the recipe for but didn't get. Taras was a serious student and always did his best. I had the pleasure of reconnecting with him in Moscow last year. He has a nice restaurant that specializes in vegetarian dishes. Taras was one of many students that I had the privilege of getting to know outside of the Institute setting.

NOMINATION FOR PROFESSORSHIP: INTERNATIONAL PEDAGOGICAL UNIVERSITY OF MAGADAN

Although this took place in 1993 after we had moved to Soldotna, Alaska, I will place it here where I talk about my teaching at MPI.

NOMINATION

For the award of the title of "Honorary Professor of the International Pedagogical University of Magadan, Russian Federation to Mr. Larry Rockhill.

Larry Rockhill belongs to those people who were the first to extend the hand of friendship to Russians during Perestroika. Working as a teacher in Soldotna, Alaska, Larry Rockhill decided to offer help and assistance to the Russian Far East. In 1989, with an invitation from the Magadan State Pedagogical Institute along with an agreement with the University of Alaska Fairbanks, he came to Magadan and began teaching English at Magadan State Pedagogical Institute. Being an experienced teacher and having a Bachelor of Arts Degree in Education and Psychology, a benevolent friend, and a reliable person, he gained the love and respect of all who knew him. With the direct participation of Larry Rockhill, the first relations between the University of Alaska and Magadan International Pedagogical Institute were established, and the student and faculty exchange program was established. He made a great contribution to the creation and development of the International Pedagogical University as a coordinator of Russian-American relations, as a member of the Committee of the development of the International Pedagogical University, as a native speaker who fostered in many students of the Foreign Language Department the love of the English Language and in that way contributed to the successful study of Magadan students at the University of Alaska. As a member of the MSPI delegation, he worked at the Ministry of Education of the Russian Federation and participated in the scientific conference of the Americanists in Moscow. After returning to Alaska, Larry Rockhill continues to cooperate with the International Pedagogical University and the University of Alaska contributing greatly to the process of rapprochement between Russians and Americans.

Based on what is stated above I ask the board of Trustees of the International Pedagogical University to present Mr. Larry Rockhill with the title of "Honorary Professor of the International Pedagogical University in Magadan."

The President of the International Pedagogical University in Magadan. Signed: E. Kokorev

MY TEACHING SALARY

In Alaska, teachers usually had their salaries deposited directly into their checking accounts or in the form of a paper check. My salary at Magadan Pedagogical Institute was 320 rubles a month after a 13% tax was deducted. This was due to my having a Master's degree which was about double the salary of an ordinary teacher at the Institute. It is interesting to note that many teachers at MPI received a lower salary than many secondary school teachers. This was in part based on the number of hours the secondary school teachers taught. My salary was more than I needed to live on being single and living alone. I had given up my full Kenai School District salary and only received the district paying into my retirement fund. Making rubles was a bit of a problem since it did not pay for my house payment in Alaska, which came out of my savings account each month. However, the reward was an unforgettable experience of two years of teaching in the Soviet Union. These were by far the most interesting years of my career in education. No amount of money could even come close to being equal to the value of all the wonderful experiences and friendships I enjoyed living there in Magadan.

All MPI teachers were paid once a month. On that day we were told when we should go to the special little window near the Financial Office to receive our pay. We did not receive a check but were paid in cash in rubles, and if you did not get to the pay window early enough you might have to take your salary in small denominations, which meant that you might get a stack of three-, and one-ruble notes. The rubles came in fifty-, twenty-five-, ten-, five-, and one-ruble notes. On payday one of the Finance Office staff had to go to the central bank and take all of our salary money in cash in a big box. As you can imagine, there were times when your wallet might be bulging with the paper rubles you needed to just go grocery shopping. This was another great memory of the unique times that were everyday happenings when I lived in the Magadan.

CHAPTER TWELVE:
ANNA AND PAUL COME TO MAGADAN

In the early spring of 1990, two of my three children, Anna and Paul came to visit me during the second year I lived in Magadan. This was the result of talking to my dear friend Roman Tchaikovski. I mentioned to him that Paul was fluent in German, and had studied at Freiburg University in Germany, near the Black Forest. Roman was a German Language Professor and suggested that Paul could come and would be welcome to visit classes. Anna at that time was doing graduate work at the University of Michigan in Public Policy, and she was well-versed in women's issues in the public discourse in the United States. President Kokorev agreed with Roman and very generously issued them both invitations and said he would pay their way on Aeroflot to come from Moscow to Magadan, still a closed Soviet city in the Russian Far East.

Roman had his son Gleb, one of my best students, fly to Moscow to meet them and bring them to Magadan. This was of course more than anyone would have expected, and I was most grateful. Gleb met them and had two days to show them around some of the historical places in Moscow, and then it was off to the Russian Far East. I had written to Anna and Paul many times, so they had some idea of what to expect.

When they arrived at the Magadan International Airport both Roman and I were there to meet them. It was a usual chilly day. Although both had traveled abroad to places in Europe, here they were entering a different land, the Soviet Union, where they only knew what they had read in the press and saw on TV. When Anna had mentioned that she was go-

174

FAMILY PICTURE, TOP ROW, LISA, DAUGHTER, MARY ROCKHILL, MOTHER, LARRY, BOTTOM ROW, ANNA, DAUGH-TER, AND PAUL, SON. SALEM, OREGON, 1980. KHLINOVSKI ROCKHILL ARCHIVES

ing to Magadan, some of her teachers at the University of Michigan told her that it was unheard of for her father, an American, to get a one-year-long Soviet visa to the closed city of Magadan. But this was the Gorbachev Era, and the time was right for us all to be able to share this memorable experience together.

Magadan was considered an international border city and secu.rity was tight. When one arrived at the Magadan International Airport and walked down the ramp from the plane, the usual Soviet Border Guard soldier was standing there with a submachine gun in his arms. Even Soviet citizens were only able to enter the Magadan region with special permission, such as if they lived there or had an officially approved reason for business. Yet as soon as you were down the ramp, through the airport terminal, and standing on Ulitsa Lenina (Lenin Street) in the town center you would find that the people of Magadan were some of the warmest and most friendly people in all the world. And they are still the same today.

I was very excited to see both of them and could hardly believe that they had arrived. The application process to obtain a Soviet visa had some problems and took the usual long processing time. We went in the MPI Volga (car) to my flat on Ulitsa Boldyreva (Boldyrev street) and got them

175

LENA TIKHOMIROVA, IRINA ALISHOVA, LARRY ROCKHILL, TONY, A STUDENT OF THE UNIVERSITY OF ALASKA AND GEOL.OGISTS AT THE AIRPORT IN THE VILLAGE OF UST-OMCHUG. SUMMER 1992 PHOTO BY PAVEL ZHDANOV

settled. They traveled light but managed to bring their Dad some interesting trivial things from the States. My one-room Soviet flat was a bit crowded in the usual Soviet way, with two single beds/chairs, and a long couch, but it was so nice to be all together and to share this experience with two of my children. Unfortunately, Lisa was not able to join us. They were to stay with me in Magadan for two weeks, so would be able to get to know the situation in the Soviet Union from the inside.

They went with me on most days to the Institute and visited my classes. Since all my students could converse readily in English, they made friends quite easily. Now there were two more Americans here, but this time much closer to the age of my students. Paul became friends with Andrei, one of Roman's best German Language students, since they could both speak German. Andrei took and showed Paul around the city, to meet some of his friends. This made Paul feel good to be part of the local group, and he also visited Roman's German classes during the day and got to know many of the students there. Paul was the first American student to participate in classes in the German Department of MPI. Even today Andrei speaks to me of the good memories he has of the time he spent with Paul.

LAWRENCE H. KHLINOVSKI ROCKHILL

Few American women had had the opportunity to visit Magadan in the past. And very few Soviet women from Magadan had been to Alaska or the US. This was the time in the US when women were discussing and changing many of the old ways of thinking related to their roles in society, the workplace, and the family. And with so many changes under Gorbachev, Soviet women were also rethinking their place in Soviet society. I told Roman about Anna's interest and involvement in social issues in the US. One year she worked part-time while attending the University of Michigan, at one of the main organizations that provided food, clothing, and shelter to those in need. She was always concerned about the well-being of the poor, particularly the Native Americans. Anna was considered by some in Magadan to be a representative of the modern American woman. This was the time, after the Hippy Movement of the 1960s, the period of the so-called liberation of the modern American woman, and the feminist movement in the US. Anna has always had a strong interest in liberal women's issues. With this in mind, Roman and Evgeny made arrangements for Anna to give lectures on the women's movement in the US to anyone interested.

Anna gave lectures at our Magadan Pedagogical Institute, and at the House of Political Education of the Communist Party, near the TV tower at the top of Lenin Street. Soviet Women held a strong interest in this topic during these changing times of Glasnost and Perestroika of the Gorbachev era. Her lecture at the House of Political Education was well attended, and there were many questions from the audience after she finished. Most Soviet women were well aware of the differences between their place in Soviet society, and that of the average American woman in the US. After her talk, the Magadan Communist Party presented her with several nice gifts, including a fur hat and a seal skin purse. The irony was that upon her return to Michigan she shared some of these nice gifts from the Communist Party with her husband's father who was an ardent anti-communist.

We were invited to several friends for dinner during their stay. Some of the most memorable times were when we were invited to dinner at Luda and Roman Tchaikovskiy's, and Evgeny and Larisa Kokorev's homes. Here were some of my closest friends and they went out of their way to make Anna and Paul feel welcome. Both had children of a similar age. This was another opportunity to see what life was like for a real Soviet family, albeit these families were somewhat above the usual working-class family in Magadan. They each had three-room flats with lots of bookshelves filled with Russian classics and Soviet literature. Each evening was filled with interesting conversations related to the differences in the daily lives of the people in both our great countries.

Somehow, Irina Alishova's Mom Alexandra found out that Paul likes chicken, which was not often available in Magadan food shops. She worked as a sales clerk in a gastronome, so one afternoon she called her boss and off we went with Irina in a taxi to that food shop, and in the back door to buy seven whole chickens. Back home we went, and later she prepared them for Paul when she invited us over to their flat for a delicious chicken dinner. Alexandra was always kind to me during my living in Magadan, at times sharing with me her homemade pelmeni and solenaia kapusta (salted fermented cabbage). Her daughter, Irina was truly one of my best students, and I can say she was quite fluent in English even as a first-year student. They always made me feel so at home whenever I visited them. Ira had the cutest little daughter Ramina who treated me as her dedushka, grandfather. I keep in close touch with Ira and her family when I am in Moscow.

CHAPTER THIRTEEN:
DIARY ENTRIES

April 1, 1990

Today was a special day for me. This morning, Roman and I rode out to the Magadan Airport to meet Anna, Paul, and Gleb when they arrived on the afternoon Aeroflot flight from Moscow. It was wonderful to see them here in Magadan. I could hardly believe that they were able to come after all the problems with their getting their visas, and my being able to pay for their tickets with rubles.

Gleb said that they almost missed their flight as they were told to go to the wrong airport and had to then go to the right one. Luda and Roman invited us all over for dinner that night. It was interesting for Anna and Paul to see their flat with all its books and pictures. Luda made a delicious dinner of pelmeni, Russian borsch (soup), and her wonderful apple pie. There were many toasts with fine Russian vodka. Paul had a nice conversation with Luda since both spoke German. Then around 11 pm, we took a taxi home, and after a long day, it was time for sleeping. So very nice for us all to be together in my little one-room Soviet flat.

April 10, 1990

Bob Williams called me at 0700, and I gave him my wish list. I called Perry and David at UAF and told them that all is ready for them to come if the weather is good with Jim Rowe of Bering Air from Nome to Provideniya and then take Aeroflot to Magadan. Anna had lunch with Vera, Larisa, Margarita, and Irina at Ode Restaurant. Paul went with three pretty

Russian girls from MPI to Ariran, the Korean restaurant. Later Anna and I went with Ira to Torgovi Shopping Center and then to the House of Political Education for Anna's lecture on the Role of the Modern American in Today's World. There were around fifty people, mostly women present. The ladies seemed very interested in what Anna had to say, and many questions followed her lecture. Ira, my colleague from the Institute did the translations for her. Anna got paid 93.40 Rubles from the Communist Party. She also received several gifts including a sealskin hat and purse. After her lecture, we all went to Kostya and Natasha's for dinner, and then next door to visit Alexie and Vera to drink chai and Armenian Konyak. Vera played traditional Russian folk songs on the accordion, and they all sang. Alexie gave me a wonderful wood carving, a face mask of an old Russian peasant with a long beard. He is a great woodcarver, and Vera teaches P.E. at our college. Came home walking in very wet and slushy snow.

April 11, 1990

Today Anna went with Dima to the Magadan Regional Museum and then to have dinner with him and Natasha. Paul, Irina, and I went to the restaurant Primorski for dinner tonight, 50 rubles. No seats were available until the doorman found out that we were Americans. It was fun, with good Russian food, and good music, and we had a good visit. For us being their Cold War enemies, some Russians often treat Americans better and with more respect than they do their own people.

April 13, 1990

This morning I had my first para. Not a day I was looking forward to since Anna and Paul came with me to the kafedra (Foreign Language Department) with their baggage. We must leave for the airport by 10:30. Anna gave some great feminist pins to the ladies in our Foreign Language Department. They very much enjoyed visiting with her as she did with them. Roman got the MPI Volga (car) for us to go to the airport. At the airport, we again had a problem with paying for their Aeroflot tickets in rubles. Luckily for us, Sasha Rus, an Aeroflot administrator, and friend was there and took care of the problem. I said goodbye to Anna and Paul, and it was very difficult to see them leave. We had a wonderful visit and shared many things with each other. I only wish we were all closer and could spend more time doing things together. I will

SANATORIUM "TALAYA". MAIN BUILDING. OXOTNIK PRESS ARCHIVES

never forget spending this time with Anna and Paul here in Magadan and I will miss them dearly. I introduced Anna and Paul to Bob and Shelly from the University of Alaska Fairbanks when they arrived here from Anadyr.

May 2nd, 1990

This morning Vyacheslav came to my flat and picked me up to go to the Talaya Health Resort for two days. We drove along the Kolyma Trassa in his new Volga sedan, a nice car. Although we could not get a translator to go with us, we used a dictionary and had a great time observing and talking about the beautiful nature of the Kolyma. It was a four-hour drive, and when we reached Talaya we went to the home of Stanislav Olefir, a well-known local natural history author. We have some of his books. Stanislav's house is a three-room flat but is one big library with book-shelves from floor to ceiling in the two main rooms. First, just after we arrived his wife Valya greeted us and served us okroshka, a cold vegetable and sausage soup prepared with kvas, a refreshing beverage made from fermented bread, an acquired taste for some. It was so delicious and is now one of my favorites. Then Vyacheslav introduced me to Stanislav and some other family members that were there. He made me feel right at

IN THE FAMILY OF STANISLAV OLEFIR. WRITER STANISLAV OLEFIR IS FOURTH FROM LEFT, FOLLOWED BY LARRY ROCKHILL, HIGH SCHOOL HISTORY AND ENGLISH TEACHER KONSTANTIN LISHENKO AND VALENTINA OLEFIR. THE VILLAGE OF TALAYA. 1990. OXOTNIK PRESS ARCHIVES

home. Afterward, we drove out into the woods and built a fire to make shashlyk (shish-kebab), with chorney hleb (black bread) and fine Russian vodka.

Shashlyk is a great favorite of all Russians and mine too. Volodya, a photographer, and his wife Tamara, family friends, drove out to the woods with us and he took many pictures of us around the big pieces of meat on the skewers cooking over the hot coals in the shashlyk firebox. Tonight, I went with Vyacheslav and Stanislav to the Talaya Resort and swam in the medicinal mineral water indoor swimming pool. It was refreshing and relaxing at the same time. What a great experience being in this famous Soviet Kolyma Resort. Then after swimming, we went back to Stanislav's, and Valya prepared more food. That evening Stanislav told some great bear stories and gave me one of his books, signed. (Note:2020, I am sad to say that this wonderful Taliya Resort has been closed down not so long ago due to economics. I am glad I had the opportunity to visit there long ago).

We stayed and slept at Stanislav's last night. Vyacheslav and I slept in the living-eating room and watched the Moscow-Kiev football until 01.00. We woke up at 0715 and after chai and zavtrak (breakfast) Valya brought us several color photographs that he took yesterday. Today Vyacheslav, Stanislav, and I visited the English Language class at the local school where Lena taught. She studied and graduated from the Gorky Institute in Moscow. I will give her the address of my school so she can be-gin a pen-pal program. Next, we went to visit the Mayor's office, and he gave me two photo panoramas of Talaya and everyone signed them. I was the first person from Alaska to visit this fine community. We discussed at some length the potential for tourism to be developed here in the Kolyma region, and I said that it was very beautiful like Alaska, but it would take a great effort to set up a tourist infrastructure that would attract tourists. Great skiing and natural beauty, plus health resort potential. After this, we went to visit the Administrator of Collective Farms. We walked over to the mineral hot springs building and tasted the hot mineral water. Not so tasty but very healthy. Then Vyacheslav decided it was time to leave and so we said our goodbyes and spacibos (thank you,) and into the Volga and back on the Kolyma Trassa. Not far down the road, our driver discov-ered that the brakes were not functioning properly so back to Taliya, and the Mayor had a young man take us back to Magadan in an old military jeep. This young man had a whole collection of girlie pictures on his dash-board. Maybe the result of the changing times. Home at 8 PM and was tired. A wonderful trip with a dear friend.

CHAPTER FOURTEEN:
GREAT OCTOBER REVOLUTION
DEMONSTRATION

During my first year of teaching at Magadan Pedagogical Institute, my students and I participated in one of the most important Soviet national holidays of the year. For me, it was a way of celebrating Alaska and the Soviet Union at the same time. After all, if it had not been for Mikhail Sergeevich Gorbachev, the General Secretary of the Communist Party of the Soviet Union, and his policy of glasnost and perestroika, I probably would never have had the opportunity to come to Magadan.

This was the Demonstratsiya, a city-wide parade and celebration of the anniversary of the Great October Revolution held annually on November 7th. It was a national holiday for the entire Soviet Union. and work stopped for several days each year when government offices and some stores were closed. The week before the holiday you would find many city workers cleaning the streets and getting everything ready for the big parade. Some workers were hanging Soviet flags from all the lamp posts along Ulitsa Lenina which made for a colorful street. Lenin Ploschad (Lenin Square) was also decked out with big Soviet flags flying from poles around the square, and a giant portrait of Lenin hung on the front of Oblispolkom, the Regional Administration Building. Although we were not aware of it at the time, this was to be one of the last two major Great October Revolution demonstrations that took place in Magadan.

A few weeks before the big event my students and I discussed in class how we could participate in this demonstration. The students came up with the idea of making banners in Russian and English that would say we all want to work for peace and friendship between Magadan and Alaska, the USSR, and the USA. We obtained some materials, and they made several banners to carry in the parade.

PROFESSOR ROMAN TCHAIKOVSKY AND DIMA POLETAEV ARE PREPARING FOR A DEMONSTRATION DEDICATED TO THE 73RD ANNIVERSARY OF THE GREAT OCTOBER SOCIALIST REVOLUTION. NOVEMBER 6, 1990. PHOTO BY PAVEL ZHDANOV

On the day of the parade, Roman, Dima, and I went to our kafedra early in the morning along with some of the students who had made banners and flags. We put the finishing touches on the banners, and then we took everything and went to where we were to meet up for the start of the parade. Most of the students were already there waiting for us. Many other Magadan Pedagogical Institute faculty members were also with our group including President Evgeny Kokorev, Larisa Kokoreva, Roman and Luda Tchaikovskiy ,Stanislav Pen'yevsky, Ludmilla Biryukova, teachers from the Foreign Language Department, and others. I would say that several thousand people participated by marching in the parade. And several thousand more people were lined up along the sidewalks to view the parade. Since it was a rather cold winter day, most people were dressed up in their fine winter coats and fur hats. It was always a pleasure to see pretty Russian ladies walking along the streets in their beautiful fur hats and coats.

Many school groups, Magadan City and Regional government departments, business enterprises, the KPSS, sports clubs, Young Pioneers, and Komsomol members, all carried flags and banners representing their organizations. Magadan city and oblast workers carried their beautiful flags. The Magadan flag is very symbolic with its portrayal of reindeer, gold, and the sea, representing the history and resources of the area. All schools and Institutes were represented in the parade by their members. The Communist Party, noticeable with its members carrying the many red CPSS and USSR flags, stood out amongst the others. The Communist Party may have had the largest turnout of marchers, which was to be expected. For many people, participating in this demonstration was not just voluntary, but there was an obligation that went with their job or position.

185

LARRY ROCKHILL IN A "HAT LIKE GORBACHEV" IS WITH CHAIRMAN OF THE MAGADAN REGIONAL EXECUTIVE COMMITTEE VYACHESLAV KOBETS AFTER THE DEMONSTRATION. IN THE BACKGROUND: TRANSLATOR DIMITRY POLETAEV. NOVEMBER 7, 1989 OXOTNIK PRESS ARCHIVES

Yet many felt it was too cold, or they had been there and done that so many times in the past that it was no longer interesting, and it was warmer to sit at home and watch it on the television.

The parade began at the top of Ulitsa Lenina by the TV tower and ended on Lenin Ploschad in front of the statue of Lenin. The signs my students had made read Alaska and Magadan Peace and Friendship, and Students and Teachers—Magadan and Alaska. They were carried by the students high above the heads of the marchers. But the most unusual for a Great October Revolution Demonstratsiya was the carrying of an American flag that I had brought to the Institute. This was the first time, and maybe the only time, that an American flag had been carried in a Great October Revolution Demonstration in the Soviet Union. I am sure it raised the eyebrows of some of the old hardline Communist Party members marching in the parade and watching along the sidelines. This was another opportunity for us to join with those trying to mend the wounds of the Cold War and to do our part in melting the Ice Curtain that still existed in the middle of the Bering Sea. Pavel Zhdanov was right there with

MARCHING IN THE GREAT OCTOBER REVOLUTION 1990 DEMONSTRATION, IN THE FIRST ROW, A SYMBOL OF
THE RAPPROCHEMENT IS TAKING PLACE: A RUSSIAN TEACHER DIMITRY POLETAEV CARRIES THE FLAG OF
ALASKA, AN ALASKAN LARRY ROCKHILL WALKS WITH THE FLAG OF THE RUSSIAN FEDERATION, IN THE CENTER
IS A STUDENT, SERGEY NECHAEV WHO CARRIES THE BANNER: "MGPI. ALASKA. WE ARE WORKING FOR PEACE
AND PERESTROIKA." NOVEMBER 7, 1989

his camera documenting the event, and he took the few pictures we have of our marching there on that day in November 1989. Today, we very much enjoy those old photos he took.

Not all Soviet people were pleased with some of the changes that were taking place under Gorbachev. And this was going to be even more so as the years progressed and when Yeltsin entered the scene. Although, as an American from Alaska, I was never aware of any individual expressing any negative feelings towards the United States, and I never felt unwelcome during the entire time I lived in Magadan. It was a warm and friendly city. These were the days of Gorbachev's policies of perestroika and glasnost, and things were changing. There was excitement and a positive spirit on the part of my students at the Institute of developing closer relations between Alaska and Magadan. We hoped a relationship would evolve into students from both sides of the Ice Curtain being able to cross over and experience life on the other side. We knew we were quite fortunate to be a small part of something that was going to change the world forever. This included going beyond what would have been unacceptable in the past under the previous Communist Party leaders. We also wondered if what we were experencing was to be the future of the new world order, and if so, how long would it last. Impermanence is the history of the world.

We had decided to go one step further, beyond the colorful banners the students had made and carried, to make a symbolic representation of the common Russian heritage shared by Magadan and Alaska. This meant that an Alaskan would carry the flag of the Russian Federation and that a Russian would carry the Alaska flag representing old Imperial Russia across the Bering Sea. Dima Poletaev carried the Alaska flag as a Russian man carrying the flag of Staraya Rossiya, which was once a part of Russia, and I carried the Russian Federation flag as an Alaskan carrying the flag of our common Russian heritage. Gleb Tchaikovski, one of my students, carried the American flag, and his father, Professor Roman Tchaikovski carried the flag of the USSR. I was able to keep the RSFSR flag that I carried and the metal finial hammer and sickle that was on the top of the pole. I have used these flags, and Pasha's photos of the demonstration, in later exhibits on Magadan. A new day was dawning in Magadan which would lead to many crossing in both directions over the melting Ice Curtain in the Bering Sea.

This change was also reflected in the fact that in the reviewing stand, at the end of the parade on Lenin Ploshad, there stood Gov. Vyacheslav Kobets, of the Magadan Region, and Gary Pascal from the Office of the Governor of Alaska, as well as members of the CPSS-Communist Party of the Soviet Union, among others. The student's peace banners and the American flag did not go unnoticed by the other VIP people standing at the reviewing stand. Many people made positive comments to us after the parade. It was a day of celebration, and after the parade, many of us went to friends 'homes for a toast of vodka to 'mir i druzhba', and to partake in some delicious Russian food.

CHAPTER FIFTEEN:
MAGADAN EXCURSIONS WITH STUDENTS

Pavel Zhdanov has always been my close friend, moi Russki brat (my Russian brother), and we enjoyed many special times together that he arranged when I lived there, and this continues twenty-nine years down the road. It was Pasha who introduced me to the wonderful nature and history of the Kolyma. My first excursion with Pasha was on a beautiful fall sunny day on Nagaeva Bay. First, it was down to the port where we went aboard the boat built by Captain Slava and headed out past the light-house to the entrance of the bay. There always seemed to be a flock of hungry seagulls following close behind on our stern that was hoping we would throw them something to eat. So not to disappoint, we threw them some of the cut-up herring pieces we used for bait. It was great to see them dive, and often catch a piece in mid-air. We did some fishing along the way, and then went ashore and made ukha, a delicious fish soup, in a large bucket over a Pasha campfire. We were surrounded by the beauty of the bay, and the forests that were on the hillsides. Being a lover of the sea and ships, this was an unforgettable day for me. After a grand day, on the way back to Magadan Captain Slava let me take the helm and steer her back to port. This was only one of many interesting excursions that I went on with Pasha.

I spent many an evening over at Pasha's when his wife Marina would prepare delicious dinners, and my being single, I appreciated her fine Russian cuisine all the more. She prepared the most delicious Russian salads, especially trubach, a clam-like dish. They had two wonderful little

AMERICAN SCHOOL CHILDREN VISITING PAVEL ZHDANOV'S FAMILY. MARINA ZHDANOVA, JUSTIN HENWOOD, ILYA KOPTILIN, ZHENYA ZHDANOVA, DIMA MALOV, PAVEL ZHDANOV, MAYA MORGENWECK, TANYA ZHDANOVA AND LENA LOSHCHININA. FEBRUARY. 1990 PHOTO COURTESY PAVEL ZHDANOV

daughters, Tanya and Zhenya. Now Pasha enjoys very much being a dedushka (grandfather) and a father at the same time. A lucky man is he.

Of course, we understood that not all learning of importance takes place in a college classroom. This was to be so for all my Magadan Pedinstitute students as well as my University of Alaska exchange students. There was much to see, experience, and learn about in the greater Kolyma Region. Nobody knew this better than Pasha Zhdanov. He knew so many interesting people from miners to Aeroflot pilots and was able to arrange for me and my students to meet them too.

Pasha had a good friend, Igor Morozov, who was an Aeroflot pilot who flew An-2 biplanes to remote villages around the Kolyma. He arranged for Igor to take two of the UAF students (Toni and Tom) and myself and 2 MPI students, Natasha Ravocheva from Ust'-Omchug, and Irina Alishova, to visit the Shkol'ni Rudnik—a gold mine near Ust'-Omchug, and then on to Butugychag.

Since flying in an An-2 had always been one of my favorite things in life, I thoroughly enjoyed the flight to Ust'-Omchug. After landing on the little dirt strip, we got up into the Ural truck and were driven over to Natasha's parent's house to meet with her family for lunch. Her Mom

LARRY ROCKHILL WITH AEROFLOT AN-2 PILOT IGOR MOROZOV. MAGADAN 13 KILOMETER AIRPORT, SUMMER, 1991 PHOTO BY PAVEL ZHDANOV

prepared a delicious Russian lunch for all of us. Then, we got back into the cars and drove over to the Shkolni rudnik - Shkolni gold mine. Here we were welcomed by the Chief Geologist, had a tour of the mine, and that night had dinner and slept in the bunkhouse with the miners. Pasha says that my ability to speak Russian increased with the number of vodka toasts we had with the miners that evening. I think this is fiction, but it was interesting to talk to them and this was the first Soviet gold mine I had visited.

Shkolni was a typical old Soviet hard-rock gold mine with underground tunneling. I have been in many old abandoned and working mines during my college days when I went on geology field trips to collect minerals in Arizona and Nevada. The conditions here that the miners lived in were quite basic but comfortable, wooden bunkhouses, a dining hall, and storage buildings for the equipment. One of the geologists gave me an excellent half-inch thick cross-section, the size of the palm of your hand, of a test sample of gold in milky quartz that I still have and use in displays. It has several dozen inclusions of native gold in quartz appearing in the cross-section. This is a fine example of gold in quartz from this region of the Russian Far North.

191

AMERICAN AND RUSSIAN SCHOOL CHILDREN BEFORE A FLIGHT OVER MAGADAN. SECOND FROM LEFT MEGAN OBRAIN WAS ONE OF ROCKHILL'S STUDENTS WHO STUDIED THE RUSSIAN LANGUAGE WHEN ENTERING UNIVERSITY IN THE USA. MARCH, 1991 PHOTO BY PAVEL ZHDANOV

In the morning we woke up in the bunkhouse, then washed up and went to the dining hall where we had the usual miner's zavtrak of man-naya kasha, known as cream of wheat, which I grew up on. We thanked the geologists and the miners with bolshoye spacibo (many thanks) for their interesting, warm, and generous hospitality, and now it was time to climb back up into the great Ural truck, and off to Butugychag. Pasha said that currently, Shkolni is no longer a working gold mine.

CHAPTER SIXTEEN:
BUTUGYCHAG, STALINIST FORCED LABOR
CAMP AND URANIUM MINE

My first trip to Butugychag was with Pasha Zhdanov in 1989, followed by a second trip some twenty years later in 2009 when my wife Lena, and I went with Pasha and Anatoly Shirokov. Anatoly is a historian and a scholar of the history of the GULag in the Kolyma region. He has written extensively on this topic, and two of his books can be found in the University of Alaska Rasmusen Library and the Cambridge University Library in England. Pasha is a writer and professional photographer with thousands of photographs documenting the changes that have occurred over the years in all the Stalinist forced labor camps in the Kolyma. No one I know has visited the many forced labor camps/mines in the Kolyma more than Pasha. My third trip to the mine was with Pasha and Andrey in 2016.

From the Skolni gold mine, it was not a long drive to Butugychag. As we turned off the main road there was a small private house-izba with a large garden next to it. If I remember correctly these people were the caretakers of the small electric sub-station that was nearby. Here lived a family that raised almost all their vegetables, and had chickens, a cow, and some goats for fresh milk. Their garden was green with the tops of potatoes, and cucumbers on the vines. We stopped and they invited us to come in, and with the usual warm and generous Russian hospitality, bid us sit down and have something to eat and drink. I remember drinking fresh cold cow's milk which was unusual for me. We had a bite to eat, tea, and a short visit. During my last visit to Butugychag in 2016, I noticed

SHOES IN FRONT OF THE ISOLATOR. BUTUGYCHAG.
2009. PHOTO BY PAVEL ZHDANOV

that this little house and garden were no longer there. As Pasha would say, it was part of the 'disappearing past'.

Then it was back into the Ural, and on the un-road up to the mine. Each succeeding time we went to this mine it was a greater challenge to go as far as we could in our big Ural cab bouncing from side to side on this almost un-road that had been overgrown with flora and washed out with winter rains. We were thrust about inside the truck cab, up and down, and then side to side. You might say it was like riding a four-wheel bucking bronco. There was a noticeable difference with advancing years in the increase in the amount of flora present along the road and riverbeds, and also inside the buildings. At times it seemed that the alders had grown over what was left of the road, and made it almost impassable. It was only possible because of the Ural being a tough all- terrain vehicle.

Butugychag (1937-1956) was important to the Soviet Union in that it was part of Stalin's first atomic bomb program and was considered to be one of the most dangerous mines, for the prisoners were exposed to the high levels of radiation, and many succumbed after being there for no more than one year. Stalin needed enriched uranium for the development of the Soviet Union's nuclear weapons arsenal since the United States had already developed, and tested an atomic bomb from the Manhattan Project, and then dropped two atomic bombs on the Japanese cities of Hiroshima and Nagasaki. This was a part of the USA/USSR arms race that had developed and continued for the duration of the Cold War up until the time of Gorbachev and Reagan.

LARRY ROCKHILL IS INSIDE THE
ISOLATOR CELL. BUTUGYCHAG
PHOTO BY PAVEL ZHDANOV.

We went as far as we could go. Today these ATV Urals are used to transport workers in rural areas to the mines or their places of work. They are big flatbed trucks with a large compartment on the back that could hold around twenty people. They have a high clearance that permits them to travel over places with rocks and boulders standing well above the level of the ground. Sometimes I felt that we could tip over when trying to drive over such large boulders. We reached a point where we could drive no farther due to the blockage from the trees and the washed-out roadbed. The old road existed up to the Concentrate Factory or the place of high radiation where uranium concentrate had been stored and could still be seen in the yellow sand-like piles on the ground outside the factory building. We walked over to the factory and looked around inside the roofless building for only a short time. Someone from our group suggested that it would be a good idea to wear lead underwear when standing here for any length of time. The person with the Geiger counter encouraged us not to linger too long here, and to start on our way up to the area of the mine. The road from here to the mine was almost completely overgrown with alder, bushes, and even young tamarack trees that would eventually take over the entire mine area. The Uranium mine closed down in 1957, and that was some 32 years ago, long enough to notice a big change in the flora.

Since we could no longer see what was supposed to be a road, we walked up the trail and the dry riverbed to the area of some old buildings that were constructed of what looked like flagstone or flat rocks. I think that from the Factory Concentrate building it was about a five-kilometer walk up to the building called the Isolator, some other administrative offices, and the guard's old living quarters.

None of these old buildings had a roof over them, nor windows, or doors, and all had alder and other bushes growing inside.

I have seen only one old photo of the mine buildings during its working days. There is one small, not very clear photo in the book 'Ten'ka 'that shows a picture that indicates that there were many buildings here, and this was a large operation that must have been operated by many Soviet officials and zeks(prisoners). This was a high-priority mine in its day, and so the operation was extensive, although the prisoners operated with the basics, a pick, a shovel, and a wheel barrel. The actual mine tunnels were located near the top of the mountain well above the Isolator and administrative buildings and the area of the old cemetery.

AT THE BUTUGYCHAG TIN MINE. LARRY ROCKHILL IS WITH RUSSIAN JOURNALISTS. JUNE. 1990 PHOTO BY PAVEL ZHDANOV

We walked over to the Butugychag cemetery which was not far from the Isolator building. The graves themselves were mounds rising a few inches above the level of the ground. I felt that this was a very sacred place for those who had suffered and died unjustly under the old Stalinist forced labor system. It was weird, but it seemed that I could feel the spirits of those who had been laid to rest so far away from those whose love they had been deprived of as zeks. A unique aspect of this cemetery is that all the grave sites were marked with a round tin can lid that has a Cyrillic letter and number punched into it, and then nailed to a small post at the head of the grave. Many graves have lost their markers, and some have been partially dug up by animals long ago. Now and then one can see a human bone lying on the ground near a grave. It may be that there are some records of those buried here in the archives in the Magadan Regional Library and Archives. Asir Sandler, who had been a zek, a prisoner here and survived, gave me four of his original black and white photos of the cemetery that show one grave site with a human skull that has the top third cut off which seems to indicate some sort of medical experiments took place here. This has also been denied by other sources.

197

MINE WORKINGS OF THE BUTUGYCHAG TIN MINE. CAMP "SOPKA". LARRY ROCKHILL WITH RUSSIAN JOURNAL-ISTS AND GEOLOGISTS. JUNE. 1990. PHOTO BY PAVEL ZHDANOV

The Isolator building is a single-story stone-constructed building where the roof had been long gone. It had been used to house those zeks who were not in favor of the guards and had either not worked hard enough or had disobeyed some of the guard's orders. There were ten small cells, five on each side. Each cell had iron bars across a small window that had no glass in the window frames. It was said that up to ten men could have been placed in one of these small cells. This would have meant almost standing room only. There were no observable toilet facilities in the building even in the area at the entrance where the guard's room was located. As was usual in these settings, the honey bucket system was employed with the lowest-ranking zek having the responsibility of collecting and emptying them each day. There was evidence of a small wood stove for heating the area of the guard's room, but not the rest of the building. When it was minus 50C outside, it would have been very cold for the zeks in the cells. This was the temperature at which the guards could release the zeks from their work details. But many guards would just look at the thermometer and say it was only -49 C and the zeks had to keep working. There was one area of the building where it appeared there was a cell under the floor area. This was a punishment cell for those zeks whom the guards wanted to punish to the extreme and to give a warning to the other zeks. Life was extremely harsh here under these severe conditions both inside and outside the Isolator. One must read authors like Varlam Shalamov, Evgenia Ginzburg, Michael Solomon, and Anatoli Zhigulin, with their first-hand experiences, to be able to get some idea of how terrible life must have been for the zeks that had to work here under such extreme conditions.

The Isolator building sits alongside the riverbank, which is usually dry until a rainstorm comes along, and then it can become a roaring torrent. It seems that eventually, the river will just erode the bank away, the Isolator building will become flooded, fall into the river, and be gone. The building is surrounded by several rows of barbed wire laying for the most part on the ground. In front of the building, and just up from the rows of barbed wire is a large pile of old leather shoes that appear to be prisoners' footwear. There must have been well over two hundred pairs of shoes in the pile. Most seem to be of hard dry leather with tire rubber attached to the soles and were curled up with the toe and heel forming the letter u. The upper and lower parts are fastened together with cobbler nails that are quite visible from the drying out of the leather which causes separation of the top from the sole. The cobbler nails alone date the shoes back many years. We took one shoe as an example of something real that could memorialize the people who suffered and died under this extreme oppression. This shoe has been part of the five International "Magadan: Life in the Russian North" exhibits that Lena and I supported with the photographs of Pavel Zhdanov and Andrey Osipov. Ever since my first visit to Butugychag, I have on my desk a small length of barbed wire from in front of the Isolator building that to me was the main symbol of oppression for the political prisoners in the GULag camps. It reminds me to not take for granted some of the freedoms we enjoy today in the United States.

It would have been almost impossible for any zek to escape from this prison camp. The location of Butugychag was remote, and the guards were always on the lookout for any zeks that were not working as was de-manded, and any zeks found thinking of trying to escape. Living and work-ing here was extremely difficult in that the high radiation, extreme cold, bad nutrition, isolation from family and friends, poor clothing, and over-work, meant that often a zek's longevity was short-lived. Not to speak of dying from hypothermia due to the extreme cold. There were several other stone buildings in the immediate area, some of which were the guard's quarters, and others the administrative buildings. Some had walls that were still upright, with the doors and windows no longer in place, and some had been almost destroyed with only the foundations showing. Most had small trees and other flora growing inside the buildings that were still standing. Some years into the future nature will just take over this entire area and the buildings will not be recognizable as they are today.

In 2019, Pavel Zhdanov published a remarkable book on the forced labor camps of the Kolyma GULag. His book, "The Disappearing Past" is a collection of the writings of survivors of the Kolyma GULag camps com-bined with his excellent photographs of the present conditions of the places where they were held prisoner and worked. It is in both Russian and English. It can be found in the University of Alaska Fairbanks Ras-muson Library, and the Scott Polar Research Institute Library at Cambridge University in England.

CHAPTER SEVENTEEN:
An-2 AEROFLOT BIPLANE

The Antonov An-2 was one of the old biplanes still in service during the latter years of the Soviet Union, but few are still in service today. However, some are used for supporting men fighting wildfires in the hot summers of the interior. There are not any An-2s still flying in a regularly scheduled passenger service that I know of. It was the main airplane used in the rural areas of the Russian Far East to carry people and supplies to and from villages and distant towns. At this time there were several scheduled daily, and weekly flights by Aeroflot from Magadan to cities like Seimchan, Susuman, Sinegoriye, Ust'-Omchug, and other towns where there were extensive mining operations still active. These old biplanes could hold twelve passengers on bulkhead seats along the side of the interior. There was both a pilot and a co-pilot for each flight. An-2s flew low and slow but were very dependable to get where they were heading no matter the weather, with some exceptions of course.

Pasha introduced me to Igor Morozov, an Aeroflot An-2 pilot. We became friends, and one evening Igor called me and asked if I would like to go to Balagannoye, a rural village about 90 min. from the Magadan Mile 13 Airport. I immediately said yes, and the next day came to meet him at the local 13 Kilometer Magadan City Airport for our flight. I had two students with me. Neither of them had ever flown in an old biplane like this, and they were excited to go for the ride. We took pictures and then Igor said to climb aboard. Igor took his place in the cockpit and soon the big old reciprocating engine's four-blade propellers began to turn, slowly at

THE LEGENDARY BIPLANE AN-2 AT THE AIRPORT "MAGADAN 13 KM". PHOTO BY PAVEL ZHDANOV

first and then extremely fast. A big cough and lots of black smoke belched from the exhaust pipe along the side of the engine. We were ready to taxi out to the runway and take off for sights unknown, at least for us. It was a nice sunny day and as we gained altitude, we had great visibility of the beauty of the Kolyma forests as they came down to the seashore below.

When we approached the dirt landing strip at Balagannoye, Igor set this old taildragger down very gently, and we were ready to jump out and look around the little village. After we landed, we were told not to take photos of a certain part of this small village as there was some contingent of Soviet Army soldiers stationed here and living in one of the two-story barracks-like buildings not far from the airport. So, we focused our cameras on the kids riding their old Soviet bicycles along the dirt streets, and the adults going into the magazines.

Except for being surrounded by beautiful nature, there just wasn't much here for the locals to be involved with, it seemed to me. Although the state was required to provide all citizens with jobs, I am not sure how many jobs there could be for people here. If it hadn't been for the Young Pioneer and Komsomol group programs connected to the school, kids might have found living here rather boring. These programs were essential for teaching cooperation and working together, and also for indoctrinating young people into the Soviet system. They also provided many opportunities for students to learn outdoor skills during the summer vacation periods in camp-like settings. Some of the teachers I talked to did not care for the Marxist-Lenin aspects but recognized that many other parts were valuable learning experiences. However, in a small community like this, I am sure they were very important to the local kids.

After the Aeroflot pilots did their business, we walked back to the plane and Igor asked me if I would like to take the controls of the An-2 and fly her back to Magadan. This was very unexpected, and I said a big DA-yes. He did the initial take-off with me in the co-pilot seat, then gave me the controls, and told me the altitude and compass heading I was to follow. Igor would check every so often to make sure I was on the correct course heading, and I was. What a wonderful experience to fly such a historical and important Soviet airplane. It took my full concentration, and I can still see the view from the cockpit window looking at the ground below through the rotating propeller blades. The sound of the big reciprocating radial engine was music to my ears. With full concentration, the time went by much too fast, and a little over an hour later the Magadan 13 Kilometer airport came into view in the distance. This was not a sight I was longing to see. It was an experience of a lifetime and one I treasure. Igor was a good friend, and I enjoyed his company during those two years. Fortunately, I took several photos of the An-2 at the Mile 13 Airport before we took off, and still have them as part of my Magadan Archive. Igor also shared with me his Aeroflot pilot's wings and insignias that we use in our Magadan exhibits. Igor knew I had taken some flying lessons years ago and had practiced with my friend Pat Treanor in Los Angeles as a young adult. Pat had an old 1944 Stinson gull-wing single-engine airplane that he let me fly with him on occasion.

Another Aeroflot friend was Victor Trezubov, the Regional Director of Aeroflot in the Magadan Region. He was the man we had to work with when developing our Soviet Alaska exchange program since Aeroflot was the only way we could bring Magadan students to Alaska and take our students there. His office was in the Avtovokzal/Bus station building with the big Aeroflot sign on the side. Every time we wanted to set up an exchange program and bring Magadan and Soldotna students together, we met with Victor to help us with the schedule and the costs. I am sure we very much benefitted from the Soviet Aeroflot subsidized aviation program. Victor was always helpful in making the cost for students as low as possible, and not restricting the amount of baggage we could carry. There were several Aeroflot pilots and administrators, including Sasha Rus, who saw the value in bringing students together and went out of their way to help us. Sasha Rus helped us to solve more than one problem and was always ready to assist. One time when I went to meet with Victor and ask him to help our students, he gave me his Aeroflot officer's hat with the "scrambled eggs" on the brim, which I always use in our Magadan e.hibits. He was a devoted friend of the Magadan and Soldotna students.

CHAPTER EIGHTEEN:
FINDING SEATS TO PROVIDENIYA

The first visitors from the University of Alaska came to MPI in April of 1990, just as Anna and Paul were leaving. They were Bob Williams, President of the University of Alaska Board of Regents, his friend Shelly, and UAF Professors Perry Gilmore and David Smith. Some of our MPI professors hosted them, and there were many meetings with President Evgeny Kokorev, Professor Roman Tchaikovskiy Gov. Vyacheslav Kobets, and Mayor Gennady Dorofeev, along with visits with other government officials. They were the ones that went back to report to UA President Don O'Dowd and, the University of Alaska Administration with positive feelings as to the possibility, and value of bringing Magadan and Alaska students and teachers together in the first University Educational Exchange Program.

Then in the spring, it was time for President Evgeny Kokorev and Dean Roman Tchaikovsky to go to meet President Don O'Dowd of the University of Alaska in his Fairbanks office. I had to coordinate this trip with his office at UAF. There were many phone calls to Irma Jean, the Administrative Assistant at UAF that took place to decide when we would come. Her coordination was invaluable in making things work out. But calling to Alaska in those days was an adventure in and of itself. Just to place a long-distance call meant that you had to order a call from the special long-distance operator, and then wait while she worked on patching it through a connection via Novosibirsk, Moscow, London, New York, Seattle, Anchorage, and then Fairbanks. The usual wait time was around three hours. This meant sitting by the phone waiting and hoping, for you never really knew when it would ring, and the operator would either say your call was ready, or they could not connect. And if the line was busy, it would mean starting all over again and feeling a little disappointed, to say the least, maybe even a bit ticked. But that was the Soviet system in 1989.

We had to make arrangements for the three of us and three MPI students to buy tickets from Aeroflot to fly from Magadan to Anadyr, and then from Anadyr to Provideniya, and then from Provideniya to Nome, Alaska via Jim Rowe's Bering Air Service. As the time for our departure approached, we found out that we had tickets and seats from Magadan to Anadyr, but we only had tickets and no seats from Anadyr to Provideniya. What to do? Late one night two days before we were to leave Roman called me and told me the situation and said that President Evgeny Kokorev wanted me to go to see Governor Vyacheslav Kobets and ask him to help us so we could have seats on the flight from Anadyr to Provideniya. I called Dima Poletaev, and we both went to see if Vyacheslav would be willing to help us by solving this problem. Who could imagine going to the Governor of Alaska if you did not have tickets on a particular flight that was full, and asked him to remove some people who already had tickets so you could go in their place? People would say you would not be able to do this ever. But this was the Soviet Union still, and of course, Vyacheslav understood the problem, and the importance of President Kokorev being able to meet with the President of the University of Alaska, and so he was willing and did make it possible for us to fly as planned. Vyacheslav also signed the Protocol that was so important for Evgeny to take to the President of the University of Alaska. This is one more of the many unforgettable memories of Magadan. Vyacheslav was always willing to go out of his way to support our exchange programs, after all, he was part of them right from the beginning when we first met in Nome and he took our gifts back to School No.1 in Magadan, and later when he first visited with my students at Soldotna Elementary School in February of 1989.

DIARY: February 12, 1990, On the morning of February 12th, I got up early and went to the Institute and met with Roman and Evgeny to make final plans for our trip to Alaska. In the afternoon I went shopping and bought three rabbit fur hats, three Vostok watches for Anna and Lisa and Paul, and some table linens. Several people brought gifts to my flat for their friends in Alaska that I just put with the others in a big box. Whenever one went to Alaska people wanted to send their friends little Russian gifts. We were always glad to help out if we had space in our boxes.

13 February 1990, I got up at 0645 and called Roman to tell Evgeny that Vyacheslav would help in solving our tickets to Provideniya problem. I finished packing, had breakfast, and cleaned up my flat. I have one large suitcase, one large box, and my soft bag for hand-carrying things. I walked down the stairs, and the Volga from the Institute was there waiting along with a truck to take my baggage to the airport with the others. I said goodbye to some friends on this crisp and beautiful morning in Magadan. I knew it was going to be a cold -33 C when we landed in Anadyr. After our four hour Aeroflot Tu-154 flight to Anadyr landed we had to drive the 22km over the ice-covered Bay of Anadyr to the city where we checked into the Anadyr Airport Hotel. I went shopping and bought fifteen Soviet Army belts and buckles for gifts to friends in Alaska. They would be unusual and interesting to people like my close friend Earl Craig in Soldotna who was interested in Soviet military things like this. We had a usual stolovaya dinner, and then to bed.

The next morning it was back out to the airport across the ice-covered frozen Bay of Anadyr to check in for our flight to Provideniya, thanks to Gov. Kobets we had seats. We flew aboard an Aeroflot An-24 for our rather short flight. After we landed in Provideniya our friend Mayor Oleg Kulinkin met us and helped us by taking us to the town where he provided us with a suite in the hotel with a kitchen, and also being able to use his office to meet in. We had met previously in Nome when he was there with Gov. Kobets in 1988.

But a big problem arose. I called Jim Rowe at Bering Air in Nome, and he had received a telegram from Soviet CAA in Moscow that no flights from Nome to Providenaya were permitted without a Soviet navigator aboard. This was not good news for us, and so what could we do, being here in a small remote Russian Arctic community? We decided we needed some friends on the outside to try and help us. I was elected to do the calling, and so I called Gov. Kobets, Jerry Mohatt, and Irma Jean at UAF, Kirill Kasatkin, at the Ministry of Foreign Affairs in Moscow, Senators Murkowski, Stevens, and Rep. Don Young many times. Well, this requirement to have a Soviet navigator on board was of course not necessary but was part of the international agreement for all flights between the US and the USSR at that time.

Bering Air was/is a small bush Alaskan air taxi and charter service based in Nome. The owner, Jim Rowe was so interested in supporting relations between Magadan and Alaska to the extent that he at one time was accepting Russian rubles as payment for his flying service. He had previously flown to Provideniya several times before this restriction was placed by both governments. It was a new challenge for us to face.

Around 10 PM we decided to stop calling, and we all went back to our hotel. We did not feel very encouraged. We had a light dinner with Oleg Kulinkin and his friend Valery Ivanovich, then pivo (beer) and vodka, and talked and talked until around 2 AM. We went to sleep not knowing if and when we would fly to Nome.

The next morning after a nice breakfast of hot cereal, eggs, Russian black bread, and chai in the hotel stolovaya it was back on the phones calling again. Everybody I had called was working on our problem. I decided to take a break and go shopping and bought several Native language books for the Alaska Native Language Center. These Evenki indigenous Native language textbooks were not so easily available in Magadan. They would be important additions to the ANLC (Alaska Native Language Center) library. I enjoyed just visiting the local shops to see what was available in this small northern community.

We ended up being stuck in Provideniya for five extra days. I did not mind for it was interesting for me since I had never been to this rather remote northern part of the Russian Far East. This is an important modern seaport town. Although smaller than Anchorage, it is similar in that it is a distribution point for supplying several of the more northern Arctic communities where mining operations are located, including Bilibino where one of the Arctic Soviet nuclear-powered electric generating station is located. (Note: The Bilibino nuclear power station is due to close down completely by 2021, and will be replaced by the new Akademik Lomonosov floating nuclear power plant project that is based on proven nuclear icebreaker technology). The port of Provideniya is a relatively modern Northern town and has several large cranes on the dock for off-floading large containers from ships. Supplies of food and consumer goods, as well as equipment, are all brought here via cargo ships. Provideniya Bay is kept open all year round and supported by Soviet icebreakers in the wintertime.

I enjoyed just walking about in this little Soviet town. It had its own unique character being built along the shores of the bay and huddled up against the base of the mountain. I could see a couple of ships that were at the docks, and one anchored out in the bay. There were the usual Soviet apartment buildings with the stores and food shops at the street level, and the polyclinic and school. Its charm to some extent was that it didn't have much other than a beautiful setting, but it was a true Arctic outpost, and important to all those living north of it. The buildings showed the color of weathering the cold, wind, and snow. But inside the flats were warm and cozy.

Mayor Oleg Kulinkin arranged for our group to visit the pivo-beer factory there. We had the opportunity to taste the 30-day, 60-day, and 90-day vats brewing beer. As we walked through the brewery, we could see very large vats that must have contained thousands of gallons of pivo. One thing I noticed was the rather old-looking pipes that went from one vat to another. Not sure how old this pivo factory was, but it seems it may have been an important part of the social scene in Provideniya for some years. Each sample we tasted seemed to me to be a good-tasting beer. Soviet beer is not pasteurized, and so does not have a long shelf life. One must drink it in a week or so. This was not a problem for most men.

Since we were just waiting there, I continued to call some of our Alaska Congressional Delegation in Juneau and Washington D. C. to see if they could help and hurry things up a bit. All long- distance calls took ages to go through, and so lots of time was spent sitting in the mayor's office around the telephones. Finally, after several hours on the phone and a few days later, we got word that Washington and Moscow had cleared the way for Jim Rowe to fly without a navigator and we would leave in two days. This provided me with the possibility of a few more adventures in this little northern outpost of the USSR.

Having some free time, I decided to visit the class of Natasha Fukes, one of the English Language teachers. I brought little gifts of candy and gum to share with the children. My class and I had previously corresponded via pen-pal letters and shared photographs and little gifts with some of these students. It was always a pleasure for me to visit with English language students, and listen to their questions about what life was like in the United States, and also, for me to learn what life was like for these fine Soviet students who were learning English. I spent several hours just talking to the students who would later be the ones to live in a world with a freer exchange of ideas as well as economics.

NOVOYE CHAPLINO

So, there was time for one more adventure for our group. Mayor Oleg Kulinkin had made arrangements for us to visit the Chukchi village of

Novoye Chaplino on the coast. It was not too far, but you could only get there by a track vehicle like a vezdekhod, a small military personnel carrier. One morning our three students, Raisa, Natasha Buhonina, Lena Nikitina, and I climbed in the back of a vezdekhod (all-terrain vehicle), and off we went across the tundra to the Native village of Novoye Chaplino. I will never forget that Raisa, who was a young Chukchi woman in her late twenties, and who had two children, was part of our group. She was unusual for our MPI did not have many Native students. Sitting in the back of the vezdekhod while bouncing across the tundra she asked if she could tell my future/fortune. Of course, I said, please go ahead and she took my hand and began to examine the lines running through my open palm. I was somewhat amazed at the accuracy of what she said in telling me what to expect in the future as well as what had been in my past. Much of what she said was rather general but still interesting. She was invited to be part of our group, since we would be visiting with members of the Alaska Native community, especially in Nome. She stayed in Nome for some extra days to meet with local Eskimo people to discuss issues related to education and the retention and fostering of Native language programs in the schools.

Looking out the little windows we saw only tundra until we approached the village. Now several wooden buildings came into view. We drove into the village and parked in front of the school building, and we all climbed out through the back hatch. From what I remember most of the buildings and houses here were of wood construction. There were no cement plants in this area for the construction of five-story apartment houses.

It seemed to me that a small remote Native Chukchi village like this was not so different from many Eskimo villages in Alaska. Novoye Chaplino was founded in 1960 by bringing residents of several coastal villages together in the present location. This was part of the Soviet sedentarisation and collectivization program where the government reorganized many Native groups into state and collective farms. It was said to be done by the Soviet state for economic reasons to consolidate the populations of several villages. Interesting to note that these changes in the traditional social and economic structure of the Native people often had devastating and long-lasting effects on their traditional culture. No longer were they able to operate with the freedom of their traditional culture as they had done in the past. Now they would be forced to enter the world of employment as a member of the dominant culture, away from their traditional subsistence lifestyle, and to enter the world of working for a salary. It was a small village of around 450 people, both Native and non- Native, mostly Chukchi and Siberian Yupik. Some local

210

Native people worked at the village store, and others at the school did maintenance work. Most of the certified teachers at the school were Russians. Almost all of the higher-level administrative and higher-paying positions were held by non-Native Russian incomers before 1991. And, as in Alaska, many of the skilled jobs were done by non-Natives, although there were programs for training Natives to do this kind of work.

An important economic enterprise of the Chukotka coastal village communities, such as Novoye Chaplino, was and still is whaling, and marine mammal hunting. With little or no support from the Russian state after 1991, whaling activities were greatly hampered for the hunting of marine mammals, including bowhead whales and walruses. From what I was told by Dr. Tom Albert, the Senior Bowhead Whale Scientist for the North Slope Borough, Department of Wildlife Management in Barrow/Utqiagvik, Alaska, extensive support for these Chukotka village whaling activities at that time came from the Alaska Eskimo Whaling Commission of the North Slope Borough of Alaska.

Tom was an important supporter of the whaling activities of the Inupiat people of the North Slope of Alaska. He was instrumental in developing, along with whaling captain George Amoak and other members of the Alaska Eskimo Whaling Commission a joint cooperative project with the Naukan Native Cooperative of Chukotka to try to establish the number of bowhead whales migrating off the coast of Chukotka, and also the extent of harvesting of marine mammals by the Chukotka hunters in the waters off the Russian coast. This was needed to determine the quota that would be set by the International Whaling Commission for all Native communities in the harvesting of the bowhead whales. Funds were provided for the Native Chukotka hunter's research by supplying a significant amount of equipment, such as boats and outboard motors to the Eskimo Society of Chukotka based in the city of Provideniya. This was also to enhance the economic situation for village hunters, like those living in Novoye Chaplino. I had the opportunity to attend several interesting bowhead whale conferences in Anchorage when Tom was the Director of Science at the North Slope Borough Department of Wildlife Management in Utkiagvik (Barrow), Alaska.

The majority of the Novoye Chaplino village workforce has always been involved in the traditional hunting and butchering of whales, walruses, and other marine mammals. But things changed when the Soviets organized hunters from different coastal villages into being members of the village kolkhoz. Whaling has been an important part of the traditional culture of most of the Native people living along the Chukchi coast from time immemorial. Now being a

Chukchi or Eskimo marine mammal hunter also meant that you were an employee of the government. This was not subsistence hunting in the traditional sense, but a job, and, you were paid for the work, hunting marine mammals. It was not only the coastal Native people but also Native people of the interior, who were affected over the years by the new changes, both Soviet and post-Soviet. Some thirty years later my friend Andrey Osipov and I visited an Even reindeer brigade who were living a nomadic lifestyle out on the tundra north of Evensk in the Magadan region. I shall talk about this journey in more detail at the end of the book.

The village store sold several types of non-Native foods such as would be found in any Soviet gastronome in a major city but with a much smaller selection of goods. Here all the modern foods that contained flour, sugar, starches, and salt, were to be found that would later have a less than positive effect on the general health of the population. The traditional diets of marine mammals and reindeer meat, fat, and internal organs were far healthier than the high carbohydrate, and sugar diet of the Russian urban population. The results would be seen in the polyclinics in these new communities where people suffered from health issues not seen before.

After parking the vezdekhod we got out and went to meet the local Chairman of the Communist Party, a very friendly woman of middle age. She said she was glad to see us, as not many visitors came here. Then we met Igor, the Director of the boarding school of 120 students. Most of the students had come from other remote villages, were separated from their families, and remained here as boarding students during the entire school year. When we visited their classrooms, the children were quite excited about meeting foreigners and being able to talk with people from Alaska, and we were made to feel very welcome. We got to talking with some of the teachers and Igor, the school Director, and learned that there were many problems faced by these Native people that were similar to those faced by Alaska Native people. We also learned that Igor was a friend of Dr. Tom Albert. He told us that the North Slope Borough Eskimos had helped the Native people here in this region with supplies of important equipment for hunting and butchering the bowhead whales. Then later we talked with the well-known Native educator Anna Anaina about some special funds that supported the advancement of Native Language programs in the schools.

The language of the school was, of course, Russian, and students had been discouraged and even prevented from speaking their Native language. The same situation related to speaking their Native language also existed for Native people in Alaska. The Russification program of the Small People of the North had been going on for years, since just after the Revolution. Although I do remember seeing in the classes Soviet elementary reading textbooks that were in Cyrillic, yet also some in their Native language. I was told that they were used by teachers in this school. Things were changing related to speaking their Native language. We have one middle-school textbook in our library that is in the Evenki Language and dated 1979. I must research this since maybe some but not all Native groups had curriculum materials in their Native language. It was always a pleasure to visit with students in their classes and this was even more so since it was the first Native village I had visited. It is too bad I do not have any of the photographs I took then.

One difference from Alaska was that most people here lived in old Soviet-style two-story wooden apartment buildings similar to those cement structures in the larger towns and cities. The central heating plant provided heat during the winter and hot water for washing. There was a coal-fired electrical generating plant for lights and power for the school, the village administration, and flats. I remember when I lived in the Eskimo community of Utkiagvik (Barrow) most individual houses were also heated from utilidor pipes running from the central heating plant.

So now after our interesting visit, it was back over the tundra to Provideniya, and hopefully on to Nome. Interesting to note that Raisa the Chukchi student had predicted that we would get permission to fly on the 17th, and sure enough we did. Our group of seven people and our luggage made it necessary for two airplanes, single-engine Cessna 185's to come and pick us up.

With one more day of waiting it was back touring the town with Sergei, a man on the staff of the Institute. We visited the interesting local Museum where the Director, Volodya showed us their collection of 130 beautiful paintings of the people and the region. I went back to the elementary school and Larisa, another English Language teacher, invited me to dinner. Her daughter received her first pen-pal letter from my student Valery Jackson, and so she gave me some letters and little gifts for Valery and my class. I enjoyed yet a little more time with the English Language students. The teachers were more inquisitive with a bit more English language to ask questions. Earlier, Natasha Fukes also showed me some of my student's pen-pal letters, one from Pearl Harvey, Virginia Harvey's younger sister. I still have some of the newspapers, little gifts, and photographs that we received from Natasha and her students.

CHAPTER NINETEEN: SAMOVARS, SOVIET LAW AND THE UNIVERSITY OF ALASKA

Mayor Oleg Kulinkin arranged for us and our baggage to be driven out to the Provideniya airport the next day. We had to have all our luggage and boxes inspected and cleared by the Soviet Border Guards. They acted as customs officials here in this remote Northern region. We had some gifts that Dr. Kokorev was taking to give to the President of the University of Alaska, professors, and administrators at UA. He had three electric Russian samovars in boxes that he was hand- carrying. When standing there in the airport one of the Border Guards approached us and asked what was in the boxes. Evgeny said he had three electric Russian samovars, which at that time were difficult to obtain, especially in Magadan. Well, the Border Guard informed Evgeny that it was not legal to take samovars out of the country. This was not good news as there was little that was interesting in the way of gifts for us to take. Then shortly thereafter the Border Guard walked up to us and asked us where we were going and if it would be possible for us to bring him a souvenir from Alaska when we returned in a couple of weeks. We said no problem, we would be happy to do this for him. Now, the laws of the Soviet Union had changed in a matter of minutes, and it was no longer illegal to take electric samovars out of the country to give as gifts. All the Soviet Border Guards were friendly, and we enjoyed visiting with them. Such Soviet flexibility one did not often experience. The samovars were greatly appreciated by President O'- Dowd and others at the University of Alaska.

After clearing Soviet customs, Oleg provided us with two old Soviet Army jeeps to take us and our baggage out to the Bering Air airplanes sitting on the ramp. What a nice sight to see two Cessna 185s waiting there to take us over and above the Ice Curtain to Nome, Alaska. After the short flight, we landed in Nome and went through US Customs, who did not inspect any of our baggage. Then out in the terminal where we received a warm Alaska greeting from Nancy and Perry Mendenhall. Nancy was the Director of Nome Community College. They had a nice reception and dinner for us that evening. There were many people there from the college. Being the first visitors from Magadan Pedagogical Institute there ensued a lively discussion regarding the differences between our two different institutions. After dinner, we all went to experience some local culture at the old Polaris bar and the Board of Trade bar near the Nome waterfront. Here we were able to experience the character and color of a true Northern Alaska old mining town. Gold had been discovered in Nome around the turn of the century. Nome is the home to the Eskimo King Islanders who moved there from the island some years ago. They are excellent ivory carvers and marine mammal hunters.Everyone enjoyed seeing their beautiful ivory carvings displayed for sale in the cabinets of the souvenir shops, bars, and hotels.

The next morning, we went back to the college and Nancy gave us a tour. Nome Community College provided many Native people with the opportunity to take college-level courses leading to a degree program. We also met and saw the TV studio that Dan Johnson operated. UAF Chancellor Pat O'Rourke had given MPI a satellite dish antenna and large screen television set so that we were able to receive live Alaska State TV—RATNET in our TV room. It was with some difficulty that Dan Johnson brought, and set up the dish antenna on the roof of the Magadan Pedagogical Institute. The wind in Magadan seemed to often blow so hard as to change the direction of the antenna and interrupt our reception. Alaska was the only state that had its own television satellite to broadcast live television programs to rural Native villages.

After lunch, Nancy and Perry helped us take all our baggage to the airport and we checked in for our Alaska Airlines flight to Anchorage. We said goodbye to our new friends and boarded our Boeing 727. I mentioned to the stewardesses that we had some special guests aboard from Russia, and if possible, could you please bring them a nice glass of wine to make them feel welcome? They brought Evgeny and Roman each a glass of wine and said many was a new experience for our group and quite a contrast to flying Aeroflot in those days.

We flew to Anchorage via Kotzebue, a large Eskimo town on the Bering Sea coast. After landing at Anchorage International Airport, we were greeted by the University of Alaska Anchorage staff members Tom Sielo, Professor Michael Karl, and Professor Gretchen Bersch. Professor Michael Karl, Dean of the Education Department was the main person we were to work with at UAA. First, we were farmed out so to speak to various host families. I was to stay, along with Sergei, another man from MPI, at the home of Gretchen Bersch, a Professor of Adult Education. Evgeny and Roman were to stay at another professor's home, an older single lady whom I think I never met.

This lady seemed to lack some of the social graces usually found in most educated people. The second day dawned, and at our morning university meeting with Michael Karl, Roman came up to me and expressed some concerns. it seems this lady had hardly spoken to them, prepared no dinner or breakfast for them, and worst of all, they had to both sleep in the same bed. I was astounded, went directly to Gretchen, and said that we would have to make some changes. She said she would be glad to have them stay at her place even if a bit crowded and so we both went to explain the situation to Michael Karl. He too was surprised and apologized. But Gretchen saved the day and joined our little Magadan team. We moved Evgeny and Roman to Gretchen's house where we all stayed, and have been close friends ever since. There is a bit more to this story that eventually came out when Evgeny discovered that he had inadvertently forgotten and left his pajamas there when they left in somewhat of a hurry. He felt he could live without them, and so he did. We never let him forget this.

With the four of us now staying at Gretchen's, it made it easy to plan our meetings with Michael Karl, the Dean of the Education Department. Every morning Gretchen was first up, the coffee pot was on, and soon would be ready for all to have a cup of her special brew. After a nice breakfast, Gretchen drove us to UAA, and we began with meetings at the UAA Education Department. There was a lot to discuss since none of the UAA people had had the opportunity to come to Magadan. First on the agenda was an explanation of the Magadan Pedagogical Institute, and its mission and programs. Rector Evgeny Kokorev and Dean Roman Tchaikovski both explained in some detail that the mission of MPI was to train teachers in all areas that were taught in the city and regional schools.

Michael Karl and the other UAA professors had many questions regarding what sort of programs MPI would be able to provide for UAA students. Dean Tchaikovsky explained that there would be Russian Language instruction at the Institute by the teachers in the English Department, and students would have the opportunity to do their student teaching in the English Language Programs at some of the Magadan city schools, They would be staying with a host family, and would therefore be able to have a unique opportunity to gain insight into the daily life of ordinary Soviet people, shopping in the local stores would provide opportunities for them to learn about some of the differences between what Soviet people had available and what the American shopper had available, and meeting and being able to make new friends would make their life more interesting. Since I was the one person who had moved

UNIVERSITY OF ALASKA PROFESSOR GRETCHEN BERSCH. THE "HEART" OF STUDENT EXCHANGES BETWEEN THE UNIVERSITIES OF MAGADAN AND ANCHORAGE. 2011. PHOTO BY ANDREY OSIPOV

from Alaska to Magadan not that long ago, I was able to elaborate on these ideas and explain what a unique and valuable experience I felt this would be for these Alaska students. After several rounds of meetings, Dean Karl and the others were supportive of further exchanges for both UAA staff and students. The future of exchanges between UAA and MPI was now assured and would continue for some years as long as the scheduled flights would continue, and the funds were available. This lasted for about ten years, and then the economics changed, and scheduled flights to Magadan and Anchorage were canceled due to the lack of passengers and cargo demand.

Gretchen Bersch has been one of the most involved people in keeping in contact with our Magadan Pedagogical Institute people for the past 25 years. I am sure she has had more students and other people from Magadan staying at her home in Anchorage than any other person in Alaska. Gretchen, Lena and I are the only three people from Alaska who still return to actively participate in the programs at the MPI, which is now called North Eastern State University. I am sad to say that the Covid 19 pandemic put an end to this, and now the war in Ukraine has made it very

DAN JOHNSON (UNIVERSITY OF ALASKA), ROMAN TCHAIKOVSKY, GRETCHEN BERSCH, LUDMILA TCHAIKOVSKAYA AND PROFESSOR MARGARET ENGLES (UNIVERSITY OF ALASKA) ENJOYING DINNER IN THE FLAT OF ROMAN TCHAIKOVSKY. PHOTO BY PAVEL ZHDANOV

complicated to travel to Russia.

Soon thereafter, I was to learn what it meant to have a single-entry Russian visa. Suddenly I realized that my first Soviet visa had been canceled when I crossed the border from Russia to Alaska. Well, now what to do? I had to get another invitation from Rector Kokorev, and send it along with my application, fees, and passport to the Soviet Consulate in San Francisco requesting a new Soviet visa for the duration of my stay in Magadan. I paid the fees for the fastest possible service and was lucky to get my new Soviet visa just two days before our scheduled return departure. One does not like to learn the lessons of life in this way, a bit too stressful.

More meetings with Professor Michael Karl resulted in a close connection with Margaret Engels, a German language professor and the Chair of the German Language Department. Roman had several meetings with her where they were able to discuss what possibilities there would be for German Language students coming in both directions. They became close friends and colleagues, and Margaret came to Magadan more than once and taught in the German Language Department with Roman. One day was spent with the President of Alaska Pacific University, a private university that is next to UAA. Although there was some interest nothing developed due to the costs involved with such a great distance.

This being our first visit to the University of Alaska Anchorage, after our meetings, we all wanted to go shopping for things that were on our lists. Since I had been there and done that, I was elected as the guide for the shopping program. For the Russians, it was getting to know the real differences between shopping in our two countries, and ice cream was one of them. Ice cream is very popular and of high quality in many cafes in Russia. So, it was necessary to find a high-quality ice cream shop since it was at the top of Evgeny's list. This was not a problem since Baskin Robbin's stores were quite available in most of the shopping malls. The problem was that Evgeny couldn't make a choice when there were 31 different flavors from which to choose. The only solution was for him to just start at the beginning and proceed down to the thirty-first. He certainly gave it his best shot and was quite far down the list by the time we had to return to Magadan. Roman and I move up with him, but it was difficult.

Since Gretchen provided us with a car, it was out to visit some of the main shopping malls in downtown Anchorage. For our guests, this was a new and interesting experience, quite different from shopping in the somewhat half-empty Soviet department stores at that time in Magadan. The selection was almost too much for them to imagine. Roman bought Luda a microwave oven and had to also buy a converter for the power difference. Evgeny bought Larisa a toaster, maybe the first electric toaster in Magadan, since toast was not so known there. He needed to buy a good pair of shoes, so we went to several stores to find a nice pair of size 14 shoes. It was a challenge, but we finally did it, and he was pleased. Of course, all our guests thoroughly enjoyed being able to purchase so many little things to bring back to family and friends. What they learned from visiting the stores in the malls could not be learned from books, and was a lot more fun. The results of their purchases were to be long-lasting and enjoyable, Alaska memories.

STUDENTS EAST AND WEST

The next day it was back to meeting with Michael Karl in the School of Education Department at UAA. After much discussion as to how many

PROFESSOR GRETCHEN BERSCH PRESENTING HER TEACHER OF THE YEAR AWARD., NORTH EASTERN STATE UNIVERSITY, MAGADAN, 2014 OXOTNIK PRESS ARCHIVES

students, and what classes would they participate in, an agreement was signed that stipulated five students from UAA would come to MPI in the second semester of 1990, and the same number of MPI students would go to UAA.

In Anchorage, Alaska, host families would be organized by Prfessor Gretchen Bersch of UAA. I always felt that what students could learn from being part of a family in Alaska and Magadan was as important as what they would learn in a classroom setting. And to this day, many of these students who took part in the early exchange programs still keep in contact with their host families from those days. The UAA students would pay tuition to UAA and get credit for their Russian language studies at MPI, and the MPI students would go tuition-free and get credit for their coursework at UAA. Since the MPI students had some fluency in English they had several options for taking a variety of courses at UAA. Some returned to UAA later and received their BA degree. In Magadan, each UAA and UAF student was assigned to an English language teacher at one of the Magadan middle schools. Most of the time they would observe, and work as a teacher's assistant in one of the English language teacher's classrooms. Here they would be able to observe the differences between the way classes were conducted in a Soviet classroom and a classroom in the United States. The Soviet teachers and students would have the benefit of being able to listen to the native English language being spoken by an American when they were the ones in charge of the lesson. As I mentioned, this was one of the main things missing from most English language classes in the Soviet Union as many classes at that time used audiotapes of Oxford English.

Not only did the Alaska students learn a great deal about the Soviet system of education, but also, they were able to see for themselves the workings of average Soviet families. This was something that few Americans had the opportunity to observe and experience, especially if they were a tourist. Most Alaskan students found shopping in the Magadan stores interesting both in the type of merchandise they carried, and in the percentage of the average person's salary that a family had to pay for such items as food, clothing, and consumer goods like electronics. Living in less space was also good for Alaskan students to see and understand. Soviet families did with a lot less than the average American family, and I did not hear a lot of complaining from anybody.

This was a time of great deficit for many foods and consumer items that were readily available in most American stores. There was some concern that the host families would have difficulties in being able to buy enough food to feed themselves and a student guest. So, the Magadan City Administration introduced a plan to help families with this problem. They had opportunities to purchase foods from some of the specialty stores for veterans.

DIARY: "After several successful meetings with people at UAA, we decided that Evgeny, Roman, and I would take a break and drive to Soldotna. It was a beautiful drive along Turnagain Arm and Cook Inlet, through the mountains, and down the Sterling Highway to the Kenai Peninsula. We were able to stay at my house in Soldotna. The next morning, I took Roman to Sunday mass at the Catholic church. His father was a Ukrainian Catholic priest who had been oppressed and sent to prison when Roman was a boy. His father survived and returned to their home in Ukraine after Stalin died. Roman said that this was the first time he had been to a Catholic church in the past forty years. After church, we three went to Sourdough Sal's Diner for a special pancake and egg breakfast. Sal, an old friend, treated us to breakfast. She was a Soldotna institution and a great supporter of our program. On our way over to Lamont's department store, we saw several moose just walking around people's yards, a curiosity for our Soviet friends. Shopping at Lamont's was eventful: Roman and Evgeny both bought their first real American jeans and flannel shirts, and Linda the Manager gave me several nice gifts for when we returned to Magadan. Then we all went with Jerry Best to meet with Fr. Targonski, the Russian Orthodox priest at Holy Assumption Russian Orthodox Church in Kenai. This is a very important and historic site, the location of the first Russian settlement on the Kenai. Then Bob Williams picked us up, and we went on a tour of the Chevron Oil Refinery in North Kenai. Bob was the Manager of the Refinery and a major actor in our University Exchange Program being the President of the Board of Regents of the University of Alaska. Afterward, we all went to dinner at Bob's house. Bob is a gourmet cook and prepared a special dinner for his guests. Then it was Russian banya time, and so Evgeny, Bob, and I all went in his banya in the backyard overlooking Cook Inlet. After each throwing of water on the hot rock's session, it was stepping outside, laying down, and rolling around in the snow. Then back into the banya for another hot steam experience. There was, unfortunately, no banschik to beat us all over with the birch tree leaves as in Magadan. After a nice dinner and visit, we said spasibo and goodbye, and drove back to my house. The next day it was another beautiful drive up the Sterling Highway through Turnagain Pass, and on to Anchorage and to see Gretchen." (February 1990)

CHAPTER TWENTY:
NORTH TO FAIRBANKS WHERE THE
PRESIDENTS MEET

The next morning, 27 February, we went to the Anchorage Airport, said farewell and spacibo to Gretchen and Michael Karl, and flew on Alaska Airlines to Fairbanks. Evgeny and Roman were both pleased with their meetings with Michael Karl, and with the agreements signed that assured the future of the exchange program with UAA. After landing in Fairbanks, we were met by Professor Jerry Mohatt who would become a close friend and colleague of Evgeny Kokorev as the relations proceeded. Jerry took us to get settled in the modern University of Alaska dorms where we each had our own room. Evgeny and Roman were well aware of the difference between where we were staying, and the Magadan Pedagogical Institute Obschezhitiye-Dormitory. Each of us had our bathroom with a nice shower. We all went to lunch at Wood Center, a nice modern stolovaya with a wide range of offerings for lunch, including a beer if one so desired. Then it was to our first meeting with President Don O'Dowd in his office. In the beginning, he was cautious about signing any protocol agreements. Evgeny gave him the protocols signed by Gov. Kobets, a Soviet flag, and a Magadan book. After some long and serious discussions, it would be up to Jerry Mohatt and Vic Fisher to work out the protocol details with Evgeny and Roman. That night we went to David and Perry Gilmore's home for a nice dinner reception. David and Perry were the first University of Alaska people, along with Bob Williams, to come to Magadan Pedagogical Institute. They presented each of us with an Alaska Cross pen and pencil set. After dinner, Jerry and Evgeny went to the banya/sauna for some relaxation. Roman was always available when Evgeny needed a translator except in one place, and that was the banya.

The next morning, February 28th, 1990, we had a breakfast meeting at the Fairbanks Miner's Association where the big four, Evgeny, Roman, Vic, and Jerry hammered out the final details of the agreement that President Don O'Dowd would sign. Then Roman and I did the final proofreading. Steve MacClean, Director of International Students, also was very helpful. They completed the protocols in the seventh-floor conference room, and that evening we had dinner and a little ceremony at the President's house on campus. Vic Fisher played a major role in drafting the protocols and letters from UA President O'Dowd to take to Gov. Kobets and the Ministry of Education of the USSR in Moscow. President O'Dowd and President Kokorev, along with Chancellor Pat O'Rourke signed the protocols of the agreement for both UA professors and students, and MPI professors and students to develop a working relationship, and for students to be able to attend classes at each university/institute. These, along with the UAA protocols and letters, were important for President Kokorev to take back to the Soviet Union and to obtain further support from the Soviet Ministry of Education of the USSR for the exchange program.

After much discussion, President Kokorev and Roman Tchaikovsky, along with the UA administrators decided that the same programs would be made available for both UAF and UAA students when they came to Magadan Pedagogical Institute. This had already been discussed with the faculty at UAA during our visit there, and so it was felt that the same would be true for the students at UAF. Then they also discussed how many UAF students would come to MPI, and an agreement was signed that stipulated five students from UAF would come to MPI in the second semester of 1990, and the same number of MPI students would go to UAF. As stated above both the UAF and UAA students would focus on Russian Language development at MPI in special classes designed for them, along with the possibility of doing their student teaching requirement in one of the Magadan schools. For both groups, I would be their supervisor during their student teaching practice, and work with the local classroom teachers.

This was the time that a young Alaska Native (Aleutiq) man named Sven Haakanson came to MPI and decided to do his student teaching at School No. 14, and I was to supervise this experience. He did very well and was one of the few UAF students who had ever completed a student teaching requirement in a Soviet school. After he graduated from UAF, he went on to further his education and took his doctorate from Harvard University. Sven became fluent in Russian and returned to Russia to pursue studies in Archaeology. He is now a Professor at the University of Washington, and the Curator of American Anthropology at the Burke Museum.

The next day we had a tour of the UAF Rasmussen Library where we had the good fortune to meet Tamara Lincoln, the Russian Bibliographer. She was very interested in our program and later had the opportunity to come and visit us in Magadan. She and her husband Darrel were to be Alaskan 'parents 'of Gleb Tchaikovsky, Roman's son when he did an MBA degree program at UAF. Tamara was a delightful Russian lady who went out of her way to make all of us feel so welcome at her university. We were sad to learn of her passing, and she will be duly missed by all those who were fortunate to be friends with her.

The following morning it was back to the University for meetings with the staff at the College of Rural Alaska: Jerry Mohatt, Ray Barnhardt, Pat Nelson, Steve Grubis, Mike Gaffney, Larry Schaffer, and others. I gave Dr. Lydia Black the North East Research Institute books from Alvina Voropaeva. Dr. Claus Naske gave Roman one of his books on the history of Alaska. Roger Pearson gave Evgeny a National Geographic World Atlas for the Institute Library. After lunch, we visited two elementary schools and one high school. It was important for Evgeny and Roman to be able to see the dynamics of elementary and secondary schools in Alaska. In the evening we had dinner at the home of Jerry and Robbie Mohatt. After dinner, there was a long, and serious discussion about the future of the exchange program. Evgeny and Roman gave Jerry and Robbie Mohatt a nice Russian samovar and some other Russian gifts.

The next day we toured the University campus, the Fairbanks downtown area, and in the late afternoon went to see the old gold dredge and Malamute Saloon at Ester. The dredge appeared to be the same as those working dredges along the Kolyma River. Ester was established in 1906 when gold was discovered by miners and prospectors on Ester Creek. In the early days, the gold was mined with a gold pan, a shovel, a wheel barrel, and a sluice box. Some years later, in the 1930s on Ester Creek, there was a large mining operation with dredges operated by the Fairbanks Exploration Company. At its, peak Ester had a population of around 5000 people.

In the evening we went to have a beer, listen to readings of Robert Service's poetry, and watched the can-can girls dancing in the old-time Malemute Saloon not far from the old dredge in Ester. I like the poetry of Robert Service very much, and it was something new for our Russian guests.

Everybody enjoyed the dancing girls and poetry readings in this old-time gold rush era saloon, and the beer and peanuts. The bartenders and all the waitresses were dressed in 19th-century gold rush era costumes which added a lot to the setting, along with the bowls of peanuts on the tables, and everybody just threw their empty peanut shells on the floor which also added to the atmosphere.

That morning I took advantage of being back in the United States and called Lisa [my daughter], and she said she had a good student teaching observation, and that she would have another 4.0 GPA at the end of the term. She was a very good and serious student at Oregon State University. It was nice to not have to spend hours calling her going through a Magadan operator. I only wished she had been a bit closer so we could have spent some time together.

Every day was full of meetings, most took place on the seventh floor near the Cross-Cultural Educational Development Program offices. Irma Jean Strickler, the Administrative Assistant had been more than helpful, and Evgeny gave her one of the Russian samovars which she liked very much. Whenever I had to call regarding our plans, it was Irma Jean whom I relied on to solve any difficulties, and she usually did. She told me that her involvement with our Russian delegation was one of the most meaningful experiences of her twenty years at the University of Alaska. She was truly a major part of the exchange program, and we could not have done it without all her help.

Then came the last day of meetings. All of us felt good about having been able to put together protocols of agreement signed by UA President Don O'Dowd, Chancellor Pat O'Rourke, and Magadan Pedagogical Institute Rector Evgeny Kokorev that there would be an exchange program between the University of Alaska and Magadan Pedagogical Institute. Rector Kokorev and Dean Tchaikovskiy were very pleased since this would not have even been imagined six months ago. It was time to say our bolshoye spasibos and dosvidanias for tomorrow we would be flying back to Nome.

4 MARCH 1990

Then the day came that we all weren't ready for, and it was up at 0430 when we all headed for the airport to check in our baggage. Jerry Mohatt, and a few others were there to bid us farewell. We first flew back to Anchorage and then changed planes for our flight to Nome. We had very little time at the airport, and Gretchen gave me fifteen baggage claim tickets for boxes of gifts for Magadan friends that she had checked in already. We all checked in and got ready to board our Alaska Airlines flight back to Nome.

I think that everyone at UAF and UAA felt that Evgeny and Roman, as well as our students, were wonderful Russian people, and they enjoyed meeting them. They all made everyone feel comfortable even without at times all sharing the same language. Evgeny and Roman were easy going, friendly people to interact with within any social setting.

And these wonderful Alaskans provided an unforgettable experience for our Russian guests. It could not have been better. Well, I could have done without having my single-entry Soviet visa canceled, and the anxiety that caused. Lesson learned.

It was important for Evgeny to return to Magadan with the signed agreements-protocols between the University of Alaska and the Magadan Pedagogical Institute. Now he would be able to take these to Gov. Kobets and the Ministry of Education in Moscow, and begin a new world of adventures that would eventually lead to many students from both our great countries being able to come together and better understand each other's way of life and culture. Later on, Evgeny would work closely with Professor Jerry Mohatt, Chancellor O'Rourke, Vic Fisher, President Komisar, and others which would result in the founding of Northern International University.

After we arrived in Nome, we sent the students and Sergei ahead on Bering Air since we had too many boxes for us to all travel together. Roman, Evgeny, and I were tired from non-stop meetings in Fairbanks and had no time just to relax. We met Ira Lepchinko, who had just arrived from Magadan. In Nome, she would spend the next six months teaching the Russian Language, a Russian cooking class, and would stay with Nancy Mendenhall. She received a $600 stipend. That night we had a delicious reindeer stew dinner with Nancy and Perry and at last a relaxing visit.

Nancy and Perry made it possible for Roman and Evgeny to do a little more shopping at Alaska Commercial and Hansen's Trading Company before they left. Both found some items on sale that they bought. It was their last chance. I was able to get two Sears and Roebuck, and two Penny's mail-order catalogs to take back to show my students. Then we went back to the airport and saw that we still had a lot of weight and were not sure if we would be able to get all our boxes on Aeroflot when we arrived in Provideniya.

The next morning, we went to the airport and Evgeny talked to Jim Rowe about his problem with taking rubles for payment, but not being able to pay for airport service or buy fuel in Provideniya with rubles. Evgeny told him he would try and help. I gave Jim a nice Aeroflot desk calendar and told him how much we appreciated his helping us, and that he was a significant actor in melting the Ice Curtain. Jim is a kind and considerate businessman who always tries to work together with his Russian counterparts so that both sides benefit.

Before we left Nome, I called Anna who was planning to come, along with her brother Paul, to visit me in Magadan in a month or so, and she said she was having some problems with getting her Soviet visa. I tried and was finally able to call Kirill Kasatkin at the Ministry of Foreign Affairs in Moscow, and he said he would try and help. She needed to send all her documents to the San Francisco Consulate. The Russian Embassy in D. C. said she needed a letter from the Foreign Affairs Office to accompany Dr. Kokorev's letter of invitation. She had nine days before she was to leave for Germany to meet up with Paul before they would fly to Moscow and then to Magadan. It was a short time of uncertainty, as usual when applying for any visa. As we know now, it all worked out, the usual Russian adventure. I was very much looking forward to them coming to see me in Magadan.

CHAPTER TWENTY-ONE:
BACK TO THE USSR

The next morning, March 7th, I got a call from Richard Storns at Bering Air that they received a telex from CAA in Moscow that we could fly to Provideniya that day. Out we went to the waiting Cessna 185, loaded our remaining baggage, climbed aboard, and off we flew back across the Bering Straits to the good old USSR. We landed in Provideniya, and the Border Guards were ready to open and inspect the goodies from America that we brought. They only opened one box of mine, the canned goods. I was very glad since I did not want to explain all the gifts I was carrying for the students. Sergei said that the Border Guards took five hours to go through all the boxes we had sent with him and the girls. I felt so good being back in the USSR/ Russia. I felt so at home with my new Magadan friends. Here they made me feel a part of their families.

I walked over to the Provideniya Hotel while Roman and Evgeny went to see about getting all the boxes that Sergei had brought on the first flight from Nome. Natasha Fukes had come out to the airport and brought me some pen-pal letters, books, and a matryoshka doll for my students. I was hoping, if we had remained in Provideniya another day, to go again to visit her class, but suddenly Roman came running up to me and said that we had to hurry and get all of our 35 boxes and baggage out to the Aeroflot An-26 cargo plane that was waiting on the tarmac to fly to Anadyr. We did not know when the next flight would be, and if it could handle all of our many boxes so we had to take what was available even if it was a cargo plane with only jump seats along the windows.

We put our bags on carts, and out to the plane, and threw them aboard just loose in the middle of the plane. There was no cargo net to cover and secure the boxes in case of high turbulence. Such a mad, and unexpected rush, but we would at least be part of the way home that day. We climbed aboard, took our jump seats along the side of the fuselage, and reached for our seat belts to buckle up. Well, I found out that I was no better off than our baggage in case of hitting high turbulence, for I only had half of a seat belt. Another interesting Soviet adventure that I will never forget. Flying in an An-26 is very loud. But we did not need to talk for a while, just sit back and relax, which we had not done for the past several weeks.

Soon we landed in Anadyr, and it was back to rechecking our boxes, and baggage for our next flight to Magadan. We checked in at the Anadyr Airport Hotel and had a room for four, a usual Soviet hotel room with four rather narrow single beds with bouncy coil metal springs under a not-very-thick mattress. But it was clean and comfortable, like a college dorm. When I was walking along the corridor a young man stopped me and asked if I was an American, and we started talking. He was a photographer who invited me to come to his room and said he would like to show me some of his photos. I said yes, of course. He could speak some English but with difficulty. We went to his room, and he showed me a selection of his very professional photos of the Anadyr region. He gave me a few of his original pictures and an ivory-carved little beliken. After about a half-hour I said I must go as I knew Roman did not know where I was. When I walked out of the room, I saw Roman and Evgeny walking towards me, Roman had a stern look on his face that said I was in trouble. Roman and Evgeny were so worried that they had one of the militsias going from room to room looking for me. They were both a bit upset. But later it became a joke, and we all could laugh about it. Their advice was just don't be so friendly with strangers. I admit sometimes I didn't feel like following some of their advice, and I didn't. So, it was late, and after going to the stolovaya for dinner we went back to our room to sleep. Another busy, and not-so-restful day, but so glad we were one more flight ahead on our way back home. In the morning after zavtrak, it was back to the airport and checked in with all our baggage. Fortunately, Aeroflot agreed to take all our baggage, and it was time to go through passport control and out to the big Tu-154 to fly home to Magadan. I was now to begin the next chapter of my life in Magadan. After arriving in Magadan, we took all my boxes of gifts from Soldotna up to my flat. It was late again, and so to bed for tomorrow would be gift distribution day.

Up, and after a chashka horoshego chaya (a cup of good tea), Evgeny's Volga came, and I took the five boxes up to the Institute. I went to my third para, and it was so nice to be back with my dear students. We had a meeting with Evgeny about writing an article on our trip for Magadan-skaya Pravda. Then I took gifts and went to Pasha and Marina's for dinner. It always felt like being home when I was with Pasha and his wonderful family. I gave them all the news, greetings from their friends in Soldotna, and their gifts. Then I walked over to see Kostya and Natasha and was greeted with open arms. They had been cross-country skiing in Snezhnaya Dolina all day and had just gotten home. It was getting late, but I had to take the Panasonic Stereo boombox and gifts over to Irina Alishova. She was quite moved, and appreciative, and would you believe gave me another samovar. Irina gave me two samovars, one for Anna and one for Lisa. Now after being a delivery man, it was back home to rest.

After returning from Alaska the rest of the year went along quite smoothly as the end of the second term was fast approaching. I found every day to be a new, and interesting experience. I did not want my first year teaching and living in Magadan to come to an end for I knew that my Soviet visa would expire soon, and I would have to leave my very close friends and return to Alaska.

Since President Kokorev and Dean Tchaikovsky had succeeded in their goals, it was time to make trip reports to both the local, and national governmental authorities regarding the agreements that were signed concerning the future of the Alaska and Magadan Educational Exchange Program.

Then there were the meetings with the MPI faculty and staff that were very interested in what life was like for those on the other side of the Bering Sea Ice Curtain. One of the main interests was what were the differences in the availability of consumer goods in the stores. This may have been the main interest of those who had to remain home in Magadan. Then there was the story about Evgeny having such a difficult time trying to decide what flavor of ice cream to have each time we went to a Baskins Robbins ice cream store.

However, there was another cross-cultural experience that never seemed to go unnoticed by visitors going in either direction, and that is the everyday experience of using the toilets in both countries. There seemed to be a noticeable difference recognized by both Alaskan visitors to Russia and by our small delegation on their visit to Alaska, particularly to the University of Alaska. The university had what we would consider modern, and usual toilet facilities both in the dorms and in the public areas, nothing special. However, in our MPI building, all the toilets were the 'squat and go' type, and this was considered a bit archaic by many Alaskan visitors. Evgeny realized this and felt that this must change before our next visitors arrive from Alaska. So not long after we returned, he had all the old squat toilets removed, and regular sit-down toilets with seats attached installed in all the restrooms in the building. In the men's restrooms, he had stand-up urinals also installed.

Well, some of us felt that the old squat toilets did add some more character to the experience, but not everyone. Now we were ready to receive our friends from Alaska.

CHAPTER TWENTY-TWO:
IMPERMANENCE IN THE SOVIET UNION

To say that Magadan and the Soviet Union were life-changing experiences would be a gross understatement. However, this is where the saying that change is permanent is so very applicable. After my first year of
living, and teaching at Magadan Pedagogical Institute, I had to return to
Alaska for my Soviet visa was about to expire. I had been asked by President Evgeny Kokorev, and Dean Roman Tchaikovsky as well as the President of the University of Alaska, to try and obtain a second sabbatical and
continue my work as a Professor of English and Coordinator of the University of Alaska and MPI Exchange Program for a second year. I returned
to Soldotna and immediately discussed this with my Superintendent Dr.
Fred Pomeroy. I gave him the letters of support for my continuation at MPI
from Evgeny Kokorev, Roman Tchaikovsky, and Jerry Komisar, and we discussed what would be fair to me, and the school district. He was willing to
let me have a second year teaching at Magadan Pedagogical Institute, and
so we both agreed that I would again receive only payment into my retirement fund, and my health insurance being paid by the district. I felt this
was fair, and so rented my house and prepared to get my second one-year
Soviet visa and return to my dear friends and students in Magadan.

I had applied and was waiting to get my Soviet visa and to fly back
to Magadan on the next Aeroflot charter flight from Anchorage, Alaska.
I remember that after applying for my visa it seemed a long time in coming. Not only my visa but there were five University of Alaska students
who would be going with me and would spend a semester studying at MPI,

as well as doing their student teaching assignment in the Magadan schools. All our visas were to come together from the Soviet Consulate in San Francisco. I became quite concerned, and so contacted Gov. Kobets, and Roman and Evgeny at Magadan Pedagogical Institute. They were all trying to contact the Soviet Consulate in San Francisco to make sure that our visas would come on time for us to take the forthcoming Aeroflot charter flight. Two days before we were to depart our visas still had not arrived. These students had made plans to be gone for a semester and had given up dorm rooms, apartments, jobs, and any possibility of classes at UAA, and so we were all a bit anxious about receiving our visas. The day before we were to leave, I again called the Soviet Consulate, and they said they were shipped, and now in the hands of the US Post Office. So, I called the Post Office, and they were able to track all six visas and said that I could pick them up tomorrow morning by 0500. This was pushing it tight since we were to depart on the Aeroflot charter later that same afternoon, and I was three hours away from Anchorage in Soldotna. I was there at the back door of the Post Office before 0500. It felt so good when I held them in my hand and knew that I would for sure be able to return to my Magadan for another year, along with my University of Alaska students. Not the kind of experience one prefers, but another Magadan memory.

As usual, when I arrived at Magadan International Airport and walked into the terminal my friends Roman Tchaikovsky and Evgeny Kokorev, along with Pasha Zhdanov, were there to greet me and say welcome home. Traditional Russian bear hugs were always included. We threw my luggage into an Institute truck and got into the MPI Volga to drive back to Magadan. Just past the airport we pulled over to the side of the road and stopped to engage in another tradition of ours. We got out of the Volga, Evgeny opened the trunk of the car and took out a bottle of fine Russian vodka, three little stopas, vodka cups, and some buterbrody, little sandwiches with kolbasa-sausage, and cucumbers, and set them on the hood. Then the three stopas were filled and our first of many more toasts to the success of our Magadan Pedagogical Institute, University of Alaska Exchange Program. You just cannot have a nicer welcome home than that. Then back in the car. What a beautiful site to see all the tamarack trees along the Kolyma Trassa. As we passed the Mask of Sorrow on the hill overlooking the city, I could see below us the familiar sight of my Russian hometown, Magadan. After my arrival, I went directly up to my cozy little flat on Boldyreva Street and opened the door to begin another wonderful year of unforgettable memories. It felt so good to be back in my own Russian home, in moi rodnoi gorod, my Russian hometown. How little then did I realize just what was in store for me, and what a truly lucky person I was. The next day I was back at Magadan Pedagogical Institute and preparing for my next year of teaching. I was a bit sorry to not be with the same first-year students with whom I had also shared the first-year experience. But my next group, second-year students, was just wonderful, and we were to have a great year of study and friendship. They were just as interested as my previous class in what life in Alaska was like, and who I was as a person. I won't go into so much detail here since it was not so different from my first year. There were other aspects of this year that were quite different, so will focus on them.

After the students returned from spending a week or so harvesting the fall cabbage crops, we began our classes, and they continued right up to the end of the year holidays. This year the Great October Demonstratsia in November was not at all like the previous year, nor was the political situation that existed between the US and the Soviet Union. Things had calmed down considerably with the extensive talks between Gorbachev and Reagan. There was a strong positive feeling in the air that things would continue to get better, but always with a bit of skepticism. We still had to use talonies, and there still existed a big deficit in the way of many food products and consumer goods.

I brought with me from Alaska several VHS tapes of good American films to use with my students in our TV room that had the large screen television given to us by the University of Alaska. These were classic American films and not the B-movies that they often saw on Soviet TV in translation. These American videotapes provided them with the opportunity to hear many different people speaking their version of the English language. I showed American cartoons on Saturday mornings on our big screen TV for little children who were interested. There was a strong interest in this program, and it provided me with an experience that I never expected.

A friend of mine from the University of Alaska had come to Magadan earlier and had left a brochure with a research scientist at the Institute of Biological Problems of the North. It had to do with genetics research that was taking place at an American university in the Midwest. It

CATCHING SALMON ON THE KENAI RIVER IN SOLDOTNA, ALASKA, SONYA, LARRY, LENA, AND KSENYA, 1993. COURTSEY OF THE KHLINOVSKI ROCKHILL COLLECTION

was in English, and the individual in question, although well-versed in English, had some questions related to its content. This person had read in Magadanskaya Pravda that a certain professor from Alaska was at MPI, and so thought that it might be possible to get some answers to questions related to this brochure. So, one Saturday morning when I was at MPI getting ready to turn on the big screen TV for the children to watch cartoons I was approached at the bottom of the stairs by a nice young lady, with her cute little daughter at her side, who introduced herself as Helen. I introduced myself, and said you mean Lena, right? She said yes and from then on change has been permanent, one adventure after the other on three different continents.

I took the brochure and said I would look it over and get back to her. As I thought about it I said to myself that this person seems quite interesting and worth meeting again in the near future. She told me that she was a scientist doing genetics research at an institute not far from mine. In a few days, I went to visit her at her population genetics laboratory and was able to answer her questions related to the brochure. We talked, and she explained her research to me. This was not a field that I knew a lot about. She had graduated in biology from Far East University in Vladivostok and had done marine mammal research at a research center on the Crimean Peninsula. Later I learned just how much she loved working with her dolphins there. The first visit only made it necessary for me to return for another visit and then another. She was a unique woman, and I felt that I would like to know her better, so I invited her and her daughter over to my flat for dinner. Then it became part of my every day. Her daughter Sonechka was so cute, and I remember later we used to play Russian lotto together, and other times I would go to pick her up after her ballet lessons, and we would walk home together. So, one thing led to another, and it was apparent that I was more than just interested in being a casual friend. After a few months, I felt that I would like to share a long-lasting relationship with this wonderful Russian woman, and her wonderful daughter. So, we decided to come together to share our lives, and whatever lay ahead. Well, a lot lay ahead that we could never have predicted, and part of that will be found in the next chapter.

CHAPTER TWENTY-THREE:
A SOLDOTNA TROIKA MOVING BACK TO
ALASKA

In 1991, after finishing my second year teaching at Magadan Pedagogical Institute, I had to return to Soldotna to continue teaching for the
Kenai Peninsula Borough School District. It is interesting to think that
I/we were going to be moving from the 'new' Russia of the Soviet Union
to a new place called Alaska that was once part of the 'old' Stariya' Russia before the days of the Soviet Union. In some ways I was ready, and, in
some ways, I wanted my Magadan life to continue as it had been for the
previous two years. But this time there would be three of us moving to
our home on Arlington Court. It was not just packing, and moving some
clothing and household effects, it was a bit more complicated. First of all,
I had proposed marriage to Helen/Lena/Elena, and to my absolute delight,
she said yes and so along with her little daughter Sonechka we had a lot
to do before the day we would leave Magadan. The first thing was to call
her mother and father who lived in Cherkessk in the Northern Caucasus
and tell them that she was going to marry an American. A long-distance
phone call with a time difference meant that we had to stay up sitting on
the floor by the phone until the early hours of the morning waiting for
the long-distance operator to call back and tell us that the call was ready.
Her Mother, Nina Ivanovna, was a retired Doctor of Science in Biology,
and a member in good standing with the Communist Party who took this
information with a bit of concern. Her father had been the Vice-Director
of the Polytechnique School in Magadan. This was not news that they had

ever expected to hear from their loving daughter. It was especially worrisome since they had recently read in the Soviet press that many Russian women had married American men who had taken them to the US and then abandoned them. Of course, we tried to assure them this would not happen, but it was later when we went to visit them, and they could meet their future son-in-law that they felt more at ease.

It was not just moving to Alaska for Lena that was on her mind. It was a very difficult decision to leave family, and close friends, to take Sonechka to another country and culture, to leave a job that she enjoyed, and where she felt success in her genetics research, leaving the city of Magadan where she had grown up, and that was a big part of her life, the flat of her parents where she grew up, and always considered home, her parents who lived only airplane hours away, her motherland, culture, and identity. This was not easy for her, but she is an amazing and very strong Russian woman and was more than up to the challenge.

She knew English from her research and scientific work but had little opportunity to use it in everyday speech. However, I felt that she did very well under the circumstances. This was to be challenging in the new land of Alaska. After our arrival, there were many not-so-evident adjustments that she had to deal with, and she dealt with them all in a very determined to succeed manner, and she did succeed. This woman always did her best in everything she attempted, and this was , even more, to be seen when she entered a graduate degree proram for her Doctorate at Cambridge University in England.

After the initial answer of yes, the real work began for her to go to Alaska. First, she had to apply for and obtain an external Soviet passport. So, it was off to the local government office to fill out the application. Nothing was guaranteed, but her external passport finally arrived after about a month. Then we had to obtain a visa from the United States Embassy for both her and Sonechka. This meant we had to go to Moscow and visit the US Embassy in person. This was an adventure.

We purchased tickets on Aeroflot from Magadan to Moscow and return. Our friends Kostya and Natasha, who had moved from Magadan to Moscow were able to provide us with a place to stay, an interesting old Stalinist-era flat in the center of Moscow. So, it was not difficult to take the Moscow Metro when we needed to go someplace such as the U.S Embassy.

We then had to focus on the main goal of obtaining a US Visa for

Lena and Sonechka to travel to the United States. We went to the US Embassy, bypassing the long line of Russian people waiting outside to be admitted since as an American citizen all I had to do was to show my passport to the security guard, and we could go right in. After we entered, we were told that she would have to go for an interview with one of the staff. She took her invitation, Soviet passport, application documents, and required fees to the clerk at the window in the embassy when she was called.

Sonechka and I were waiting on the street outside the embassy, and after a while when I saw her coming out from her interview, I knew that things had not gone well. She was quite upset and said that the clerk told her that she could go but that she would have to leave Sonechka behind in Russia.

So, what to do? I decided to bite the bullet, so we went back inside the Embassy, and I requested to speak directly with one of the embassy staff. Understandably, I was quite upset as this would mean that all our plans would have to change. One of the Embassy staff came, and I explained to him in great detail that Lena had been working with me in the exchange program between MPI and the University of Alaska, and my reasons for requesting a visa for her, being that she needed to go to the University of Alaska, and become more familiar with our exchange program, but now from the Alaskan side. Then I showed him a copy of a recent article in the Anchorage Daily News, April 24, 1991, that described the University of Alaska and Magadan Pedagogical Institute exchange program and mentioned my name as the coordinator. He then seemed to understand my reasons and told us that the US Embassy was not in the business of holding children as hostages when a parent would leave to go to visit the United States. He was a bit apologetic and said that he would reconsider this decision and that we needed to return to the embassy the next morning. My blood pressure must have risen more than a little, but I hoped, prayed, and presumed that he would not have told us to return the next morning if he had not already decided to change the decision and issue Lena a visa for both she and Sonechka. My mind was going a mile a minute trying to figure out what to do, who could I call in Alaska for help? A good night's sleep was not in the cards for that night. But after morning coffee it was back on the Moscow Metro, and to the US Embassy.

With my US passport in hand, we went back inside to see what the counselor had decided. He met us and told Lena to go to the window for

FAMILY PICTURE, LARRY, SONYA AND LENA, SOL-
DOTNA, ALASKA. 1994
KHLINOVSKI ROCKHILL COLLECTION

MY DEAREST LENA, SOLDOTNA, ALASKA 1995.
KHLINOVSKI ROCKHILL COLLECTION

her next interview, and so this time I waited inside for her to return. Slava Bogu! (Thank God!), we were two very happy people to see the official US Visa entered into her Soviet passport along with Sonechka's approval. We thanked the counselor very sincerely and left the embassy to enjoy a much more relaxed lunch than we did the day before.

We had been advised by Sasha and Gretchen Sagan, the first Magadan-Alaskan couple to be married, that since we were planning to be married it would be much better to do so in the United States than in the Soviet Union. With the visa in hand, it meant that now our future plans could be realized, and the continuation of an interesting, loving, and challenging 30 years of being together. First, we called and told her parents about our plans. Then we made arrangements to come to Cherkessk and visit them since we did not know when the next time we would be back in the Soviet Union. It was great for me to meet them, and we had many interesting conversations regarding what life would be like when we went to Alaska. I tried to make them feel at ease and to know that I loved their daughter and Sonechka more than anything and would never abandon them. We talked a lot about life in Soldotna, our house, my teaching job, getting around, Alaska in general, prospects for Lena as far as work, and hoping that they would come and visit us there. I liked them both very much, and as the years went by Lena's Mamochka became my Mamochka too. She lived with us for several years and added so much to our family. Nina Ivanovna was a great Russian lady who shared many interesting family stories with us of growing up in Astrakhan at the mouth of the Volga River. We truly miss her dearly. Sadly, Lena's father could not join us in our travels as he had a heart condition that prevented him from flying long distances.

They had retired in Cherkessk after living for 30 years in cold Magadan. It is an interesting city in the Northern Caucasus. The climate was much warmer than Magadan, and life was much easier for retired folks,

LARRY ROCKHILL IN FRONT OF THE TRINITY-SERGIUS LAVRA. SERGIEV POSAD, 2011. PHOTO BY ANDREY OSIPOV

but the political situation with the local people deteriorated after the end of the Soviet Union. Unfortunately, Lena's father passed away, and we felt it was not safe for Mamochka to live there any longer, so we looked for an alternative in Russia. After she came back to Moscow, we looked at local communities and found that Sergiev Posad, formerly known as Zagorsk, seemed to offer the best and most convenient location for someone like her. She purchased a flat, and for around twenty years she was able to enjoy a decent life in her two-room flat. It was comfortable, convenient, and safe. It was so nice when we came to visit her, and often when we arrived, she had fresh borsch and a fish pie waiting for our hungry family.

We moved from Magadan to Soldotna via Aeroflot and Khabarovsk in the fall of 1991. Sasha Sagan and his wife Gretchen met us at the Anchorage International Airport, and we went to the Europa Bakery for breakfast where Sonechka ordered her first real American meal, a giant omelet that was impossible for her to finish. So, I had to offer to help her out. Then it was a drive down the Sterling Highway to Soldotna and our house on Arlington Court. Although our house was somewhat ordinary it was quite a contrast to Lena's flat in Magadan. I had rented it out, and all our furniture was stored in one of the bedrooms. Out came the furniture, and we 'officially 'moved in. It took a little time to get settled in, and we

TWO MOOSE FEEDING IN OUR SOLDOTNA BACK YARD IN 1995. KHLINOVSKI ROCKHILL COLLECTION

needed to buy some additional furniture. Sonechka got settled into her own room, for the first time in her life. The decor of her room was to change drastically with the addition of new bunk beds, and a large family of cute stuffed toys that she accumulated.

I had been given a new position teaching sixth grade at Redoubt Elementary School which was less than a mile away from our house. We had decided that we would work to continue the Magadan Exchange program with our friends at Magadan School No.14. I would resume teaching my old Soviet Studies program and Beginning Russian Language in my sixth-grade class. It was not difficult for me to get back into the sixth-grade routine, and I especially enjoyed the time each school year when I began again my Soviet Studies Program. This was a year of getting it together and planning to take my class to Magadan the next school year and host a group from School No.14.

Our first year in Alaska meant a lot of adjustments for our family in that it was a whole new culture and setting for Lena and Sonechka. Lena took in everything that she encountered from new friends and acquaintances to having headaches for the first six months while trying to listen to and understand what everybody said in their version of English. She spent many a time in the local Pay and Save and Lamonts stores just go-

244

ing around and looking at all the available merchandise, in big contrast to the same departments in Magadan stores. The idea that stores were having the end-of-month sales was new to her, and not one she overlooked. She was always a very thrifty and generous person, and never materialistic in any way. When first going to explore the local stores, she was very hesitant to ask a sales clerk for help for fear of being yelled at, which was often the case in Magadan shops. But soon she felt more comfortable interacting with the sales clerks and became more familiar with the marketing system in this capitalist country.

She is a very quick learner and was always willing to help explain things to people who came from Magadan to visit us. But Lena remained a true Russian in her heart and soul and never bought into the lust for money and consumer goods culture of the United States. For Lena, home was, and always will be Russia, with all its good aspects, and its difficulties.

Lena and I had some concerns when we first moved into our house in Soldotna. We were not sure how our dear Sonechka would make the adjustment with her lack of English language. After moving into our Soldotna home, we found out that there were four girls around her age on the street. She was a little shy at first but soon she went out to see who they were. Sonechka became the darling new Russian girl on the street, and they all wanted her to play with them. She was instantly popular with the girls, and they made her feel like a part of the group. To our amazement, it was not very long before she was beginning to pick up the English language from the other children, and was able to talk to them and understand what they were saying. It was a good neighborhood, near the schools where there were many nice kids to play with.

In September Sonechka entered the third grade at Redoubt Elementary School where I was teaching, and in six months she was able to function quite well on her own in her class. Mom did give some assistance for the first few months. She was a very bright girl and did fine in all her subjects. She took up the flute in the school band and was soon able to play quite well. It was such a pleasure to hear her practice. I was a lucky Dad to be able to have my dear daughter in my class when she reached sixth grade. She was right at the top of the class academically, and the only thing that I still have to remind her of is that she still owes me her autobiography from that year. I still have hopes, for she became a very good writer, which carried on all through her University of Oregon college days and beyond. She continues to do just fine in both English and Russian.

In the second year, we were fortunate to add one more daughter to our family when Sonechka's cousin Ksenia (Ksyusha) from Magadan joined us. Ksenia is six months younger than Sonechka. She had been having some health problems, and we offered her mother, Lena's cousin, that she should have a thorough medical examination in the West. She was told that she could not play sports or engage in any strenuous games on the playground. Lena and I were willing to help and were able to take her to see a pediatrician in Anchorage for a complete examination. The results were positive, and the doctor said the condition was minor, and should not inhibit her from playing sports at all. We were all glad to hear that she was in good health all around.

We discussed this with her mom and decided that it would be nice if she could stay the year and go to school with Sonechka at Redoubt Elementary where I was teaching. She had almost no English, as Sonechka did when she first arrived. But Lena was happy to help her to adjust, and she was just like Sonechka, in six months she was able to speak and read English to the point she needed little extra help with her schoolwork. She too was bright, and soon rose to the top of her class. She had no trouble making friends, and within a year after their arrival, she and Sonechka were both quite fluent in English. Ksenia lived with us for five years. I was fortunate for the second time to have my other Russian daughter in my class when she reached sixth grade. Then in 1998, we moved to Cambridge, and Ksyusha had to return to Magadan.

Our street had several families with children around the same age as our girls. I am sure we were thought of by Sonechka and Ksyusha as being quite strict at times. Fortunately for our girls, other parents were not so strict, and they could engage in activities that we did not have at home like Nintendo and other computer games. We also refused to buy a trampoline because we felt it could pose too many problems. Fortunately for the girls, two doors down from us a family with a girl of the same age had a nice big trampoline that they were most happy to share with Sonechka and Ksenia. We usually knew where they were with the sounds of the kids having a good time jumping up and down. Arlington Court was safe, a dead-end street, and so there was little traffic. Both girls had their own bicycles, and it was not dangerous for them to ride in the street.

The girls had their room and shared it with their large family of

FAMILY PHOTO, LENA, SONYA, KASUSHA, AND LARRY, IN OUR SOLDOTNA, ALASKA HOME, 1994.
KHLINOVSKI ROCKHILL FAMILY ARCHIVES

friendly and lovable stuffed animals. And each time a new member of their 'family' arrived it had to have its own special name.

Mikhailka, the little brown bear was one of Sonechka's favorites along with Moomik. At night it seemed that there was hardly enough room in their beds with all their family members having to be right there with 'mom'. They had vivid imaginations, and big old cardboard boxes were made into indoor houses for all their animal family members, and also for their Barbie dolls, including the father of the family, Ken. Our dog Barchuk, a Russian wolfhound (Borzoi), seemed to think he was just one of the kids and wanted to be part of everything the girls were doing. He especially liked to open his own Christmas gifts of doggie treats when they were wrapped in pretty paper. Often, when we were having dinner Barchuk would sneak up beside you, and you would find your napkin being chewed up into small pieces in the living room. In summer the sunset was very late, and we could play croquette out on the lawn even as late as midnight. Then, for the girls, it was a bicycle ride down to Dairy Queen for a nice cold Slurpee. Sleep was for late mornings, and not for late evenings.

SONYA HOLDING BARCHUK, OUR LITTLE RUSSIAN
WOLFHOUND, AFTER WE JUST ARRIVED IN ANCHORAGE,
ALASKA FROM MOSCOW, 1992. KHLINOVSKI ROCKHILL
FAMILY COLLECTION

Our street often had large moose strolling along the yards looking for some nice-tasting flowers. One time the girls coaxed a cow moose right up to the front porch and were hand-feeding it some carrots. But Moose are very dangerous, and we always gave them the open space they needed, and that we needed, to be safe. We knew whenever a moose was near our backyard, for Barchuk could sense them a long way off and would go to the door, and want to go outside and start barking at them to try and scare them away. But they were much bigger and just ignored him most of the time. It was great in the spring to see a mother cow moose with her newborn calf walking around the houses. Not many places can you experience such beautiful nature up close like this. Barchuk was part of our family from the second year we lived in Soldotna. In 1992 we flew Aeroflot from Anchorage to Magadan, and then from Magadan to Moscow and London. We had special British Rail passes to visit interesting cities, their wonderful museums, and bed and breakfast homes. After leaving England we returned to Moscow. Our return flight was a direct Aeroflot flight from Moscow to Anchorage, Alaska. This schedule only lasted a matter of a couple of years since the market was just not there.

When we were in Moscow, we visited a family that raised Russian Wolfhounds, and we fell in love and bought the cutest little Russian Borzoi from this family. We went to some trouble to get all his vaccinations, and papers needed to go through the Russian authorities, and get permission to take him with us. At the airport, when going through Russian customs the officer expressed some concern regarding whether a Borzoi was a state treasure, and had to have special permission to leave the country. This caused us some anxiety, especially for our little daughter Sonechka. But it all worked out with the help of some tears from our little Sonechka who had already adopted little Barchuk into our family. We were able to take little Barchuk back with us in a box under the seat of an

Il-62 long-range Aeroflot passenger jet. Our concern was he might whine all the way, so we gave him a tiny piece of a Dramamine pill, and he slept quietly all during the flight. Now we joke that we just drugged the poor little fellow so he would be a good puppy.

Since I was teaching at Redoubt School, we were able to go to the school gym on cold, snowy winter days, shoot baskets, and play tetherball. Then we would go into the faculty room where the big popcorn machine was sitting and make a pot full of fresh, hot popcorn. These were the little perks that we teachers could enjoy at times. Even though Redoubt Elementary was only a half mile away from our house, in the winter the girls always preferred to ride in a nice warm 'chauffer Dad' driven car just out of the garage to school.

When we moved from Magadan to Alaska in 1991, we continued our quest for mushrooms. On one of our first drives along the Sterling Highway outside Soldotna Lena spotted mushrooms growing not far from the side of the road. We stopped and went over to see if they were the same species of mushrooms that we were picking in Magadan, Russia. Lena knew of at least four species of mushrooms that were safe to eat. In Alaska, we had little competition, and Lena, Sonechka, Ksyusha, Mamochka, and I would go out into the forest on the Kenai Peninsula and be able to gather several pounds of mushrooms in just a couple of hours. After picking we would take them home, and she would marinate them in jars for future delicious dinners. It was the same here as in Russia, where many dedicated, knowledgeable people appreciated delicious mushrooms.

One had to be careful of the brown bears in the area, and so I made a lot of noise as we were picking mushrooms. Lena always thought that forests were for peaceful silence and didn't care for my singing and whistling that much. I could understand that. I can also remember one time when we were out walking very quietly in the peaceful forest around the Soldotna Bible Camp when all of a sudden, we found ourselves on a collision course, being only about 100 feet away from a medium-sized female brown bear and her cubs crossing our path. We stopped and just looked for a few seconds. Now, what should we do was the question? Then the mother bear started to charge us. I had read that the worst thing one can do is to run since the bear will instinctively think you are prey and try to catch you. She was also chasing us in defense of her cubs. So, what did we do but turn around and run. I decided I could not outrun this bear and

A MORNING OF PICKING MUSHROOMS IN THE FOREST NEAR SOLDOTNA. NINA IVANOVNA "MOMECHKA", LARRY AND LENA.

prepared myself mentally to fall on the ground and play dead and hope for the best. Then I remembered what I had read, and I just stopped, turned around to face the oncoming bear, raised my small blue briefcase waving it high above my head, and screamed to the top of my lungs waving my arms. I tried to make myself as big as possible as this was what I had read was the best way to avoid being mauled. Thank God it worked. My heart was just pounding inside my chest as the bear turned and ran into the bushes back towards her cubs. Lena was just ahead of me, and we very quickly walked in the direction of our car. All the doors of the camp buildings were closed as the opening was not for a few weeks.

That was an Alaskan experience we will never forget. When in the wilds of Alaska, I usually took my old 1911 45 cal. Colt automatic along just in case, but not then. I am sure I would have only used it to frighten a bear, for I certainly would not be able to kill it with such a small weapon.

For all of our family, the Kenai River provided some wonderful outdoor adventures and eating delights. Each summer and fall we spent many a day fishing for red and silver salmon on the banks of the river. Being a Russian family, Lena was very interested in catching female salmon for they contained the roe that she was very skilled at making into ikra or salmon caviar. Lena would ask the girls to go to people who had just caught a female salmon and ask them for the salmon eggs.

Of course, the girls were a bit embarrassed to do this, but now and then we had some extra salmon eggs, not from our fishing. We were able to fill our freezer each year with fresh salmon, and also to can some fifty-pint jars with salmon that we would use for salmon spread and salmon chowder. Sometimes when we fished on the river there were not enough salmon to go around, and it was the girls who caught the fish and the parents got skunked. And too often the Pixie lure found a snag when we cast out. A bit annoying it was.

Our friend Bob Williams had a beautiful log house with a Russian banya on Island Lake in Nikiski and used it as a bed and breakfast. Once he had a group of oil people from Texas who came to stay for a week, and he asked Sonechka and Ksyusha to please help him with taking care of his clients. Both girls were very excited to be hired to help Bob with his food service, and cleaning responsibilities, and get paid for having fun too. One day the oilmen had chartered two planes to take them across Cook Inlet to fish for salmon and ask the girls if they would like to go along. Of course, the girls were more than happy to have a real Alaska wilderness experience. So early one morning on Bob's Island Lake they hopped into the old De Havilland Beaver, taxied across the lake, took off, and flew out over Cook Inlet to a remote fishing sight. Not only did they see schools of salmon swimming up the river to spawn, but to their surprise, there were several Alaska Brown bears, some with little cubs, in the vicinity. It was an experience they have never forgotten, and maybe they could list this on their resumes as their first real job.

During the first four years, we had season tickets to the Anchorage Civic Light Opera Program and looked forward to seeing our favorite Nutcracker ballet by Tchaikovski at the Music Center. We would get in our nice Volvo station wagon for the three-hour drive up the Sterling Highway through the beautiful snow-covered mountains via Turnagain Pass, and then down along Turnagain Arm and Cook Inlet to Anchorage. We always looked forward to staying and visiting with our dear friend Gretchen Bersch in her lovely home. Soon after arriving, it was time for the girls and Lena to change into their pretty theatre dresses, and we were off to the ballet. It was so enjoyable to be sitting in this beautiful auditorium and to listen to a live orchestra play for the ballet. One year they did a replica of the original Nutcracker ballet first performed in St. Petersburg at the famous Mariinsky Theatre on December 17, 1892. The dancer's costumes were just so beautiful and very Russian of the period. Every performance we attended, and there were four a year, was wonderful. However, one year we had left Soldotna to go to Anchorage for another ballet performance at the Music Center when going over and down Turnagain Pass we noticed that there seemed to be a long line of cars stopped up ahead. Well, to our surprise mother nature had other plans for us that day. There was a large avalanche that had come down the side of the mountain and was covering the Seward Highway and preventing any cars from going any farther. So, we turned around and went back to Soldotna. Not many can say that they were prevented from going to a ballet by an avalanche. Alaska memories.

After coming to Soldotna Lena and I decided to continue the Magadan-Soldotna Student Exchange Program with School No.14. I was glad to have a new sixth-grade teaching position at Redoubt Elementary School not very far from our house. I talked to my Principal Larry Nauta, and he was agreeable to doing this. School No.14 had been participating in the exchange program along with School No.1, from the start and we were good friends with Valentina Sud'ina, the Director, and Ludmila Popova, one of the English Language Teachers. Both were interested in continuing the program and led the way at their school. We looked forward each year to their visit and the latest news from our Russian hometown of Magadan. We discussed having the next exchange in the spring of 1992 when they would come to Redoubt Elementary for two weeks, and I would take my students to Magadan one month later. Some other Soldotna schools were also continuing the exchange program with Magadan School No.1, and School No.17. All the Magadan students were from their English Language classes. The annual exchange programs were my favorite time of the year since this was when I began again to teach my Soviet Studies and Russian Language classes. I would bring out all of our collection of Soviet artifacts, and make my room appear like a Russian museum with the samovar on the shelf next to the windows, and the Soviet flag and propaganda posters hung all along the walls. The atmosphere was definitely Soviet/Russian, and I think helped to generate a strong interest on the part of my students. The samovar was hot each day during Russian Language lessons, and Russki chai was enjoyed by all. We jokingly called this a collective study environment.

I sent an invitation with the names of the Russian teachers, usually two, and the students who had been selected to come for the exchange on Redoubt school letterhead to School N.14 and received an invitation from them with the Redoubt students and teacher's names. To get their US visas they had to submit their invitations to the US Consulate in Vladivostok, and for our Russian visas, I had to submit our invitations to the Russian/Soviet Consulate in San Francisco. This all took some time, and we had to start several months in advance. As the time approached for the arrival of our Russian guests my fellow teachers and I had a lot of work to do in preparing a list of home parents that the students would stay with, as well as the activities that they would participate in while here. All participating students were carefully selected and had to be good representatives of their school, culture, and country. Lena and I usually hosted one or both teachers.

Each day the Magadan students would come to my classroom and take part in some of the daily lessons, and then go out with their host parents to the larger community to visit other schools and experience visits to the local MacDonalds, Sal's Sourdough Cafe, local stores like Lamonts and Trustworthy Hardware, Safeway, and the Soldotna Visitor's Center. We made sure that they would be able to experience their Russian 'Staraya Rossia 'culture with a visit to the Holy Assumption Russian Orthodox Church in Old Town Kenai. This was the site of the first Russian settlements on the Kenai Peninsula in the eighteenth century. Father Targonski was always very gracious and happy to see some of his fellow countrymen. There was usually a field trip to Homer to visit and explore the local tide pools on a low tide day, and to also dig for gooeyduck razor clams at Clam Gulch for a clam feast the next night at somebody's house. The Pratt Museum in Homer was also on the list to see their fascinating displays of marine life, commercial fishing, and local history. All this was new to them, and they went with eyes wide open. Usually, on another day there would be a trip down the Sterling Highway towards Homer to visit the Old Believer village of Nikolaevsk. A colony of Old Believers had settled there in 1960, and now it was a small village of a few hundred souls, along with a church and school. Old Believer children were first-language Russian speakers but in Old Church Slavonic. This was always interesting for our guests since they never had the opportunity to meet Old Believers.

Some of the students said that they could not believe what they

IT HAPPENS THAT REAL FRIENDS IN AMERICA DROP BY WITHOUT A WARNING TO VISIT. BOB WILLIAMS AND LARRY ROCKHILL. KEIZER 2019 KHLINOVSKIROCKHILL COLLECTION

saw when they went shopping in the local stores. It was always fun to go out with our guests and to see their reactions when visiting stores. Wherever they went they received a warm welcome. All the sales clerks were very friendly and went out of their way to show them anything they might want to see. MacDonalds and Sal's gave them free lunches as their special guests. The host parents made sure that the students had some spending money to be able to purchase things needed, and that were of interest. All host parents were very generous and understood that these students were coming from a different world where less was available, and affordable under the present economic situation there.

My students were happy to host their new Russian friends and had such a fun time sharing daily adventures. With only a little Russian language they were limited in what they could say to them. But the Magadan students usually had at least a few years of studying English, and so were able to speak English quite well. For them to be able to listen to and practice speaking English was one of the main goals of the program. For our two daughters, Sonechka and Kseniya, this was an opportunity to be able to speak their native Russian with the Magadan kids their age and to share their lives in Alaska. We also felt that it was important for the Russian kids to experience life with an average American family since this could not have been taught in a book. The reverse of this was also true when I took my students to Magadan, and they were able to stay in the homes of their Russian host families. Understanding life in each other's countries, homes, and cultures was considered to be an important part of ending the Cold War, Peace, and Friendship. We continued this program with School No.14 until the time I retired, and we moved to Cambridge, England for Lena to start work on her graduate degrees.

Soldotna was a good place for our kids to grow up but for us, not a forever place. I retired in 1998, and it was Lena's turn to decide our next adventure. She had been corresponding with people we met at Scott Polar Research Institute at Cambridge University and applied there for a Master's Degree Program. She was accepted. So, we decided to head across the pond for a year, or more. We packed up all worldly possessions and hauled them to our friend Bob Williams big garage at Island Lake Lodge in Nikiski. There seemed to be a neverending supply of boxes, and we continued to look for the last one, finally, it was filled with more of our household goods, and we made our last trip to Bob's Island Lake garage. Our household goods and furniture were to be stored for a year which turned into something like fourteen years later when we finally moved to our house in Keizer, Oregon.

It is now going on 30 years since our first visit to the U. S. Em.bassy in Moscow, and relocation to Cambridge, UK, an MPhil, a Ph.D., and her book, "Lost to the State: Family Discontinuity, Social Orphanhood and Residential Care in the Russian Far East", published by Berghahn in 2010, and the adventures continue.

CHAPTER TWENTY-FOUR:
ACROSS THE POND. GORBACHEV

Soldotna was a good place for our kids to grow up but for us, not a forever place. I retired in 1998 and then it was Lena's turn to decide our next adventure. She had been corresponding with people we met at Scott Polar Research Institute at Cambridge University during a previous visit to England, and applied there for a Master's Degree Program. She was accepted, and so we decided to head across the pond for a year, or more. We packed up all worldly possessions and hauled them to our friend Bob Williams 'big garage at Island Lake Lodge in Nikiski. There seemed to be a never-ending supply of boxes and we continued to look for the last one, and finally, it was filled with more of our household goods and we made our last trip to Bob's Island Lake garage. Our household goods and furniture were to be stored for a year which turned into something like fourteen years later when we finally moved into our house in Keizer, Oregon. It is now going on 30 years since our first visit to the U. S. Embassy in Moscow, and relocation to Cambridge, England, an MPhil, a Ph.D., and her book, "Lost to the State: Family Discontinuity, Social Orphanhood and Residential Care in the Russian Far East", published by Berghahn in 2010, and the adventures continue.

The day of departure from Soldotna finally came, but not before we all, Lena, Sonechka, Ksusha, and I, went to Hawaii for a couple of weeks to rest and, relax after all the stress and hard work of putting our things in storage and packing for what we thought might be only a one year program at Cambridge University. Hawaii was very relaxing and we all en

15 MARCH 1999 MIKHAIL SERGEIVICH GORBACHEV SIGNS COPIES OF HIS "MEMOIRS" AT WATERSTONES BOOK STORE, CAMBRIDGE, ENGLAND. KHLINOVSKI ROCKHILL COLLECTION

`joyed the daily swimming at the Hilton Hawaiian Village beach and the sights of Waikiki, including the Cheese Cake Factory, snorkeling at Hanauma Bay, a drive around the island with a stop at the Dole Pineapple Plantation, dinner under the majestic banyan tree at the historic Moana Hotel along with some little gifts, as well as fresh pineapple and mangoes each morning for breakfast. The girls had their special evening at the Hard Rock Cafe where somehow they couldn't find one of their two ten dollar bills. No matter, they still had a great time. Then there was the time they wanted to go on a catamaran ride. Both girls walked over and talked to the handsome young man who was on the beach in front of the catamaran selling tickets and found out that they were in luck and were told that today there was a special for twin sisters, two for the price of one. So, they hop aboard and set sail for the deep water of Waikiki. We did not want to leave Hawaii, but Lena had to be in Cambridge soon. So back to Soldotna and on to the Lower Forty-eight and off across the pond.

When we moved to Cambridge, England we departed from Vancouver, BC aboard a giant Air Canada Boeing 747 and were seated in the smaller, upper deck area. We were surprised to be seated in this special area usually reserved for First Class passengers. Being interested in aviation in general, I asked one of the stewardesses if it would be possible for the three of us to visit the pilots in the cockpit to see just what this area looked like. They were happy to oblige and so we were taken up front and were allowed to come into the back area of the cockpit. The door to the cockpit was not locked at those times. The Pilot and co-pilot were in their respective seats just below us. Both of them said welcome and asked if we had any questions. We did, and they happily replied to them. This certainly would not be possible today.

After this rather long flight, we landed at London Heathrow and had to get our luggage and moving boxes. There was a lot and necessitated getting one of the famous large black taxis that are well known to everybody in London. We were just barely able to get our boxes and luggage in the taxi, and I remember I could not move my feet being stuck in the back seat behind one of the large boxes. After what seemed a rather long ride to Cambridge, we finally pulled up into the little parking area in front of this famous old building of the Scott Polar Research Institute. We went inside and introduced ourselves to the welcoming staff who were expecting us. We had to leave our boxes and luggage at SPRI since that night we would sleep in the small Darwin College guest rooms, where Lena was a member. We had to spend that night being very uncomfortable when Lena and I had to sleep head to toe in a very narrow single bed, where Sonechka had all the space she needed, but it was on the hard floor. We managed and were glad the next day to move into our three-bedroom flat above the garages at Fen Causeway. This was University Housing, quite comfortable and not far from the River Cam.

Not far from our flat we often enjoyed watching people going up and down the River Cam punting in the flat-bottomed boats, as well as each spring watching the swans, who laid their eggs in rather large nests that they attached to the river bank. When the eggs hatched and the little signets appeared from under the spacious wings of the mother, it was so beautiful. They were just the cutest little balls of fluff with wings. Walking around Cambridge was always interesting with the old college buildings scattered around the city. Some like Jesus College were over 500 years old.

Darwin College was one of the newer colleges established in the 20th century. All of them had very lovely grounds with flower gardens which we often walked through on our way to the Institute from home. Cam-

bridge is a small town and we walked wherever we were going, whether to SPRI, the store for groceries or to visit friends. We did not have a car for the ten years we lived in Cambridge or the next three years. This was good for health reasons and also financial reasons.

Living in Cambridge was not all new since we had previously visited England and Scotland a few times over the years when we lived in Soldotna. We immediately felt at home at Scott Polar Research Institute, and

259

we became part of a small group of like-minded scientists with interests in the Polar Regions. Lena was fortunate in being able to be one of the last M.Phil. students to have some of the early Antarctic and Arctic scholars and explorers as her professors. I had the privilege of sitting in on many of her lectures with old-time explorers like John Heap, Bob Headland, Gordon Robins, Peter Wadems, William Mills, Harry King, and others. Soon they would all be retired. The next few days were times of getting to know the staff and just what was expected of her in the MPhil program. It was all interesting, demanding, and challenging for Lena, but she was certainly up to doing the work and doing it at a high level. Every Friday at 5 PM she had to hand in her 2000-word essay for that week, and she was never late. Sonechka and I were her little helpers at the Xerox machine making copies.

The 15th and 16th of March 1999 were special days for us. I had heard that Mikhail Sergeivich Gorbachev was visiting Cambridge University where his Gorbachev Foundation was located at King's College. He was scheduled to deliver an address at the West Ridge Concert Hall on the 15th and admission was by ticket only. I knew that there was limited seating in this small hall and so I immediately applied for three tickets for Lena, Sonechka, and me. We were fortunate and were able to attend his address. After the program we were, along with many others, able to briefly meet him, shake hands, and say a few words. Of course, being able to meet such an important political world figure of the 20th century was very meaningful, to say the least. Then the next morning he was going to be at Waterstones Book Store in Cambridge signing copies of his biography. I went and bought three copies for us to take to him the next day. I was also able to get several copies of Pravda from the late 1990s with his picture on the front page. So, we each took a copy of his biography and two copies of Pravda for him to sign/autograph. We went early the next morning and were close to the front of the line when the store opened. When we went in we could see him sitting at a table waiting for people to come and bring him the books they wanted him to autograph. I first introduced myself, shook hands, and handed him the biography and two copies of Pravda. I said, in my limited Russian, spasibo for his life's work of fostering peace in the world and his policies that contributed to the ending of the Cold War. Sonechka was right behind me with a biography and two Pravdas. I then said that this is our daughter Sofia. She introduced herself and said a few words to him, then handed him the same items to autograph. He replied to her that she certainly could speak better Russian than her father. What could I say, it was true. Then Lena followed with her biography and two copies of Pravda. So we did have a few autographed copies of Pravda to share with some of our friends who shared our interest in the old USSR, like Hilton LaZarr, a student of Soviet History whose family had strong ties in the city of Odessa. We also donated one autographed biography and one Pravda to the Scott Polar Research Institute Archives.

The next night we had tickets and went to hear a speech given by Professor Stephen Hawkings. He was unable to speak in a normal manner and did so via his computer. He was such an amazing scientist. We never had in the ten years that we lived in Cambridge such an interesting weekend of attending lectures given by such significant world leaders.

CHAPTER TWENTY-FIVE:
MAGADAN FRIENDS

GENNADY DOROFEEV

After moving to Magadan, I became good friends with Gennady Dorofeev, the Mayor of Magadan. Gennady was a man dedicated to the wellbeing of the people of Magadan. He was very supportive of both of our exchange programs, and it was through him, that MPI was able to provide me with a one-room ordinary Soviet flat. During the Soviet times, all flats were state-owned, so he made an agreement with Dr. Kokorev to provide me with a flat, and Magadan Pedagogical Institute would provide all the furniture, appliances, dishes, and cookware. Soon after we first met, he expressed concern that an American, who usually had little trouble when shopping in Alaska, might find it too difficult under the present Soviet conditions. I said that I came to Magadan to teach English at MPI, and to learn just what it was like to live under the same conditions as ordinary Soviet people. Gennady asked me if I was a veteran, and I said yes that I had been in the US Air Force as an instructor in survival techniques for pilots and aircrews of downed aircraft. He said that since I was a veteran, I would be eligible to use the special magazine available to Soviet veterans. In the Soviet Union veterans were held in high respect and received some special privileges. Here veterans were able to buy foods that were not always available to the average person, such as cheeses, tea, coffee, candy, sausage, meat, and fish.

He gave me a letter he signed that I could take to the Veteran's special magazine and be allowed to shop there. I said bolshoye spasibo and told him that I did not want to have this special privilege. Standing in lines was to some extent getting to be an old Soviet tradition, so I wanted this to be a part of my life for the next two years.

Sometime later I went to see him with his good friend Galina Schlagman, a fellow teacher at School No. 17, which was known as the best English school in Magadan. This was the time that Gennady gave me a Vostok Komandirski wristwatch. These were in a very big deficit, and I was quite surprised to receive such a gift. I had tried to purchase one in Moscow in 1988 and found none were available in a regular watch store. I still have this watch with its black face and use it on special occasions. He was a great Mayor, and for the next ten years, all student exchange groups would come to meet him upon their arrival in Magadan. Unfortunately, Gennady passed away a few years back. We all miss him dearly.

ROMAN TCHAIKOVSKY

From the beginning when I first met Roman in June of 1989, I realized this was a special person, and I would be privileged to work with him. He expressed a strong interest when I first mentioned the possibility of an exchange program with the University of Alaska to both him and President Evgeny Kokorev. Over the years we three worked very closely together in developing our student and teacher exchange program. Roman and I traveled together in 1990 with President Evgeny Kokorev on the first visit to Alaska to meet with the President of the University of Alaska. Roman was friendly, easy to get along with, and had a good sense of humor. He made many long-lasting friends with people from Alaska. He, and his wife Luda were always willing to host dinners for visiting guests from Alaska and Germany. They probably hosted dinners for every Alaskan who came to Magadan Pedagogical Institute during the first couple of years and beyond.

Roman Tchaikovsky was the Dean of the Foreign Language Department and a professor of German Language at Magadan Pedagogical Institute. He was my supervisor and close friend during the two years I taught there and for the next twenty-five years. I spent many an evening visiting with him and his wife Luda. Luda would usually prepare a nice dinner for her guests from Alaska which would include delicious borsch, pelmeni, and my favorite apple pie. Roman would be sure and open a bottle of fine Ukrainian or Russian vodka, and we would share many toasts during dinner to peace and friendship, to Alaska and the Soviet Union, success in our work in bringing University of Alaska students together with our students, and of course always a toast to our wonderful women. This last toast was always a bottoms-up one since I was known to sip my vodka during dinner. I always said I liked fine Russian vodka and just wanted to enjoy it a little at a time. 'Moi tost't (my toast), when this was said it was usually a time when something serious would be expressed by the individual making the toast. This was when a person could express his/her true feelings about family, close friends, an important event in life, and the future. A toast was not taken lightly by those for whom it was intended. It was a way of expressing your appreciation for those around you, for what they had shared with you, for the good things that were part of your life, and for the hopes that you all shared for the future. A toast brought us all closer together, and I am thankful for all of them that we shared between us over the years, Roman, Evgeny, and me.

Whenever my vodka glass was empty it was the obligation of the host to immediately take the bottle and refill it. And Roman did this in the true Russian tradition.

After dinner, Roman would sit in his big, comfortable armchair, and we would discuss life in Alaska and the Soviet Union, the future of our exchange program, the upcoming visit from the University of Alaska and professors, and at times he would tell me stories about earlier times in the Soviet Union. I remember once when I gave him a copy of Solzhenitsyn's GULag Archipelago in English, he said that not so long ago he could have been put in prison for just having this book. He admired President Kennedy and showed me a book about this President.

Roman grew up in Ukraine where his father was a Ukrainian Catholic priest. This was a time when there was severe oppression by the Soviet authorities on all religious people, especially priests, and nuns. When Roman was quite young his father was arrested, and imprisoned by the Soviet government authorities. He, along with his brothers and their mother, was sent from Ukraine in railroad cars for days on end to the Far East, and placed in a camp where he grew up and went to school for the repressed near Khabarovsk. His father was released after some years and returned to their home in Ukraine. After finishing school in their oppressed settlement, he entered Khabarovsk Pedagogical Institute and graduated. Then he applied, and was accepted as a teacher of German Language at Mag.dan Pedagogical Institute where he taught, and became a Professor, and the Dean of the Foreign Language Department until he retired.

Roman was fluent in Ukrainian, his native language, and also in Russian and English. He was a very serious scholar and a very serious book collector. When you came into their nice three-room flat one was not sure if it was a home or a library. He had hundreds of books filling all the floor-to-ceiling bookshelves in their flat at the bottom of Lenin Prospect. He was a lover of the poetry and music of the great Russian bard Bulat Okudzhava

ROMAN TCHAIKOVSKY, MAGADAN OX-OTNIK PRESS ARCHIVES

and had his every book and recording. At least twice Roman visited the widow of Bulat when he was in the process of writing his Okudzhava bi-

THE GREAT MAGADAN POET ALEXEI GARIPOV, ROMAN TCHAIKOVSKY, AND LARRY ROCKHILL. 2016

ography. He has written many works on the teaching of foreign languages, translating, books on Bulat Okudzhava, Erich Maria Remarque, and a biography of his mother, and his father, as well as many articles published in scientific journals.

Roman was very strict in that he had high expectations for both his teachers and his students. This was reflected in the high level of academic teaching by the teachers in his department and the high level achieved by the students. When Roman spoke, we followed his instructions, at least most of the time. He always supported his teachers and encouraged them in their pursuit of advanced degrees. He gave countless hours of help to his teachers who were in the process of writing their thesis for their candidatskaya, and doctoral studies. Roman was instrumental in encouraging his teachers to pursue their graduate studies.

Our friendship has endured over the many years and chut'-chut 'celebrations that we shared with our dear friend President Evgeny Kokorev.

EVGENY KOKOREV

In June of 1989, I had my first meeting with President Evgeny Kokorev at Magadan Pedagogical Institute, and I knew it was to be a close friendship from then on. He had a great sense of humor, and it was always pleasant to be around him. After our first meeting, Evgeny was interested in my proposal to have students and professors be able to study at each other's institutions, from the University of Alaska and Magadan Pedagogical Institute. Evgeny, who had his doctorate in Sociology, was a pioneer in leading the way for the development of the MPI and University of Alaska exchange programs which lasted around ten years. When we first met in his office in June of 1989, he invited me to come and teach at his institute. This was a new idea, and it was almost unheard of to have an American teaching, and living in a Soviet city like Magadan. He was the first educator from the Soviet Union to meet with the President of the University of Alaska and sign protocols of agreement that set the exchange visits in motion in 1990. As these relations progressed, he worked with administrators from the University of Alaska and was able to raise the status of Magadan Pedagogical Institute to that of Northern International University. He also reached out and was able to develop relations

DR. EVGENY KOKOREV PRESIDENT, NORTHERN INTERNATIONAL UNIVERSITY, MAGADAN OXOTNIK PRESS ARCHIVES

with Hokkaido University in Japan and to have a Japanese Language Program at his university in Magadan. Evgeny was a very progressive and experienced administrator who was a true leader in the melting of the Ice Curtain that separated Alaska from Magadan.

He and his wife Larisa were both outgoing and friendly people who hosted dinners for visiting professors and students from the University of Alaska. I have spent wonderful evenings over dinner at their home. Larisa was very kind and would always go out of her way to help me and any of our guests from the University of Alaska. She prepared delicious Russian dishes that I certainly enjoyed. She also taught English at the Institute and was a big help to me in being able to understand our students and appreciate the Soviet system of higher education.

As of the time of this writing, Evgeny, Roman, and Luda are no longer with us. It was a great shock, and with deep sorrow when we learned of their passing. We miss our dear friends with whom we worked so closely in developing good relations with the University of Alaska and beyond.

LAWRENCE KHLINOVSKI ROCKHILL LIVES IN TWO COUNTRIES, STRIVING TO BE AT EVERY RED SQUARE BOOK FESTIVAL IN MOSCOW. LARRY AND PAVEL ZHDANOV. RED SQUARE. JUNE 2015

PAVEL ZHDANOV

Pasha was there at the Magadan Airport from the first time we stepped off the Aeroflot TU-154 Flight 2315 from Alaska in February 1989. He was part of our Magadan and Soldotna exchange groups right from the beginning and was always with us wherever we went. He was one of our biggest supporters and always would do all he could over the years to make sure that Soldotna students and teachers had the best possible experience when in Magadan. He would often take his students on nature walks along the hillsides of Nagaeva Bay on weekends, and they loved it. He is an experienced outdoorsman with extensive knowledge of the natural history of the Kolyma region. Pasha is also well versed in the history of Magadan and the Kolyma during the Soviet days, and in particular, the system of the Stalinist forced labor camps, the GULag, strung out along the Kolyma Trassa.

Pasha Zhdanov knew that I was interested in having some Soviet military hats, so he gave me several Soviet Navy hats and belt buckles. I keep on my desk one of the Soviet Navy belt buckles that he gave me back then. These Soviet Navy buckles were rare items in the US at this time.

Later as time went on, I was able to share my US Air Force flying suit,

ON ONE OF OUR OUR JOURNEYS ALONG THE KOLYMA HIGHWAY WE STOPPED AT THE OLD SOVIET ENTRANCE SIGN TO THE VILLAGE OF ATKA. 2009 PHOTO BY ANDREY OSIPOV

and pilot's sunglasses from 1960 when I was an Air Crew Survival Specialist. Pasha is also an airplane history buff, so it has been a pleasure to share books and military items with him over the years.

I enjoyed many an evening visiting with Pasha and his family, and the delicious dinners prepared by his wife Marina. He always made me feel right at home and treated me as one of the family. Pasha always went out of his way to make sure that everything was going as it should, and if I needed anything he would do his best to take care of it. On one occasion I had no place to stay when I came to Magadan, and with a simple phone call, Pasha had taken care of the problem.

Pasha was a very important part of our exchange program and went to Soldotna twice with students and teachers from School No.1. He has many friends in Alaska from those days of the Exchange Program. Thirty years later we continue to often communicate since it is Pasha who will be responsible for the publication of this book. He is more than just a friend and has been ever since I stepped off the Aeroflot Tu-154 in February of 1989. Pasha is truly a part of our family, and we cannot imagine this would ever change.

LARRY ROCKHILL AND ANDREY OSIPOV IN MONUMENT VALLEY. NAVAJO NATION, USA, 2014 PHOTO COURTESY OF ANDREY OSIPOV

ANDREY OSIPOV

Even though Andrey was not there in the Magadan airport to greet us back in 1989, he has been a major part of our Magadan adventures for years, and that continues to this day. Andrey is a professional ethnographic photographer, writer, and art designer of books. He has many awards for his great artistic ability in designing books that were published by Oxotnik. But more than this Andrey has been a very close friend and colleague on both continents. Lena and I have had the pleasure of working with him on many projects, both in Magadan and in Alaska, Oregon, New Mexico, Arizona, and England. He is a close member of our extended family, and I treasure the many interesting adventures we have shared over the years and hope to continue for many more years to come. As Oxotnik Art Director it is Andrey who will be the person that will turn my book into a work of art and an heirloom for our family. A kinder and more giving person would be difficult to encounter wherever you go. He is a true friend, and this will be so for the duration.

APPENDIX

It was Andrey Osipov with whom I made that memorable trip to an Even reindeer herding brigade, which I mentioned earlier when describing my visit to Novoye Chaplino. Let me share some of my memories of this expedition with you.

EVEN REINDEER HERDERS

I arrived back in Magadan in July of 2016, the city that I first moved to from Alaska almost 25 years ago. I can say that many things have changed since those old Soviet days. No longer do we have to use food ration coupons to buy food in the local gastronomes. Now Magadan food stores are filled with products, and you can buy almost anything you like. Back then it was a challenge to just exchange dollars for rubles, and now in most retail stores, you can use your Visa credit card to make purchases. The modern era is upon us even 8000 miles east of Moscow.

Although not always so visible, there is a strong presence of the cultures of the Indigenous people of the Russian North who have resided in this region for thousands of years. This is demonstrated by the two annual spring celebrations of Hebdenek and the Day of the First Fish held near the Native community of Ola, some 60 kilometers up the coast from Magadan on the Sea of Okhotsk. I have attended both celebrations and enjoyed seeing the traditional Native dresses, and the dancing which is so colorful. Then being invited by Even group after group to share in their tasty ukha fish soup, and other dishes make this an unforgettable experience.

I am fortunate to be able to share my interest in the cultures of the indigenous people of Russia with my dear friend Andrey Osipov, an ethnographic photographer who is never without his camera around his neck. He has been interested in the Even reindeer herders of the Severo-Evensk District of the Magadan region for the past several years, and from his mini-expeditions, he has made an extensive collection of photographs of their daily lives. In 2016 he decided to return on another mini-expedition to the Even herder's base camp Irbychan, and then on to their main camp of Brigade 10 where a herd of 1500 reindeer grazes far out on the tundra. Andrey asked me if I would like to go along and there was no possible answer to his question but yes. I have had a lifelong interest in the anthropology of indigenous peoples of both Alaska and the Russian North.

For me, it was an opportunity to experience something that I could only dream about. The weather was good, and so we were able to spend part of the ten days with the Even reindeer herders in their remote camp out in the middle of the tundra, as well as with their families and friends living in the communities of Evensk, Garmanda, and at the herders 'base camp Irbychan.

On the morning of August 3rd. we walked to the Magadan Bus Station on Ulitsa Lenina in Magadan. Here we met Martene, Sophie, and Alla, the other three people going with us, and took the bus 52 km to the Magadan Airport and checked in for IrAero flight 131 to Severo-Evensk. Our adventure began aboard an old Soviet-era An-24 ex-Aeroflot turbojet passenger plane. The one- and-a-half-hour flight was very smooth over the beautiful Kolyma mountains and along the Sea of Okhotsk. But the beverage service was a bit limited with just a plastic cup of cold water. The roar of the turbo engines was so loud that it was difficult to talk to the person sitting next to you. But then it was looking out the window at the beauty of the Kolyma that one did not want to miss. When we landed, I hoped that the end of the runway was far down the way since these An-24s touch down at a rather high speed. The Antonov 24 is a tried and true old Soviet bush plane that has a tradition throughout the Kolyma Region of getting people safely to where they want to go. IrAero is the main airline providing service to the rural communities of the gold mining region. Most people go via the Kolyma Trassa in cars and trucks.

SOVIET TIMES

The Severo-Evensk region is an administrative municipal district in the eastern part of the Magadan Oblast. The community of Evensk is beautifully situated right on the coast of the Sea of Okhotsk. Times have changed this community drastically since the collapse of the Soviet Union. Prior to 1991, everybody here worked for the Soviet government, and the government subsidized everything from housing to health care to food, vacations, transportation, reindeer herding, and more. Most of the time food shops were well stocked with many local products from around the region, such as milk, kefir, and cheese from local dairy farms, and those products that came from distant regions, even as far as Moscow, and the Caucuses. Almost everybody had a job, and they could count on receiving a monthly salary from the state, and prices were affordable based on their incomes. Most everybody had a decent flat, even if a bit small, that had heat, hot water, and electricity, and was comfortable against the cold winters. And the rent was a small percentage of their monthly income. There was a polyclinic that was staffed with doctors and nurses who provided decent health care, and it was free to everybody. It was a small community where you could walk from one end to the other in no more than fifteen minutes, and many people knew each other by face and by name.

Before 1991, the Soviet government operated many enterprises in Evensk that no longer exist. Now, almost everything from food shops to flats is privately owned. No longer are most people able to rely on the state to provide a monthly salary, except for those who are retired, and their pensions are barely enough to keep body and soul alive today. The schools and the polyclinic are the few leftovers still staffed by the state.

FORCED MIGRATION

How many people lost their jobs because of the collapse of the Soviet Union one can only guess. The year 1991, and some years after, were exceedingly difficult times for Soviet people from all walks of life. The devaluation of the ruble caused many people to lose their life savings, all that they had saved up to have a decent future when they retired. These were extremely difficult times for the people living in Evensk, and through-

ON THE WAY TO THE BASE CAMP OF THE IRBYCHAN REINDEER HERDERS. 2016

out the Kolyma Region. Families often had to sell their personal belongings such as books, dishes, tools, and clothing just to get money for food.

Companies often could not pay their workers in rubles and either didn't pay or paid in some form of manufactured goods that they produced. There was not enough coal delivered to provide adequate heat for the flats, and food supplies became much less, especially in faraway places like Evensk.

Many people had to leave Evensk to find jobs in other towns, some in the materik, the mainland, if possible, and even in Magadan. This was the time that Dr. Elena Khlinovskaya Rockhill, focused on in her study of what was termed 'state-induced migration'. In her in-depth study, she interviewed many people in the Kolyma region. She found widespread out-migration from many of the Kolyma communities, including Magadan. Today one can observe abandoned and semi-abandoned communities as one travels up the Kolyma Trassa from Magadan. The city of Kadykchan is a classic example of a ghost town and is today just a forest of abandoned four and five-story cement slab apartment buildings with even the floors, doors, and windows removed. The state turned off the heat, water, and power, and the residents were forced to leave their friends, homes, schools, and employment, and find work wherever they could. A minimal amount of financial assistance was provided by the State and the World Bank. Even in Evensk, one can see several four-story old Soviet apartment buildings completely abandoned. But somehow Evensk has survived, at least up to now.

Evensk does not appear like a ghost town yet, but it certainly is dwindling in the number of abandoned buildings, and residents that one sees when out walking along Ulitsa Pobeda. During the late Soviet period, the population of Evensk was around 8,275 with a significant percentage of the population being non-Native, mostly Russians and Ukrainians. Today the present population has been significantly reduced even since the census of 2010 stated that there were 2,667 residents. It is estimated that less than 1000 people are presently living there. Now, at least half of the people living there are Even Natives.

However, not everybody wants to live in these modern Soviet/Russian towns with all the conveniences of the times, a flat with electricity and hot water, steam heat from the radiators, easy access to food shops, public transportation, sports halls, public health clinics, air transportation, and jobs. There were other men and women who for many years chose not to live in a prefabricated cement flat with all these conveniences. These were the indigenous people of the Small Nations of the Russian North, Even reindeer herders. Their home was the great outdoors of the Kolyma, with all the beauty, and subsistence that nature could provide.

The Magadan Region is inhabited by several groups of indigenous people. The Even, although not large in number, occupy a large area of the Magadan region. Today, fewer Even than previously still practice their traditional lifestyle of nomadic pastoralism, herding domestic reindeer throughout the year. There are many problems facing the reindeer herder's brigades today, one of the main being trying to manage the reindeer with so few herders. According to many people that I have spoken to, both Native and non-Native, most men are not interested in the lifestyle of a reindeer herder. It is exceedingly difficult with many hardships encountered, not the least of which are the extreme weather conditions in the tundra, working 24/7, summer and winter, and the isolation from modern communities.

TO THE IRBYCHAN BASE CAMP

We had come to visit and to see for ourselves just what it meant to be a nomadic reindeer herder in the present. The base camp of Irbychan is a thirteen-hour grueling drive from Evensk on an un- road through flowing streams and riverbeds, across the tundra, through forests, and over large boulders, bouncing up and down, and throwing you uncontrollably from side to side while you try to hold on to something to keep from banging your head, or any part of your body on the truck. It was an experience of constant motion, in all directions, but not of your choosing. There was not one flat section of road, or un-road all the way from Evensk. We had to stop several times to just have a rest from the road and a bite to eat.

After thirteen hours we finally arrived at the base camp. We never did get used to all this jerking and bouncing around in the truck. But we were very glad to get out of the big Kamaz and stand on terra firma. We looked forward to a hot meal and a good night's sleep in the bunkhouse. Here at the Irbychan base camp were storage buildings for food supplies, a garage for the repair of the track vehicles, bunkhouses for the people who live and work here, and a kitchen and dining hall. The Sovkhoz stores mainly foods with long expiration dates, such as dried foods, and instant foods, but no fresh veggies or fruits. Mostly stored here were things like butter, flour, cooking oil, rice, buckwheat, canned milk, canned meat, dried potatoes, dried onions, and dried carrots. All these foods added to or supplemented the reindeer meat and fish that the herders in the camp usually ate. During the winter the herder's main diet consisted of reindeer meat, and in the summer and fall, they ate fish. They ate berries when available but did not rely on nature to provide much in the way of food.

No heat in the bunkhouse, so getting up that next morning meant that you had to go over to the kitchen if you wanted warmth, and a cup of hot coffee. Washing up was at the outdoor sink on the way to the kitchen. As it often happens, breakfast was the leftovers from dinner last night. After breakfast, it was out to the storage buildings where we loaded the supplies that the reindeer herders had requested we bring. When walking around, I noticed in one of the storage buildings was an old Even wooden reindeer sled sitting on the floor. It is interesting to note that all the parts of the sled were held together with straps of reindeer hide, and there were no screws, nails, or metal of any kind in the construction of this small sled.

Now it was time to get back in the truck for another three-hour ride from here to the herders if we could find them. But today we had a not-so-long ride, and so it was just grin and bear it. We left the forest area of the base camp and were driving out in the vast open tundra where visibility was measured in tens of miles if unobstructed. Yuri, the Sovkhoz Brigade Director, had some idea as to where out on the tundra the herders would be, and they knew we were coming. But this is a very big wide-open country, and they could be far away, and out of view. It took some time for us to find them in the area Yuri thought they would be. After driving around several valleys we finally spotted a marker in the middle of the dirt path we were on, and it had an arrow pointing in the direction of their camp. Yuri took out his binoculars and looked in that direction, and sure enough, there were two white dots, white tents in the far distance. We

REINDEER HERDING BRIGADE NO. 10 OF THE IRBYCHAN STATE FARM. ON THE RIGHT BANK OF THE RIVER THERE IS A LARGE HERD OF REINDEER. 2016 PHOTO BY ANDREY OSIPOV

then headed down and across the tundra in that direction. As we came closer to their camp we could see that they were waiting for us. The big Kamaz pulled up and parked near the old tractor, and we all got out with great pleasure. After introductions to the Brigade Chief Andrey Amagachan, we were welcomed and invited to come into one of their tents where Andrey's wife Oksana had prepared bowls of freshly cooked reindeer meat for all of us. We had no trouble sitting down on the reindeer hides laid on top of the tamarack tree bows that covered the floor and enjoyed the delicious, boiled reindeer meat, a cup of hot chai, and Even flatbread. I can say that we did not eat just a little reindeer meat, we ate a lot, and it was so delicious. Once again it felt so good to sit on something that did not move or jerk from side to side. We thanked Oksana profusely for the delicious lunch.

HERDER'S CAMP

The main camp of the reindeer herders was in a wide valley at the base of a low-rising hill out in the middle of the tundra. It was where the two families stayed and consisted of two large white canvas tents, and one small camping tent where two summer helpers had a temporary place to stay. Since the herders had to move everything in their camp frequently, they did not have much more than they needed to just be safe, and comfortable. However, it must be said that since they were supplied with what they needed from the base camp, and were able to place all their tents, household goods, food items, metal stove, generator, and tools into the enclosed sleds that they pulled by the small diesel tractor when they moved camp, they were able to have a great deal more material possessions and comforts than in earlier times when they were only able to travel with reindeer hauling their gear. With moving the camp fairly frequently, the floor just gets replaced with new tamarack bows each time. I think that the degree of comfort is relative, and when compared to our living condi.tions, theirs is very sparse, and not one that most of us would choose for our livelihood.

Their tents are modern and made of heavy white canvas with straight sides, and a sloping roof. The floor of the tent was just flat ground that was covered with the bows of tamarack tree branches. The bows of the trees made for a reasonably clean feeling, and a soft cushioning area to sit, and sleep on when covered with reindeer hides. There is just enough space for two adults' single beds along the sides and a small table in between for eating. On each side against the tent wall was placed the bedding that was covered with reindeer skins, with the fur showing. The bedding looked like regular blankets that were on a thin kind of foam mattress laying on top of the tree bows covering the floor. In between the beds was a small low table against the back wall of the tent that had a CB radio for calling the base camp to give the four daily reports on the herder's situation, or in case of an emergency. They also had a laptop computer sitting there that was used for showing DVD movies in the evenings. The laptop was run off the electric generator that was turned on for three hours each evening. Their living conditions are quite modern as compared to the living conditions that Andrey's father and grandfather experienced as reindeer herders fifty, or more years before.

Just inside the entrance to each large white canvas tent is the cooking area where sits a metal wood-burning stove, with a metal chimney poking out of the top of the tent. This stove is used for cooking and heating on frigid days. Oksana must be very skilled in knowing how to control the fire for heating the tent for comfort, and for preparing meals. Even with a fire burning in the stove, the tent may not be very warm on a very cold windy day.

Oksana, Andrey's wife, is a full-time cook and prepares all their meals on the wood stove. It is not easy to cook on the small surface area of the stove. There may be space for just two pots or pans. She must constantly bend over with the low ceiling and limited space inside the tent. Oksana knows just how to keep the fire going at the right temperature, but not to burn the wood too hot or too fast. Wood is not very easy to get out on the treeless tundra, and they must store as much as they can when the supplies come from Irbychan. This was one of the reasons we made a tree-cutting stop on the way from the base camp to the herders.

Cooking, and doing the usual home tasks is full-time job that takes up most of Oksana's time each day. Their diet is governed by the availability of reindeer meat and fish from the streams. Most of the reindeer meat is boiled, with some roasted, and served with rice, grechka (buckwheat), or dried potatoes, along with Even flatbread, butter, chai, condensed milk, and sugar. When a deer is butchered Oksana may cut some of it into small pieces, and dry them on the racks for later. Dried reindeer meat is used by the herders as snacks when they go out hunting, gathering, or on their twelve-hour shifts when watching the herd.

Winter is the time of reindeer meat being the main dish on the table. The men kill a deer by holding it down when one man inserts a long knife into the heart of the deer. This is the traditional way of killing a deer. It is no easy task to butcher a two-hundred-pound animal. After killing the deer, the men will take their knives and skin the hide off the deer, being careful when cutting the fur around the legs that is valuable, and used by people who make parkas and do skin sewing. Then it is Oksana and the helpers that cut the animal carcass up into different parts. Oksana does not waste any parts of the reindeer. In the summer she will hang some of the smaller pieces of meat up to dry. The tongue, liver, bone marrow, and heart are delicacies, to be shared and enjoyed by all. For most meals, she will boil small cut-up pieces to eat in a soup with rice, buckwheat, dried vegetables, and Even flatbread. And of course, tea, and sugar are always served.

In the summer Oksana prepares meals that center around fish from the local streams and rivers. It is not difficult to catch enough trout or salmon to make ukha fish soup, or to fry fish in oil for a tasty dinner. She will also vary these dishes by adding rice, grechka, and sometimes dried vegetables brought from the stores in Evensk. Even flat bread, made by frying the dough in hot oil is also usually served with all meals.

To wash their clothes, she takes a large pot filled with soapy water and places the clothing in it. Then, heats the pot on the stove in the usual way. The agitator is a wooden spoon or a stick for moving the clothes around in the hot water. Rinsing and drying can certainly be a bit more of a task without a spin dryer. Drying the clothes is not too difficult in the dry air of the interior. But it all takes time and energy. The added tasks of taking everything down, and then setting it up at the next site to be where the new pasture is for the reindeer takes a lot of extra work.

Then, for some Even women, on top of this, there is the role of the mother trying to raise children out on the tundra under these less-than-glamorous conditions. There are very few mothers bringing up children in the five brigades while living out with the reindeer herders. Not a popular choice by the standards of modern Even women. One can easily understand the reasons why most young women of today are not interested in sharing the life of a reindeer herder. They all are quite aware of the more comfortable circumstances in the communities not far off.

Andrey, Chief of Brigade 10, has been a reindeer herder most of his life. He told us that his father and his grandfather were both reindeer herders, and so he grew up out on the tundra with families of reindeer herders. He went to the Soviet Internat (boarding school) during the school year and returned each summer to be with his family learning how to herd reindeer. For people like Andrey, this is not just a job, it is a way of life, one that he has known since he was a little boy. He is well aware of the fact that there is another, maybe more comfortable and easier lifestyle.

He has no plans until old age sets in to do anything but to be doing what he loves best and has chosen for his life's work. Andrey is getting older, and like many other herders of his age, they wonder who will take their place when they are no longer able to be out with the deer. Will this part of the Even culture die out with the older herders? Or is there a way to change the ways of reindeer herding that will make it a more modern, and viable economic area for young people to want to be a part of in the future? It is one of the few lifestyles that a person can choose to be part of that is not directly related to living in a modern urban apartment with all the amenities, and conveniences of the world of the consumer.

Before the collapse of the Soviet Union in 1991, most reindeer herders like Andrey worked for the Soviet state as part of a sovkhoz, or state farm.

Now, most of the herds across Russia have been privatized. This is not the case here in Severo-Evensk, where the ten brigades are jointly owned by the Magadan Regional Government seventy percent, and the Brigades thirty percent. This reindeer economics is the same as a sovkhoz in the old Soviet times. The herders are paid a salary each month of around 40,000R or $600. They are supplied with their food, and equipment by the Sovkhoz from the Irbychan base camp. They have a 56-day vacation each year with full pay along with paid travel to a resort in the materik. The herds are not up to being big enough to be profitable with the butchering, and selling of meat, antlers, and hides, and so this is questionable economics on the part of some local officials. The future of reindeer herding at least here in this region contains a lot of uncertainty.

Andrey would like to be able to pass all that he knows about herding reindeer on to his two sons. His oldest son is a student at Far East State University in Vladivostok, and his younger son is a high school student in Evensk. However, he realizes that they are part of the younger generation, know that reindeer herding is a very hard life, and that they can make more money, and be more comfortable by having jobs in the modern towns and cities of post-Soviet Russia. The city offers many job possibilities with higher pay, more comfortable living conditions in modern flats, easy access to food, transportation, and recreation, better health care, and, of course, all the negative aspects that are the main reasons why the reindeer herders like Andrey and others prefer to live out on the tundra with their reindeer.

REINDEER HERDING

To say that reindeer herding is intensive work is a gross understatement. The deer are out in the tundra every day of the year and in all kinds of weather summer and winter. The ideal situation is to have at least six people involved with the herd, depending on the size. There are two twelve- hour shifts every twenty-four hours. There should always be two herders with the reindeer every day and night, no matter the season of the year. The first shift begins at midnight when two herders go out to be close to the reindeer that are held down bunched up for the night. They stay close to the herd all night so they can protect the reindeer in case any predators like wolves or a bear are nearby. Sometimes they must be out in the freezing cold, rain, blowing snow, and strong winds.

They have no choice. Both herders will usually get some sleep being close to the herd until sunrise, and then get up, go back to camp for breakfast, and return to start the herd grazing. They stay with the herd until noon when their shift ends. At noon the second shift goes out to the the reindeer. They watch the herd as it is grazing over the pastures and move it along when one area has been exhausted. They return to camp for dinner around sunset, and then back to the herd to be near until midnight when the shifts change. There are no weekend breaks or days off to rest and relax. If one of the herders becomes ill, it can be a big problem for the rest of the herders, especially if there are only four herders in the brigade. Getting enough workers to support a brigade is difficult because their salary is low, and the working conditions are not to everybody's liking.

The reindeer herders must move from camp to camp so that the deer have fresh pasture to graze upon. This means that they must pack up everything in their camp around every five days, and place everything in the covered sled that is pulled by the small tractor. Then they move the camp gear and the herd to the next area for grazing.

Andrey Osipov knew these herders from previous visits at other times of the year. So, he brought some gifts from all of us to give to both families. He knew what they could use under the conditions they had to live in all year round, and so selected two pairs of good binoculars, ten very bright headlamps, and plenty of extra batteries. Yuri and the herders were very pleased and said bolshoye spacibo.

It was very interesting just to be with the herders and their families, and to observe them involved with their daily activities of managing the reindeer and taking care of the camp. As we stood there in the camp next to the tents we could see the 1500 reindeer all bunched up down by the little river about a half mile away where they were grazing on the grasses and lichens. Two herders were keeping them together, along with their dogs who would chase any animal that tried to stray away from the group. Andrey, the Brigade Chief said he was going to bring the herd right up close to the camp so we could have a closer look, and they could do some maintenance on the herd. As the reindeer approached it was very impressive to feel the closeness of so many large animals. They were majestic with their antlers rising high above their heads as they began to

CHIEF BRIGADE 10 REINDEER HERDER ANDREY AMAGACHAN THROWS A LASSO OVER THE ANTLERS OF A LARGE BULL THAT HAS A BELL AROUND IT'S NECK.2016 PHOTO BY ANDREY OSIPOV

move swiftly in a circle right in front of us. They were running very quickly in a tight circle that we could almost reach out and touch as they went flying by. They were kept close together so we were not worried about being trampled.

Then suddenly I could see Andrey and one of the other herders running towards the herd. He was chasing one of the largest bulls with a lasso swirling over his head ready to throw at the running deer. Out the lasso went and over the antlers of the bull, and it came to a sudden halt, but not for long as it bucked, and tried to get away. Andrey and the other man quickly were on the deer, grabbed onto the antlers, and soon threw the deer to the ground when others came running to help them hold it down. It was a task and a half to keep a large animal like this from getting up. Then Andrey took out his knife and proceeded to cut the rope that hung around the deer's neck that had a small bell hanging from it. They were de-belling the bulls since it was now mating season, and the bells would tend to scare off the females when the bulls approached trying to mate. The bells were hung on some of the bulls to keep the wolves, bears, and other predators at bay during the rest of the year. Bells are a very important part of herding, especially at night when visibility is limited. This is why Andrey Osipov brought the ten very powerful headlamps for their use. The rest of the herd was still bunched up in a tight circle, and moving quite quickly in a clockwise direction. It was a very impressive sight to see so many large animals going so fast and being so close. We took a lot of photographs, and Andrey even took some movies with his camera.

The colors of their fur varied from dark brown to black to white. Since their hairs are hollow, they can endure the extreme cold of the winters out on the tundra. This meant that sleeping under a reindeer hide for a blanket one could also feel quite warm and cozy. One of the ladies gave me a reindeer hide that she had dried stretched out on the ground in the sun and dry air. Later I gave it to Andrey, and he had it properly tanned, and it is hanging in his flat along with a beautiful set of medium-sized reindeer antlers from Yuri the Sovkhoz Director.

As we climbed up into the big blue Kamaz truck to head back to the base camp we said our dosvidaniyas and bolshoye spasibos to these hospitable and generous Even people who made us feel very welcome out here on the tundra where they live, and lead lives quite different from ours. This was an unforgettable experience that I will always treasure.

TO CONCLUDE

The two years I lived and taught in Magadan set me heading in a specific direction for the rest of my life. I am ever so thankful for all the wonderful people that I have been able to call my friends and colleagues. Life is too short for a bad cup of tea, and Magadan for me was the finest of champagnes.

MAGADAN IS CALLING. (LARRY ROCKHILL IN NAGAEVO BAY, JULY, 2016

TABLE OF CONTENTS

LAWRENCE H. KHLINOVSKI ROCKHILL

ALASKA AND MAGADAN.
THE COLD WAR
AND CITIZEN DIPLOMACY

Editor:
Elena Khlynovskaya-Rockhill

Design and layout:
Andrey Osipov

Photos:
Lawrence Khlynovsky-Rockhill,
Betty Leonard, Pavel Zhdanov,
Valeriy Ostrikov, Roy Shapley,
Andrey Osipov, Rasul Mesyagutov